How to File for Divorce in Minnesota

HOW TO FILE FOR DIVORCE IN MINNESOTA

with forms

———

Thomas Tuft
Attorney at Law

SPHINX® PUBLISHING
AN IMPRINT OF SOURCEBOOKS, INC.®
NAPERVILLE, ILLINOIS

First edition, 2001

Published by: **Sphinx® Publishing, An Imprint of Sourcebooks, Inc.®**

<u>Naperville Office</u>
P.O. Box 4410
Naperville, Illinois 60567-4410
630-961-3900
Fax: 630-961-2168

This publication is designed to provide accurate and authoritative information in regard to the subject matter covered. It is sold with the understanding that the publisher is not engaged in rendering legal, accounting, or other professional service. If legal advice or other expert assistance is required, the services of a competent professional person should be sought.

From a Declaration of Principles Jointly Adopted by a Committee of the
American Bar Association and a Committee of Publishers and Associations

This product is not a substitute for legal advice.

Disclaimer required by Texas statutes.

Library of Congress Cataloging-in-Publication Data
Tuft, Thomas.
    How to file for divorce in Minnesota / Thomas Tuft.
      p. cm. -- (Legal survival guides)
  Includes index.
    ISBN 1-57248-142-0
    1. Divorce suits--Minnesota--Popular works. 2. Divorce--Law and legislation--Minnesota--Popular works. I. Title. II. Series.

KFM5500.Z9 T84 2001
346.77601'66--dc21

    2001031377

Printed and bound in the United States of America.

VHG Paperback — 10 9 8 7 6 5 4 3 2 1

CONTENTS

Using Self-Help Law Books

Before using a self-help law book, you should realize the advantages and disadvantages of doing your own legal work and understand the challenges and diligence that this requires.

THE GROWING TREND

Rest assured that you won't be the first or only person handling your own legal matter. For example, in some states, more than seventy-five percent of divorces and other cases have at least one party representing him or herself. Because of the high cost of legal services, this is a major trend and many courts are struggling to make it easier for people to represent themselves. However, some courts are not happy with people who do not use attorneys and refuse to help them in any way. For some, the attitude is, "Go to the law library and figure it out for yourself."

We at Sphinx write and publish self-help law books to give people an alternative to the often complicated and confusing legal books found in most law libraries. We have made the explanations of the law as simple and easy to understand as possible. Of course, unlike an attorney advising an individual client, we cannot cover every conceivable possibility.

COST/VALUE ANALYSIS

Whenever you shop for a product or service, you are faced with various levels of quality and price. In deciding what product or service to buy, you make a cost/value analysis on the basis of your willingness to pay and the quality you desire.

When buying a car, you decide whether you want transportation, comfort, status, or sex appeal. Accordingly, you decide among such choices as a Neon, a Lincoln, a Rolls Royce, or a Porsche. Before making a decision, you usually weigh the merits of each option against the cost.

When you get a headache, you can take a pain reliever (such as aspirin) or visit a medical specialist for a neurological examination. Given this choice, most people, of course, take a pain reliever, since it costs only pennies; whereas a medical examination costs hundreds of dollars and takes a lot of time. This is usually a logical choice because it is rare to need anything more than a pain reliever for a headache. But in some cases, a headache may indicate a brain tumor and failing to see a specialist right away can result in complications. Should everyone with a headache go to a specialist? Of course not, but people treating their own illnesses must realize that they are betting on the basis of their cost/value analysis of the situation. They are taking the most logical option.

The same cost/value analysis must be made when deciding to do one's own legal work. Many legal situations are very straight forward, requiring a simple form and no complicated analysis. Anyone with a little intelligence and a book of instructions can handle the matter without outside help.

But there is always the chance that complications are involved that only an attorney would notice. To simplify the law into a book like this, several legal cases often must be condensed into a single sentence or paragraph. Otherwise, the book would be several hundred pages long and too complicated for most people. However, this simplification necessarily leaves out many details and nuances that would apply to special or unusual situations. Also, there are many ways to interpret most legal questions. Your case may come before a judge who disagrees with the analysis of our authors.

Therefore, in deciding to use a self-help law book and to do your own legal work, you must realize that you are making a cost/value analysis. You have decided that the money you will save in doing it yourself outweighs the chance that your case will not turn out to your satisfaction. Most people handling their own simple legal matters never have a problem, but occasionally people find that it ended up costing them more to have an attorney straighten out the situation than it would have if they had hired an attorney in the beginning. Keep this in mind if you decide to handle your own case, and be sure to consult an attorney if you feel you might need further guidance.

LOCAL RULES   The next thing to remember is that a book which covers the law for the entire nation, or even for an entire state, cannot possibly include every procedural difference of every county court. Whenever possible, we provide the exact form needed; however, in some areas, each county, or even each judge, may require unique forms and procedures. In our *state* books, our forms usually cover the majority of counties in the state, or provide examples of the type of form that will be required. In our *national* books, our forms are sometimes even more general in nature but are designed to give a good idea of the type of form that will be needed in most locations. Nonetheless, keep in mind that your *state*, county, or judge may have a requirement, or use a form, that is not included in this book.

You should not necessarily expect to be able to get all of the information and resources you need solely from within the pages of this book. This book will serve as your guide, giving you specific information whenever possible and helping you to find out what else you will need to know. This is just like if you decided to build your own backyard deck. You might purchase a book on how to build decks. However, such a book would not include the building codes and permit requirements of every city, town, county, and township in the nation; nor would it include the lumber, nails, saws, hammers, and other materials and tools you would need to actually build the deck. You would use the book as your guide, and then do some work and research involving such matters as whether you need a permit of some kind, what type and grade of wood are available in your area, whether to use hand tools or power tools, and how to use those tools.

Before using the forms in a book like this, you should check with your court clerk to see if there are any local rules of which you should be aware, or local forms you will need to use. Often, such forms will require the same information as the forms in the book but are merely laid out differently, use slightly different language, or use different color paper so the clerks can easily find them. They will sometimes require additional information.

CHANGES IN THE LAW

Besides being subject to local rules and practices, the law is subject to change at any time. The courts and the legislatures of all fifty states are constantly revising the laws. It is possible that while you are reading this book, some aspect of the law is being changed.

In most cases, the change will be of minimal significance. A form will be redesigned, additional information will be required, or a waiting period will be extended. As a result, you might need to revise a form, file an extra form, or wait out a longer time period; these types of changes will not usually affect the outcome of your case. On the other hand, sometimes a major part of the law is changed, the entire law in a particular area is rewritten, or a case that was the basis of a central legal point is overruled. In such instances, your entire ability to pursue your case may be impaired.

Again, you should weigh the value of your case against the cost of an attorney and make a decision as to what you believe is in your best interest.

INTRODUCTION

A divorce can be among the most stressful events in a person's life. No one enters into a marriage anticipating that it will end. The causes of divorce are many-domestic abuse, drug use, adultery, and most recently, Internet affairs.

This book is intended to provide an answer to basic questions and help you work with your attorney. For those who choose not to hire an attorney, this book contains forms and explanations to assist you in representing yourself, referred to as proceeding *pro se*.

This book is set up to guide you through the divorce process and also provide you with the substantive law. Chapter 1 outlines the process of the divorce, while Chapter 2 provides an explanation of the forms and directions on how to complete them.

Chapter 3 discusses issues to consider in deciding whether to represent yourself. If you decide to hire an attorney, it goes through some resources available to help you select an attorney and discusses fee arrangements and ethical rules for attorneys. It also touches on the psychological issues of a divorce. Finally, it addresses services available to help you resolve your divorce without the need for the courts.

Chapters 4 and 5 deal with custody, parenting time (formerly called visitation) and the new parenting plans. Chapter 4 focuses on the traditional concepts of physical custody and legal custody and parenting time. Chapter 5 goes into the new statute that encourages the use of parenting plans and downplays the importance of the "custody" labels.

Chapter 6 deals with child support and provides information on how to calculate child support and how to collect it. It also deals with medical support and daycare. On the other hand, Chapter 7 addresses the issue of spousal maintenance (formerly called alimony) and provides the factors the court must consider in setting the amount and duration of spousal maintenance.

Chapter 8 covers property including issues of marital versus nonmarital property; valuation of property; and how to divide property.

Unfortunately, not all marriages have a friendly end. Chapter 9 deals with domestic abuse and discusses the procedure for obtaining a domestic abuse restraining order as well as what you can ask for as part of the restraining order. Chapter 9 also covers harassment restraining orders if the issue is harassing behavior rather than domestic abuse.

Finally, sometimes issues linger on beyond the divorce. Chapter 10 deals with post-divorce issues including enforcement of the terms of the divorce decree such as child support, maintenance, property division, parenting time, etc. Chapter 11 addresses modifying your divorce decree when there has been a change in circumstances affecting ability to pay child support or maintenance, or when there is a need to seek a change in custody or parenting time.

This book is best used as a resource for someone contemplating divorce or someone working with a lawyer who needs answers to certain basic questions on the law. Rather than calling your lawyer first, you can look up the question here. Then, you can ask the question from a more educated position. If you are not represented by an attorney, this book can provide forms and assist you in representing yourself. The cost of an attorney may seem too great for your case. However, you may be jeopardizing a great deal if you do not seek an attorney's assistance. It is likely a lawyer can save you thousands of dollars on issues you may not even have considered. For example, judicious use of income tax exemptions and spousal maintenance can create significant benefits to one or both parties.

Throughout the book, there are citations to the statutes and cases so that you can review them in more detail. The glossary right before the appendices should help you with terms, and Appendix A will help you fill out most forms in Appendix B. The hypothetical case in the beginning of Appendix A is what is used to fill in the sample forms. Refer to these facts whenever you wonder where certain information came from in the samples.

Preliminary Considerations 1

Marriage is treated as a civil contract between spouses. (Minn. Stat. Sec. 517.01.) A *divorce* is a lawsuit to terminate the contract. Rules of procedure are essentially the same as those used in any other civil lawsuit with some significant exceptions. While this book is designed to help you successfully complete your own divorce, procedure is the lawyer's art. You will decide how to handle substantive issues such as custody, support, and property division. If your divorce gets complicated, your attorney will handle most procedural issues. The divorce process can follow many different paths. Some cases are settled with no court involvement and some cases require years of litigation with years of post-divorce motion hearings after that. Below, and in the rest of the chapters, is the basic information you need to work alone or with an attorney.

Initial Requirements

Grounds for Divorce

Historically, there has been a requirement of proving grounds for divorce. Grounds included adultery, abuse, desertion, among others. Present law requires only that one party claim that the marriage is *irretrievably broken*. (Minn. Stat., Sec. 518.06, Subd. 1.) If one party denies that the marriage is irretrievably broken, the court is required to determine whether the marriage is irretrievably broken and that there is no reasonable prospect of reconciliation. (Minn. Stat., Sec. 518.13, Subd. 2.) For the court to determine that there has been an irretrievable breakdown of the marriage relationship, there must be evidence that: (i) the parties have lived separate and apart for a period of at least 180 days immediately preceding the commencement of the proceeding, or (ii) there is serious marital discord adversely affecting the attitude of one or both of the parties toward the marriage. (Minn. Stat., Sec. 518.13 Subd. 2.)

If both parties agree that the marriage is irretrievably broken, the court is required to find that marriage is irretrievably broken. (Minn. Stat., Sec. 518.13, Subd. 3.)

RESIDENCY

Sept. 17 02
Aug 1, 03 Gone 04 -
Jan 8, 04 Present
Bob 1-10-04 -

In order to begin a divorce in Minnesota, a party must have resided in Minnesota for at least 180 days before commencing the action or one of the parties has lived in Minnesota for no less than 180 days before commencing the action. (Minn. Stat., Sec. 518.07.)

VENUE

The next issue to address is the question of *venue*—where the case will be heard. Generally, the case may be venued in the county in which either party resides. However, the parties may agree to venue the matter in a different county. (Minn. Stat., Sec. 518.09.) There are a number of reasons to carefully consider venue. Some counties may have a reputation of being more favorable to men or more favorable to women. At least one county has a tendency not to approve joint custody agreements, which is difficult to overcome. Heavily populated counties may be slower, but lesser populated counties may offer fewer services. Some counties block your case to one judge. In other counties the judge will be different every time you go to court.

NAME CHANGE

no legal name change upon Marriage

A party may request a name change as part of a dissolution. The court is required to grant the change unless the court finds that there is intent to defraud or mislead. The new name is to be designated in the divorce decree. (Minn. Stat. Sec., 518.27.)

DIVORCE PROCEDURE

There are many ways to proceed in a divorce. Whether you need to argue about certain points, or whether you agree on all the issues with your spouse, there are always certain forms, questions, hearings, or decisions that need to be made.

CONTESTED VS. UNCONTESTED DIVORCE

The divorce in which there are no contested issues is quite rare, just as the divorce in which every issue is contested is quite rare. The level of contest can be measured by the number of issues in dispute and the amount of procedure it takes to get to the end. Some would say that if a divorce does not go to trial it is uncontested. That ignores the contentions, facts and legal arguments raised in a temporary relief hearing;

the agonizing mediation sessions; the posturing for the court at the pre-trial; and letters and communications leading up to a written settlement agreement. Another measure is the cost—the more procedure that is required, the more issues that are contested, the greater the cost.

Uncontested Divorces. In uncontested cases, only a few documents are necessary. They include:

- ❏ SUMMONS (form 3)

- ❏ PETITION FOR DISSOLUTION OF MARRIAGE (form 4)

- ❏ MARITAL TERMINATION AGREEMENT (form 15)

- ❏ WAIVER OF COUNSEL (form 16)

- ❏ FINDINGS OF FACT, CONCLUSIONS OF LAW, ORDER FOR JUDGMENT, AND JUDGMENT AND DECREE (form 18)

- ❏ PARENTING PLAN (form 17)

Those are the basic documents. You will only use the last one if there are children involved. If you and your spouse reach agreement, those four (or five) documents are the only things you will need to agree upon. If you have an uncontested and very simple case, you may be one of the few to qualify for the streamlined SUMMARY DISSOLUTION PROCEDURE, discussed later in this chapter.

There are a few other documents that the court administrator will require for basic information. To prove that the documents have been served, you will need to provide an ADMISSION OF SERVICE (form 5) signed by your spouse or an AFFIDAVIT OF PERSONAL SERVICE (form 19) signed by the person who serves the document. The court will require a DEFAULT SCHEDULING REQUEST (form 21) to indicate whether a hearing is necessary. Finally, in order to keep your Social Security number confidential you will file a separate CONFIDENTIAL INFORMATION FORM allowing that information to be pulled out of the file when someone goes to review it. (see form 22, p.275.)

All of these forms are discussed in more detail in the following sections. Appendix A has a sample *hypothetical case,* or an example case for you to follow, and forms filled in based on that hypothetical case. These filled-in forms will help in filling out the blank forms in Appendix B.

Contested Divorces. In a contested case, you must be prepared for everything discussed in this book including a trial. In Appendix A you will see many of the documents you may need to prepare. In a contested case, you may have to prepare virtually all of the forms included in this book.

SUMMARY
DISSOLUTION
PROCEDURE

There is a streamlined divorce procedure available to people in certain limited circumstances. If you qualify and you and your spouse agree on terms, you may simply complete a form joint declaration. In order to qualify you must meet each of the following:

- no living minor children have been born to or adopted by the parties before or during the marriage, unless the court decides someone other than the husband is the father;

- the wife is not pregnant;

 - the parties have been married fewer than eight years as of the date they file for the summary dissolution;

- neither party owns any real estate;

- there are no unpaid debts in excess of $8,000 incurred by either or both of the parties during the marriage, excluding encumbrances on automobiles;

 - the total fair market value of the <u>marital assets</u> does not exceed $25,000, including net equity on automobiles;

 - neither party has nonmarital assets in excess of $25,000; and

- neither party has been a victim of domestic abuse by the other. (Minn. Stat., Sec. 518.195, Subd. 1.)

The necessary forms are available from the district court. You must essentially provide the following:

- the name, address, social security numbers, and any previous names of the parties;

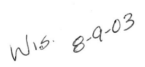 - the place and date of the marriage of the parties;

- that either the petitioner or the respondent or both:

  - has resided in this state for not less than 180 days immediately preceding the filing;

  - has been a member of the armed services and has been stationed in Minnesota for not less than 180 days immediately preceding the commencement of the proceeding; or

- has been a resident of this state for not less than 180 days immediately preceding the commencement of the proceeding;

- that the parties meet the qualifications for the summary dissolution process as stated above;

- each parties' nonmarital property;

- how the assets and debts of the parties are to be divided;

- both parties' income and preserving their right to spousal maintenance; and

- that there has been no domestic abuse of one party by the other. (Minn. Stat., Sec. 518.195, Subd. 2.)

There is also a requirement that you watch an educational video, if available. If the papers are in order and all statutory requirements have been met, the court administrator is directed to enter a decree of dissolution thirty days after the papers have been filed.

If you believe you qualify, you should go to the Family Court Administrator in your county and ask for the necessary documents to use the Summary Dissolution process.

LEGAL SEPARATION

A *legal separation* is a court determination of the rights and responsibilities of a husband and wife arising out of the marital relationship. A decree of legal separation does not terminate the marital status of the parties. (Minn. Stat., Sec. 518.06, Subd. 1.) You do not need to enter into a legal separation before going forward with a divorce.

Generally, legal separations are discouraged. A legal separation is often converted to a divorce before a decree is entered. In addition, if the decree is entered and either part wishes to seek a divorce, you must start almost from the beginning.

However, there are reasons for a legal separation. If it is clear that you and your spouse cannot remain together and you have religious or other convictions against divorce, a legal separation may be necessary. Another reason for a legal separation, is related to medical insurance. If you need to remain on your spouse's medical insurance through his or her employer, a legal separation may be an option for you.

TRIAL

Sometimes divorces go to trial, especially when there are disputes that are not resolved any other way. More about the trial process is discussed throughout the book. However, you should know that the trial is open to the public although the court does have discretion to close the hearing. (Minn. Stat., Sec. 518.13, Subd. 4.)

If there are children involved, and the court finds that a public hearing would be detrimental to the child's best interests, the court may exclude the public from the hearing, but may admit any person who has a direct interest in the particular case. (Minn. Stat., Sec. 518.168, Subd. (c).) In addition, if the court determines that some part of the proceeding should be kept secret to protect the child's welfare, the court may seal part of the record. (Minn. Stat., Sec. 518.168, Subd. (d).) Custody proceedings take priority in being set for hearing. (Minn. Stat., Sec. 518.168, Subd. (a).) The court makes the decisions of fact and law without a jury.

INTERVIEWING CHILDREN

There is a strong preference for avoiding direct involvement of the children in the divorce proceeding. Courts will prefer to receive input from a guardian *ad litem*, court services officer, or psychologist in addition to the parties and any other witnesses rather than having children testify. However, there are circumstances in which the court will take testimony from the children of the parties.

If the court determines that the children are of sufficient age to express a preference, the judge may interview the children privately to determine which parent the child prefers to live with. The court is required to permit counsel for the parties to be present and must permit counsel to provide questions either directly or through the judge. The court is required to make a record of the interview and include the interview in the record, unless waived by the parties. (Minn. Stat., Sec. 518.166.)

PRIMARY DIVORCE FORMS 2

Although there are other forms discussed throughout the book, the main ones you will need are discussed now. All the instructions for these forms are provided here, so if you find that you will need to fill out one of these forms later, you can refer to this chapter. These are generally the forms for all divorce proceedings, but each case has its own variances.

SUMMONS, PETITION FOR DISSOLUTION OF MARRIAGE, AND ANSWER

The SUMMONS and the PETITION FOR DISSOLUTION OF MARRIAGE (PETITION) are the documents that are served upon you or your spouse to begin the divorce. The SUMMONS advises your spouse of the requirement to respond to the PETITION within thirty days. (see form 3, p.191.) The PETITION is a general statement of the facts of the case and the *relief*, or assistance through money or property, requested. (see form 4, p.193.)

SUMMONS (form 3)

The SUMMONS is mostly form language. (see form 3, p.191.)

☞ The top portion of the form is referred to here as the *caption*. (All of the pleadings will have this, and it should be identical for each form except the name of the document.) In the top left portion of the form you will need to complete the county in which the case is filed. The next line is for the name of the petitioner and the next line is for the name of the respondent. On the right side of the caption, you will have to cross out the line that does not apply. If there are no children, cross out the top line. If there are children, cross out the next line. The next line is for the judicial district number. (You can simply call the court administrator to determine the number of the judicial district.) It will be one through ten. (Hennepin County is the Fourth Judicial District. Ramsey County is the Second Judicial District. The remaining districts are made up of multiple counties.)

The next line of the caption is for the court file number. This number is assigned after the case is filed. (The SUMMONS can be served before being filed. In the initial papers, there may be no file number and this is left blank.) The next line is for the judicial officer. This may be a referee or a judge in Ramsey County or Hennepin County. (Some courts will not assign a specific judicial officer to your case. If you receive a notice of judicial officer assignment, you must include this on all subsequent pleadings.)

☛ If you or your spouse own real estate, complete the second paragraph with the county of the real estate and the legal description of the real estate.

☛ Finally, complete the date, your name, address and telephone number.

☛ The SUMMONS must contain the following restraining language:

NOTICE OF TEMPORARY RESTRAINING AND ALTERNATIVE DISPUTE RESOLUTION PROVISIONS

UNDER MINNESOTA LAW, SERVICE OF THIS SUMMONS MAKES THE FOLLOWING REQUIREMENTS APPLY TO BOTH PARTIES TO THIS ACTION, UNLESS THEY ARE MODIFIED BY THE COURT OR THE PROCEEDING IS DISMISSED:

(1) NEITHER PARTY MAY DISPOSE OF ANY ASSETS EXCEPT (i) FOR THE NECESSITIES OF LIFE OR FOR THE NECESSARY GENERATION OF INCOME OR PRESERVATION OF ASSETS, (ii) BY AN AGREEMENT IN WRITING, OR (iii) FOR RETAINING COUNSEL TO CARRY ON OR TO CONTEST THIS PROCEEDING;

(2) NEITHER PARTY MAY HARASS THE OTHER PARTY; AND

(3) ALL CURRENTLY AVAILABLE INSURANCE COVERAGE MUST BE MAINTAINED AND CONTINUED WITHOUT CHANGE IN COVERAGE OR BENEFICIARY DESIGNATION.

IF YOU VIOLATE ANY OF THESE PROVISIONS, YOU WILL BE SUBJECT TO SANCTIONS BY THE COURT.

(4) PARTIES TO A MARRIAGE DISSOLUTION PROCEEDING ARE ENCOURAGED TO ATTEMPT ALTERNATIVE DISPUTE RESOLUTION PURSUANT TO MINNESOTA LAW. ALTERNATIVE DISPUTE RESOLUTION INCLUDES MEDIATION, ARBITRATION, AND OTHER PROCESSES AS SET FORTH IN THE DISTRICT COURT RULES. YOU MAY CONTACT THE COURT ADMINISTRATOR ABOUT RESOURCES IN YOUR AREA. IF YOU CANNOT PAY FOR MEDIATION OR ALTERNATIVE DISPUTE RESOLUTION, IN SOME COUNTIES, ASSISTANCE MAY BE AVAILABLE TO YOU THROUGH A NONPROFIT PROVIDER OR A COURT PROGRAM. IF YOU ARE A VICTIM OF DOMESTIC ABUSE OR THREATS OF ABUSE AS DEFINED IN MINNESOTA STATUTES, CHAPTER 518B, YOU ARE NOT REQUIRED TO TRY MEDIATION AND YOU WILL NOT BE PENALIZED BY THE COURT IN LATER PROCEEDINGS.

The restraining provisions apply to both parties to the case. (Minn. Stat., Sec. 518.091.)

PETITION FOR DISSOLUTION OF MARRIAGE (form 4)

The **PETITION FOR DISSOLUTION OF MARRIAGE** (**PETITION**) is broadly drafted so there are likely issues addressed that do not specifically apply to your case. Though you can use the form, this document should be retyped or cross out the items that do not apply. (see form 4, p.193.)

☞ Complete the caption as instructed on page 7 under the SUMMONS.

☞ Paragraph I: Complete your name, address, date of birth, age, social security number, and any former names.

☞ Paragraph II: Do the same as Paragraph I for the respondent.

☞ Paragraph III: Insert the date, city, county, and state of marriage. If any of these do not apply, simply leave it blank, e.g. you married in a foreign country.

☞ Paragraph IV: Insert the names, birthdates, and ages of the children. Cross out the incorrect statements concerning the care of the children. If you intend to use the custody process, check the line concerning custody and cross out the incorrect information concerning custody. If you intend to follow the parenting plan, path, check that line.

☞ Paragraph V: If you are seeking custody, indicate that respondent should pay child support.

☞ Paragraph VI: If this is a spousal maintenance case indicate who should pay. If not, indicate that neither should pay.

☞ Paragraph VII: Indicate who presently provides medical insurance for each party and the children. It would not be unusual for one party to cover the entire family.

☞ Paragraph VIII: Do nothing with this paragraph—it is general language regarding personal property.

☞ Paragraph IX: Simply fill in the county in which you reside.

☞ Paragraph X: State that the wife is not presently pregnant if she is not.

☞ Paragraph XI: Leave the standard language there.

☞ Paragraph XII: This is the grounds paragraph. The language "irretrievable breakdown" is all that is required.

☞ Paragraph XIII: If either party is in the military service, you should consult a lawyer to ensure that you comply with the law in this area.

☞ Paragraph XIV: Insert the date of separation. If you and your spouse are not separated, indicate that here.

☞ Paragraph XV: Indicate the occupation, employer, and net monthly income for the petitioner.

☞ Paragraph XVI: Indicate the occupation, employer, and net monthly income for the respondent.

☞ Paragraph XVII: Indicate whether there is real property and, if so, the address, county, state, and legal description of the real estate. If there is no real estate owned by either party, check that box.

☞ Paragraph XVIII: Indicate the year, make, model, VIN, value and debt on the car. If you do not know the specifics, a general description is acceptable. The VIN is helpful in transferring title. The value can be obtained from a "bluebook."

☞ Paragraph XIX: Leave the standard language, but delete any of the types of accounts you do not own.

☞ Paragraph XX: Indicate the date of separation, if applicable.

☞ Paragraph XXI: This is the most recent addition to the statutory requirements of the PETITION. Simply indicate whether there is an order for protection in effect. You do not need to indicate whether there has been domestic abuse in the past.

☞ WHEREFORE: the next section is often called the "wherefore clause." This section states the relief requested. Simply check the boxes that are relevant to your case and delete provisions that do not apply.

☞ Complete the signature block, ACKNOWLEDGMENT, and VERIFICATION in front of a notary.

After being served, the respondent has thirty days to submit a response. The response must include an ANSWER and may include a counterpetition. The ANSWER simply addresses the allegations of the petition by admitting, denying, or claiming to lack sufficient information to admit or deny.

The counterpetition is essentially a petition by the respondent, which sets out the respondent's version of the facts. The petitioner need not answer the counterpetition. By statute, the allegations of the counterpetition are denied. (Minn. Stat., Sec. 518.12.)

However, it is not unusual for the attorneys to agree that the respondent need not submit an ANSWER or agree to an extension of time to answer.

ANSWER   If you have been served with papers, you will need to serve an ANSWER. (see form 7, p.203.) The ANSWER is due within thirty days of service of the initial papers. Often an attorney will draft an ANSWER and counter-petition. This ANSWER should be sufficient in most cases. If you have a complex case requiring a counterpetition, you should hire an attorney.

To complete the ANSWER:

☛ Fill in the caption as instructed on page 7 under SUMMONS.

☛ Fill in the name of the petitioner on the first line.

☛ In paragraph 2, indicate which of the provisions of the PETITION you agree are true.

☛ In paragraph 3 indicate which provisions include information that is unknown to you.

☛ In paragraph 4 indicate which provisions you deny.

☛ Fill in the signature block and date the form.

SERVICE

Once the SUMMONS and PETITION FOR DISSOLUTION OF MARRIAGE (or legal separation) have been drafted, the documents must be delivered to your spouse. (Minn. Stat., Sec. 518.11 Subd. (a).) If your spouse does not reside in Minnesota, he or she may be served in any other state or foreign country by *personal service*. (Minn. Stat., Sec. 518.11(b).) Service may be made by any adult **other than a party to the case.** (Minnesota Rule of Civil Procedure 4.02.) However, a deputy sheriff or professional process server is often used.

AFFIDAVIT OF
PERSONAL
SERVICE

The process server signs an *affidavit* (or Certificate of Service for a sheriff's deputy) which is filed with the court to prove service has been made. There is an AFFIDAVIT OF PERSONAL SERVICE in Appendix B. (see form 19, p.272.) Remember, you must have **another party serve the papers.** Fill in form 19 as follows:

☛ Fill in the caption as instructed on page 7 under SUMMONS.

☛ In the "County of" line state the county in which the affidavit is signed. This may be different from the county where the documents were served or where the case is filed.

☞ The next line if for the person serving the papers followed by the date.

☞ After the word "attached" insert the title of the document that is being served.

☞ Next state who it is served upon.

☞ The person serving then signs the document in front of a notary.

SERVICE BY ALTERNATE MEANS

If the location of your spouse is unknown, the court may order service by *alternate means*. (Minn. Stat., Sec. 518.11, Subd. (c).) To seek service by alternate means you must apply to the court. (see form 23, p.276.) The **APPLICATION FOR SERVICE BY ALTERNATE MEANS** is filled out as follows:

☞ Complete the caption as instructed on page 7 under **SUMMONS**.

☞ List the last known address of your spouse.

☞ List where, when, and how you have had contacts with your spouse.

☞ Insert the last known location of your spouse's employment.

☞ At the next two lines, insert the names and locations of your spouse's parents, siblings, children, and other close relatives.

☞ Give the names and locations of other persons who are likely to know the your spouse's whereabouts.

☞ Describe the efforts to locate those persons listed as knowing where your spouse is.

☞ Sign the document in front of a notary.

You should send this document to the court. The judge will decide whether you can proceed, and will issue an order indicating how to serve the **SUMMONS** and the **PETITION**.

The court may then order service by sending the **SUMMONS** and **PETITION** by first class mail, forwarding address requested, to any address at which respondent may receive notice of the proceeding, including relatives. (see form 20, p.273.) If there is no such address, the papers must be sent to respondent's last known address. (Minn. Stat., Sec. 518.11, Subd. (c).) The court may order publication in a legal newspaper if it is reasonably likely to succeed in notifying the respondent of the divorce proceeding. (Minn. Stat., Sec. 518.11, Subd. (c).) If the case involves real estate, the court must order that the SUMMONS be published in a legal newspaper. (Minn. Stat., Sec. 518.11, Subd. (c).)

Service either by first class mail or by publication is deemed complete after twenty-one days. (Minn. Stat., Sec. 518.11, Subd. (c).) The respondent then has thirty days to respond to the SUMMONS or is deemed to be in default. (Minn. Stat., Secs. 518.12 and 518.13.) The court may hear the case as a default.

After service (or before in some cases) the petitioner may file the documents with the court along with the proof of service (either an AFFIDAVIT OF PERSONAL SERVICE (form 19) or Certificate of Service from a Sheriff.)

NOTE: *After the initial personal service, each party may serve documents by mail or by delivery to the other side's home or place of business. Personal service is not required.*

AFFIDAVIT OF
SERVICE BY
U.S. MAIL

When a document is served by mail, the person serving must complete an AFFIDAVIT OF SERVICE BY MAIL. (see form 20, p.273.) (Fill this form out like the AFFIDAVIT OF PERSONAL SERVICE discussed on page 12.) When a document is served by mail, three days must be added. For example, motion papers must be served fourteen days before a hearing. If served by mail, the documents must be postmarked seventeen days before the hearing. Remember, you must have someone else serve the papers. If you serve the papers yourself, service is not valid.

ADMISSION OF
SERVICE

If you and your spouse are sufficiently agreeable, he or she could sign an ADMISSION OF SERVICE. (see form 5, p.201.) If respondent will agree to accept service, he or she can simply sign this document. Fill in the caption as instructed on page 7 under SUMMONS, and the name of the respondent under the caption. Have the respondent sign the document. This is in lieu of having the papers served by a sheriff or process server.

CERTIFICATE OF REPRESENTATION AND PARTIES

This is the document that the court uses to make a record of the addresses of the parties. (see form 6, p.202.)

☞ Fill in the blank for the county of the case and the number of the judicial district.

☛ Fill in the date the case was or will be filed.

☛ Complete the name of the case (petitioner's name v. respondent's name).

☛ At the bottom of the form complete the name of the petitioner, then the address and telephone number.

☛ Next, do the same for the respondent.

☛ Make a copy of this for your spouse and send the original to the court when you file your documents.

SCHEDULING INFORMATION STATEMENT

The SCHEDULING INFORMATION STATEMENT is a form the court uses to schedule the case. (see form 8, p.204.) It indicates the level of complexity and the amount of time it will take the parties to prepare the case. This document is to be filed within sixty days of filing the case. If there is a temporary hearing, it must be filed within sixty days after the hearing. Within thirty days of filing this document, the court will issue a scheduling order.

☛ Complete the caption as instructed on page 7 under SUMMONS.

☛ Paragraph 1: Indicate whether both parties have been served.

☛ Paragraph 2: Usually both parties do not join in filling out the form. Attorneys are supposed to file jointly. Indicate that the parties have **not** joined in filing the form.

☛ Paragraph 3: Usually a case is not ready to settle at the time this form is completed. Check "no" and move on if your case is not ready to settle. However, if it is, check "yes." If there are children, you must check the next two lines indicating that there must be a hearing. If there are no children, you are not required to have a hearing, and you should check the line that says so.

☛ Paragraph 4: Indicate which issues are in dispute. On line "a" indicate whether there are minor children and, if so, the number. On line "b" indicate whether there is a custody dispute. If so, write in a quick summary of what each party wants. On line "c" indicate whether there is a visitation dispute. If so, write in a brief summary of what each party wants. You should attach your detailed proposal for visitation and custody on a separate sheet In line "d" indicate whether there will be a property dispute. If so, indicate generally who will get what property. For example, "each party shall be awarded all property in his or her name or possession as presently divided". In line "e" indicate whether either party will make non-marital property claims. If so, write in the basis for the non-marital claim and who should get it. In line "f" indicate whether there are complex valuation issues.

☛ Paragraph 5: This addresses the discovery process. Usually it takes three to four months to complete discovery—sometimes more due to third parties being slow in forwarding documents. Write in the number of months you want to allow. In line "a" indicate whether there will be depositions. If the answer is yes, you should hire an attorney. In line "b" indicate whether there will be medical or vocational evaluations. If the answer is yes to either of these, the case is too complex to handle yourself. These evaluation are often used when spousal maintenance is an issue, but can arise in other circumstances. In line "c" indicate whether there will be any experts such as appraisers. Usually you will not know who, if any, experts will be involved in the case. If this case involves difficult discovery issues, you need to hire an attorney.

☛ Paragraph 6: Indicate the dates by which certain things should be done. Generally, the court will set a schedule based upon its own calendar more than anything you provide. In line "a" the date for temporary relief may be indicated. In line "b" indicate the deadline date for property evaluations. This is usually at least six months out. In line "c" indicate deadline for completion of custody/parenting time mediation. This will usually be three to six months out. In line "d" indicate the deadline for completion of the custody visitation evaluation. This usually after mediation breaks down. It is usually six months out. Line "e" is a catch-all, and is only necessary for miscellaneous items. In most cases you will write in "not applicable." In line "f" indicate the proposed date for a pretrial hearing. This will usually be six to twelve months out. In line "g" write the date for trial. This is usually a year out.

☞ Paragraph 7: It is common for trials to take anywhere from one-half day to three days. Longer trials happen, but they are exceptions. (If you anticipate a trial you need to hire an attorney.) Write in your estimate.

☞ Paragraph 8: Alternative dispute resolution is required in virtually all but domestic abuse cases. Mediation is the most common and cost-effective method. Write in which method is used and the date by which this must be completed.

☞ Paragraph 9: This is the place to indicate whether there has been domestic abuse, disabilities or the parties or children, or anything else that may require the court to treat the case differently.

☞ Complete the date, name, address, and telephone number (signature block).

This document must be served within sixty days after filing the case with the court. Send a copy to your spouse and file the original with the court. You will need to attach an AFFIDAVIT OF SERVICE (form 19 or 20).

DISCOVERY

Discovery is the process of gathering information to make an informed decision about a case. There are a number of forms of discovery, including written questions, asking to admit to certain facts, inspecting property, seeking psychological, medical or vocational evaluations, and depositions. The most common forms of discovery are INTERROGATORIES (a list of questions) (form 12) and REQUEST FOR PRODUCTION. (see form 13, p.221.)

Your attorney may agree to informal discovery in some cases. This means both sides will exchange documents without formal written demands. If the case is too complex or there is a likelihood of deceit, formal discovery processes will be used.

Formal discovery can be quite expensive. Usually INTERROGATORIES and REQUEST FOR PRODUCTION are served first with an AFFIDAVIT OF SERVICE (form 19 or 20). Then, the responding party must compile documents and other information to respond. The next step may be a deposition which can be used to obtain additional information, pin down a party on an issue, provide information for further investigation, prove that some-one is lying, or expose weaknesses in the other side's case. The attorney may then send **REQUESTS FOR ADMISSIONS**. This is a list of statements that the other side must admit. If a party denies something that is later found to be true, the party will be sanctioned.

INTERROGATORIES

INTERROGATORIES are lists of questions that can provide important information in evaluating a case. (see form 12, p.215.) The questions contained here are fairly standard. An attorney would tailor them more specifically to the case depending on the situation. You are permitted to ask fifty questions. The subparts to these questions could be construed as additional questions so sending the complete list may result in an objection from the opposing party.

You only need to complete the caption as instructed on page 7 under **SUMMONS**, the line indicating the name of your spouse and cross out whatever does not apply as to petitioner or respondent. There are several blanks throughout, which you can simply fill in as to how many years back the question applies. Finally, you must complete the signature block.

REQUEST FOR
PRODUCTION

REQUEST FOR PRODUCTION requires little to complete it. (see form 13, p.221.) Like **INTERROGATORIES**, an attorney would tailor the questions to the case. However, these basic questions should provide you with a significant amount of information. Complete this form like the **INTERROGATORIES** using the form in Appendix B.

TEMPORARY RELIEF

HEARING

A divorce may take a year or more to resolve. In the meantime, certain issues must be resolved on a temporary basis. It is important that you pursue temporary relief effectively as it will certainly affect the final outcome of the case. *Temporary relief* is monetary assistance for a lim-ited amount of time to help relieve the burden of going through the divorce. For example, if you are awarded temporary custody, when the matter finally goes to trial many months (or even a year) later it may be difficult for the court to award custody to your spouse. However, the statute does specifically provide that a temporary decision shall not prejudice the rights of the parties at subsequent hearings. (Minn. Stat., Sec. 518.131, Subd. 9.) The terms of the temporary order remain in effect until it is amended, vacated, the case is dismissed, or, most commonly, until the entry of the final decree of dissolution. (Minn. Stat., Sec. 518.131 Subd. 5.)

The parties may raise virtually all of the issues of the divorce at the temporary relief hearing including custody and parenting time with the children, spousal maintenance, child support, attorney fees, and possession of property (including exclusive possession of the home and cars). In addition, the court may restrain the parties from using or disposing of certain property, from harassing or criticizing the other party, and from removing the children from the jurisdiction of the court. Violation of these restraining provisions is punishable as contempt of court and as a misdemeanor. (Minn. Stat., Sec. 518.131, Subd. 10 and Minn. Stat., Sec. 518.62.)

The legal standard the court uses in deciding the issues are the same as the standard for deciding issues in the final determinations. (Minn. Stat., Sec. 518.131, Subd. 7.) The information is submitted to the court by affidavits and arguments of counsel. (Minn. Stat., Sec. 518.131, Subd. 8.) It is possible to request testimony, but this is rarely done and even more rarely granted. (Minn. Stat., Sec. 518.131, Subd. 8.)

A temporary order may not do the following:

- deny parenting time to a noncustodial parent unless that parenting time is likely to cause physical or emotional harm to the child;

- exclude a party from the family home unless the court finds there is immediate danger of physical or emotional harm the other party or the children of either party or that the exclusion is reasonable under the circumstances; or

- vacate an order for protection. However, the court may hear a motion under an order for protection concurrently with a temporary relief motion or other motion in a divorce proceeding. (Minn. Stat., Sec. 518.131, Subd.2.)

In extraordinary circumstances you may seek relief without notice to the other party (*ex parte*). This is rarely done, but is available if the circumstances warrant. This may be done when there is a concern for the safety of the party or the children. It may also be done where there is considerable risk that property may be taken, damaged, or destroyed. As this is extraordinary relief, it may be granted only in extraordinary circumstances.

There is considerable risk in pursuing a temporary order. Unlike a final order, it is not appealable. A judge will be making a decision based upon a brief review of documents submitted and argument of your attorney. This decision will very likely affect the outcome of the case. Finally, the decision cannot be appealed to a higher court (except in the case of a referee's decision which may be appealed to a judge).

NOTE: *A referee's decision in Ramsey County is not appealable to a judge.*

It is possible that circumstances will change during a case or there is a need to change the temporary order. You can go back to court to seek a change in the temporary order. (Minn. Stat., Sec. 518.131, Subd. 9(b).) There is no requirement that there be a change in circumstances. However, the court may very well question why you are back again and there is some risk that attorney fees will be awarded against you.

PROCEDURE   Information to support a motion for temporary relief is supplied by serving and filing a NOTICE OF MOTION AND MOTION (form 9), an APPLICATION FOR TEMPORARY RELIEF (form 10), and an AFFIDAVIT (form 11). See Appendix A for filled-in samples of these. The motion papers must be served and filed fourteen days before the hearing (seventeen days by U.S. Mail). If the papers have been served upon you, you must serve and file a response at least five days before the hearing (eight days if serving by U.S. Mail). If you are raising issues not raised in the other party's papers, you must serve and file the documents ten days before the hearing (thirteen days by U.S. Mail) so that the other party can respond to these issues no later than five days before the hearing. You will also need to complete an AFFIDAVIT OF SERVICE BY MAIL (form 20) or an AFFIDAVIT OF PERSONAL SERVICE (form 19) for the person who serves the documents. See Appendix A for an example of these documents and Appendix B for blank forms.

NOTICE OF MOTION AND MOTION. This is the document that notifies the other party when a hearing is scheduled and what relief is requested.(see form 9, p.207.) There is a sample form in Appendix A.

Complete the NOTICE OF MOTION AND MOTION as follows:

☛ Fill in the caption as instructed on page 7 under SUMMONS.

☛ After "To" fill in the name of the other party.

☛ Cross out the petitioner or respondent whichever does not apply.

☛ Write in the address on the next line.

☛ Complete the next paragraph with the date and time of the hearing. Then, enter the name of the judge (if not known write in "Presiding Judge"), the address of the court, and the room in which the hearing will be held, if known.

☛ On the numbered lines indicate the relief requested, (e.g. temporary custody, child support, maintenance, possession of the home). (See the sample in Appendix A for guidance on completing this section.)

☛ Finally, complete the motion signature block and the Acknowledgement signature block.

You will need to draft an AFFIDAVIT OF PERSONAL SERVICE (form 19) or an AFFIDAVIT OF SERVICE BY U.S. MAIL (form 20) and have the person who serves the documents complete it. The NOTICE OF MOTION AND MOTION, the APPLICATION FOR TEMPORARY RELIEF (below), and AFFIDAVIT must be served fourteen days before the hearing (seventeen days if by U.S. Mail).

APPLICATION FOR TEMPORARY RELIEF. The APPLICATION FOR TEMPORARY RELIEF is used when there is a hearing to resolve issues on a temporary basis pending the final settlement or trial of the case. (see form 10, p.209.) If there is a temporary hearing scheduled, both parties must prepare their own APPLICATION FOR TEMPORARY RELIEF. The application is generally accompanied by a supporting AFFIDAVIT that explains any circumstances beyond the bare numbers presented in this document. If you need a temporary relief hearing, your case is probably too complex to handle without an attorney.

Fill in the APPLICATION FOR TEMPORARY RELIEF as follows:

☞ Complete the caption, as you did for the SUMMONS, page 7.

☞ The next blank line is for the county in which the form is signed. (This is not necessarily the county of the case, but the county in which you actually put pen to paper.)

☞ The next line is for your name, then cross out either petitioner or respondent, and wife or husband, whichever does not apply.

☞ Paragraph 2: Indicate the number of months separated and who paid how much to whom.

☞ Paragraph 3: Indicate the number of children, their ages, who is caring for them and where they are staying.

☞ Paragraph 4: (This is a poorly designed portion of the form.) Indicate the assets in the wife's name in the first column, then the husband, then the assets in both names. Then indicate the encumbrance on the items in the far right.

☞ Paragraph 5: (This is similarly confusing.) You may list only secured debts—those with some collateral. This may include a credit line against a car, a cabin mortgage, etc. Credit cards and credit lines are usually unsecured.

☞ Paragraph 6: List your expenses. It is best to convert all expenses to monthly. Try to be very accurate and thorough. If you have unusual expenses, you should attach a copy of the billing statement or other evidence of the expense. Some of the expenses here will also be listed as expenses in your paycheck, (e.g. medical and dental insurance.)

NOTE: *Do not count the expenses twice. The court may scrutinize this carefully if there is a spousal maintenance issue. If someone inflates their budget it can hurt their credibility with the court.*

☞ Paragraph 7: It is best to convert all figures to monthly as indicated in Chapter 6 Child Support. If you have done the net income calculation for child support you should be able to insert the figures here quite easily. On line (5) include those deductions that are not included in the child support statute such as disability or life insurance. On line (d) indicate reimbursements from an employer. This can include a credit for meals, car, travel, clothing, etc. The "other income" lines under line (e) can be taken from tax returns or account statements. Do not forget to attach copies of one month of your paystubs.

☞ Paragraph 8: This is like the "wherefore" clause of the PETITION in which you finally get to state what you want.

☞ Paragraph 9: Indicate if any money has been paid to attorneys.

☞ Paragraph 10: This is where you can add in more information for the court. Generally, you would want to use a separate affidavit to go into detail.

☞ Finally, as with an AFFIDAVIT (below), this document must be signed before a notary public to validate the signature.

NOTE: *Do not forget to attach documents as requested, (e.g. paystubs).*

This document must be served upon your spouse with the NOTICE OF MOTION AND MOTION and the AFFIDAVIT (below, if any).

AFFIDAVIT. The AFFIDAVIT fills in the details for the court. (see form 11, p.214.) For example, if custody is at issue, you will want to explain why you should be awarded custody, under each of the best interest factors as described in Chapter 4. If there are special circumstances concerning the children or a party, this is where you explain those circumstances.

This is a sworn statement in which you can present the facts that you want the court to understand. You will have to retype this form.

☞ The caption through the first sentence goes first. (Fill in the caption as instructed on page 7 under SUMMONS.)

☞ Then, add in your story—everything you want the court to consider.

☞ The signature/notary block goes at the end.

☞ Remember the AFFIDAVIT must be notarized.

This document must be served upon your spouse with the NOTICE OF MOTION AND MOTION.

JUDICIAL OFFICER

In most counties, a judge will be assigned to hear your case. However, if you live in Ramsey or Hennepin county, the individual hearing your case may be a referee. Referees are hired by the district court to hear cases. In Hennepin County they hear the initial stages of a case including the temporary relief hearing. A trial is heard by a judge. Once the matter is resolved, either through trial or settlement, the matter goes back to a referee to address any issues that may arise after the divorce is finalized. If you disagree with a referee's decision, you can appeal it to a judge. In Ramsey County, you may be assigned a referee or judge. There is no appeal to a judge from a referee's decision in Ramsey County.

PRETRIAL

PREHEARING
STATEMENT

A *pretrial* is a hearing. It is an opportunity to settle a case with some input from the judicial officer. If settlement is not likely, the court will use this opportunity to determine the issues that must be tried. If the court believes further discussion may result in settlement or that the issues are not ready for trial, the court may set another pretrial. If settlement is not likely and the case is ready for trial, the court will set a trial. Each party must prepare a PREHEARING STATEMENT. (see form 14, p.224.) This document must be served and filed at least ten days before the pretrial. There is a filled-in sample in Appendix A.

This is the document the court uses to prepare for the pretrial. (see form 14, p.224.) This is the last stage before trial and the court needs to have a quick reference to get a grasp of the case and try to narrow the issues for trial. This form is very similar to the APPLICATION FOR TEMPORARY RELIEF. Please refer to the completed PREHEARING STATEMENT in Appendix A.

NOTE: *A number of the questions ask you to attach documents (e.g. custody/access proposal for the children, budget, paystubs, nonmarital claims). There are forms included with headings to assist in preparing a complete*

PREHEARING STATEMENT. This document must be served on your spouse and filed at least ten days before the hearing (thirteen days by mail).

☛ Fill in the caption as instructed on page 7 under SUMMONS.

☛ Paragraph 1: Indicate for both parties their full name, address, employer, employer's address, date of birth and age, date of the marriage, date of the separation, and the date of any temporary order in the case.

☛ In the next section, provide information about the children including their full name, date of birth, age, and which party they are living with. On the next line indicate whether the wife is pregnant and, if so, indicate the due date. Next indicate whether custody is contested. Finally, you must attach a separate sheet indicating your proposed custody and parent access schedule.

☛ Paragraph 2: Provide employment information for each party including name of employer, length of employment, income and deductions. This information can be taken from the CHILD SUPPORT CALCULATION WORKSHEET (form 1). In part (b) indicate the other available employment benefits and indicate whether medical or dental insurance will be available to your spouse. In party (c) indicate whether there is any other type of income for either spouse.

☛ Paragraph 3: Indicate whether child support or spousal maintenance is received from a separate proceeding. If yes indicate the amounts, who receives it, the county of the court that ordered it, and the date. In part (b) indicate whether either party is paying child support or maintenance to someone in a separate case. Finally, in part (c) indicate the amount of support paid in this proceeding.

☛ Paragraph 4: state your monthly living expenses. Then attach as Exhibit 4A a detailed budget. (There is a blank form provided.)

☛ Paragraph 5: For the homestead fill in the date the property was acquired, the purchase price, the present value, the mortgage balance, the second mortgage balance, if any, the net value, the monthly payment, and any rental income. Do the same for any other real property. If there is more than one such additional property, provide the information in a separate sheet.

☛ Paragraph 6: For the husband in line (a) indicate value of household contents in his possession, the value of stocks and bonds and other investments, the value of checking and savings and checking accounts, the value of receivables and claims, and a blank for other property. Then do the same for the wife in the next column and for joint property in the third column. In part (e) you address the cars. For each car indicate the make and model, market value, amount owed, net value, monthly payment, and which party has the car. In part (f) do the same for any recreational vehicles. In part (g) do the same for power equipment, tools, guns, valuable animals, etc.

☛ Paragraph 7: Indicate any claimed items of nonmarital property and the value of the claim. In a separate sheet which you will call "Exhibit 7A" provide the basis for the nonmarital claim.

☛ Paragraph 8: For each life insurance policy, provide the name of the company, the policy number, the type of insurance (term, universal life, whole life, etc.), the face amount of the benefit, the cash value (if any), outstanding loans against the policy, the name of the insured party, the name of the beneficiary, and the name of the owner.

☛ Paragraph 9: Pension or profit sharing plans are addressed. Part (a) addresses plans through your employment. For the husband's plan indicate the cash value and whether the plan is vested or unvested. In part (b) indicated the value of any other retirement assets. In part (c) indicate the value of any other deferred compensation plans. In part (d) indicate whether there is any military disability or pension plan.

☛ Paragraph 10: In part (a) indicate any other secured debts other than those indicated earlier. *Secured* debts are those that have collateral. Most people do not have secured debts other than those on their real estate or motor vehicle. In part (b) state the debts owed by the husband, the wife, and the parties jointly. You will attach a separate sheet detailing debts as Exhibit 9B. (That form is included.)

☛ Date and sign the document. Cross off either petitioner or respondent, whichever one you are not.

☛ Fill out the necessary Exhibits that are included (Use the sample in Appendix A as your guide.)

MARITAL TERMINATION AGREEMENT

A MARITAL TERMINATION AGREEMENT (MTA) is the settlement agreement between the parties. (see form 15, p.234.) It must state in detail the terms of the agreement. It must be done right as it is difficult and expensive to make changes. Some items are virtually impossible to change if you later believe the terms are unfair.

In Appendix A there is a completed MARITAL TERMINATION AGREEMENT to assist in drafting your agreement. All issues must be addressed. Any issues not addressed may be waived.

This is the contract that dissolves the marriage, determines the child-rearing arrangement, division of assets, and all other issues in the divorce, you should review the completed MARITAL TERMINATION AGREEMENT with an attorney.

This document incorporates a broad range of situations. However, if you simply use it as is, the deletions and modifications may become cumbersome. It is advisable to retype this document. (see form 15, p.234.)

☞ Fill in the caption as instructed on page 7 under SUMMONS.

☞ Initially, the "Whereas" clauses are standard.

☞ Insert the date of service of the SUMMONS and PETITION on the second "Whereas" clause, and the rest of this section is left intact.

☞ Paragraphs 1-5 are fairly standard and will be left as written in most cases. Review them carefully. Delete paragraph 5 if there are no children.

☞ Paragraph 6: This paragraph allows you to consider either a custody arrangement or a parenting plan. If you select the first paragraph 6 on the blank form, you will need to complete a PARENTING PLAN (see form 17, p.249.). If you select the second version, indicate who will have physical custody. In the next sentence indicate who will have legal custody. Then attach as Appendix B a parenting time schedule for the noncustodial parent. If custody will be joint make Appendix B an access schedule.

☞ Paragraph 7: This section is for a couple using a parenting plan. If it is not appropriate to your situation, simply delete it.

☞ Paragraph 8: This is standard language, unless the parents and court agree otherwise, or there is domestic abuse.

☞ Paragraph 9: This paragraph sets forth a requirement of mediation. This paragraph should not be used in cases of domestic abuse. Child support is excluded from mediation in this version. However, you can delete that provision to allow for mediation of child support issues. This clause all but prohibits the parties from going to court until they try to mediate first.

☞ Paragraph 10: Child support should be awarded as set forth in Chapter 6. If there is a joint custody arrangement, child support still must be addressed. It is possible to create triggers for termination of support in the order. However, that requires very detailed drafting, depending on the number of children, that cannot be accomplished here. There are two paragraphs to choose from. If you chose the second, indicate who will be paying. Next, fill in the amount of support. In the next paragraph indicate who will be paying and who will be receiving support directly until Automatic Income Withholding Commences.

NOTE: *If you do not intend to use Automatic Income Withholding, simply delete the references to it and indicate that the parties have agreed that it is in the best interests of the children that child support be paid directly.*

☞ Paragraph 11: It is common practice to include some arrangement for insurance in the event of either parties' death. A common amount is $50,000-100,000 depending on the income, age, and number of children. As drafted, both parties are required to maintain the same amount of insurance. However, this could be modified to address specific concerns.

☞ Paragraph 12 and 13: The issue of medical insurance for the children must be addressed by law. The statute suggests that uninsured expenses should be apportioned between the parties based upon their income. However, as a practical matter parties often agree to divide the cost. You must indicate who will provide the coverage. In paragraph 12 select a paragraph and indicate who will provide insurance. In paragraph 13 select a paragraph and indicate the proportions that each party will pay if you chose the second paragraph.

☞ Paragraph 14: There are two versions of this paragraph. You can delete the paragraph that does not apply. If there is no maintenance, temporary maintenance, or permanent maintenance, you must so indicate by using the first paragraph 14. The first version waives maintenance forever. The second version allows you to select a permanent or temporary award. There are a number of other arrangements that can be considered. If spousal maintenance is at issue you should consult an attorney in drafting this agreement. (Remember: the two versions of paragraph 14 are mutually exclusive. You may pick only one. You may also want to include insurance for spousal maintenance like child support in paragraph 10. You may simply write this provision in here.)

☞ Paragraph 15: This section addresses the right to continued medical coverage through a spouse. This right is guaranteed by law, but it sometimes helps to have the language in the divorce decree. Simply indicate which spouse will need the coverage through the other's plan.

☞ Paragraph 16: This section contemplates the home being awarded to one party and the other being awarded a lien interest for some period of time. There is some risk in granting a lien as it may be discharged in bankruptcy in some, very limited circumstances. This section also contemplates the occupant refinancing to remove the other spouse's name from the mortgage.

In part (a) fill in the street address and county of the case. You will also need to fill in the legal description. Next indicate who has the lien, the amount, and when it is payable. Then indicate that the party in possession shall release the other from any obligation on the land or delete this sentence. In part (e) fill in the county in which the property is located in the two blanks.

If you chose the second paragraph, fill in all blanks as instructed.

☞ Paragraph 17: This is standard language.

☞ Paragraph 18: You should separate property by the time you enter into an agreement. If that is not possible, it is important to include a list of exactly what items are to be exchanged or that opportunity may be lost forever. Choose the paragraph that best fits your situation.

☛ Paragraph 19: Fill in the petitioner's vehicle in the first part and the respondent's vehicle in the second. The blank space is to add additional motor vehicles.

☛ Paragraph 20: (It is best to divide accounts before settlement.)

☛ Paragraph 21: (Again, it is best to divide accounts before settlement. However, you can select the second option to state the division if that has not been done and indicate which account is awarded to each party.)

☛ Paragraph 22: If you need to divide pension plans it is essential to have an attorney to draft this provision. If you intend to simply leave the plans as divided, use the recommended language. If not, indicate in the second version of paragraph 22 who is to get which plan.

☛ Paragraph 23: You can elect to divide the exemptions equally, award all to one parent, award an odd numbered exemption to one parent in even years and the other in odd, etc. If this issue is not addressed, the custodial parent gets the exemptions.

☛ Paragraph 24: Pick one of the two options or create another. Consult your tax advisor on the most beneficial filing status.

☛ Paragraphs 25 and 26: These are standard in most cases.

☛ Paragraph 27: List the debts in the blank space including amount owed then assign the debts in the following part a or b.

☛ Paragraph 28: Choose one of the paragraphs to indicate whether or not anyone's name will change.

☛ Paragraph 29-32: These are standard paragraphs.

☛ Paragraph 33: This is a complete release. If you have any potential claims against your spouse for abuse or other misbehavior, consult an attorney.

☛ Paragraph 34 and 35: These are standard paragraphs.

☛ Both parties must sign the agreement before a notary. (You must also sign the WAIVER OF COUNSEL, discussed next.)

☛ "Form 3: Appendix A" **must** be attached. (It is at the end of form 15 on page 244.)

WAIVER OF COUNSEL
(form 16)

You must also sign the WAIVER OF COUNSEL. (see form 16, p.248.) If either or both parties are not represented by counsel he, she, or both must sign a WAIVER OF COUNSEL before a notary.

☞ In the first paragraph write in petitioner's name, then the petitioner must sign before a notary.

☞ Then fill in respondent's name and have respondent sign before a notary.

PARENTING PLAN

If your case is going to include a PARENTING PLAN (see Chapter 5), you will need to complete one. (see form 17, p.249.) Complete the caption and then fill in the remainder of the form as appropriate to your case. (See Chapter 5 for more details.)

DEFAULT

Most cases are resolved by default in some form. A *pure* default is one in which the opposing party simply fails to respond and the divorce is resolved without the other side participating in the process in any way. The more common form of default occurs when the parties reach an agreement that is submitted to the court by one party as a default. This type of default is purely technical in nature and does not harm the defaulting party as the defaulting party has approved the agreement and the terms of that agreement are approved by the court.

ADMINISTRATIVE DISSOLUTION

In certain situations, the matter may be submitted to the court for approval without a hearing:

● if there are no minor children and the parties have reached an agreement;

- if there are no minor children, the respondent has not answered the petition, and twenty days have elapsed in addition to the thirty days as stated in the SUMMONS;

- if there are children, the parties have signed an agreement, which is **acknowledged**, and the parties are represented by counsel. (Minn. Stat., Sec. 518.13, Subd. 5.)

DEFAULT
SCHEDULING
REQUEST
(form 21)

If your case is resolved without a·trial, you must complete the DEFAULT SCHEDULING REQUEST (see form 21, p.274.) This document tells the court administrator how to schedule your case. Generally, if there are children, there will have to be a hearing. If not, a hearing can be avoided.

☞ Complete the caption as instructed on page 7 under SUMMONS.

☞ If there is a signed agreement and no minor children, check the first and third line.

☞ If this is a pure default and there are no children, check lines one and four.

☞ If there are children check lines five and six and schedule a hearing.

☞ Fill in the signature block and date. This document must be filed with the court and a copy sent to your spouse.

JUDGMENT AND DECREE

The final document dissolving the marriage and awarding property to the parties is the FINDINGS OF FACT, CONCLUSIONS OF LAW, ORDER FOR JUDGMENT and JUDGMENT AND DECREE. (see form 18, p.258.) Each of these terms has significance. The *Findings of Fact* are important in that they are a statement of the factual determination either agreed to by the parties or decided by the court. Even in a case in which there is agreement, the findings are very important. They could affect a later award of child support or spousal maintenance. The *Conclusions of Law* set out the terms of the agreement or decision of the court including specific amounts of child support, maintenance, custody, parenting time, property division, and all other issues between the parties. The *Order for Judgment* is the direction by the court to the court administrator to enter a judgment. **The *judgment* reflects the fact that the decision is for money such as child support, maintenance, or transfer of valuable property.** The term *Decree* reflects the finality of the decision. This final document is often simply called the *Judgment and Decree* or *Decree*.

A decree is final when the court administrator enters it. (Minn. Stat., Sec. 518.145, Subd. 1.) Issues within the divorce may be appealed, but the divorce itself is granted. Only in very limited circumstances may a party reopen a decree. (Minn. Stat., Sec. 518.145, Subd. 2.)

The JUDGMENT AND DECREE must contain the following notice:

A person may be charged with a felony who conceals a minor child or takes, obtains, retains, or fails to return a minor child from or to the child's parent (or person with custodial or visitation rights), according to <u>Minnesota Statutes, section 609.26</u>. A copy of that section is available from any district court clerk.

This document is created by putting together the facts alleged in the PETITION with the terms of the MARITAL TERMINATION AGREEMENT. The Findings of Fact are far more specific than the general allegations of the petitioner. The agreement language of the MARITAL TERMINATION AGREEMENT is changed to commanding language of the court in the *Conclusions of Law*. (Minn. Stat., Sec. 518.177.) There is a filled-in sample in Appendix A. If you follow the directions from the PETITION and the MARITAL TERMINATION AGREEMENT, you will be able to complete this document. (Don't forget to attach "Form 3: Appendix A" found on page 244 after form 15.)

CERTIFICATE OF DISSOLUTION

In addition to the JUDGMENT AND DECREE, a separate CERTIFICATE OF DISSOLUTION may be prepared. (Minn. Stat., Sec. 518.148.) (see form 24, p.278.)

Fill out the CERTIFICATE OF DISSOLUTION as follows:

☞ Fill in the caption as instructed on page 7 under SUMMONS.

☛ In the first "Whereas," fill in your present name.

☛ In the second, fill in your maiden name.

☛ Indicate that the marriage of the parties is dissolved and the date will be filled in at court.

☛ In the "ORDERED" blank, fill in your legal name after divorce (usually maiden). The judge will then sign and date. (Minn. Stat., Sec. 518.148, Subd. 2.)

This document should be sent to the court with the JUDGMENT AND DECREE.

The CERTIFICATE OF DISSOLUTION is often used when there is a name change involved. For example, when changing names on accounts or to perform other acts which may require proof of a name change or divorce. Rather than providing the entire JUDGMENT AND DECREE, you may simply provide a certified copy of the CERTIFICATE OF DISSOLUTION.

REPRESENTATION, RESOURCES, AND RESOLUTION 3

If you are considering representing yourself, you should at least consider having an experienced family law attorney review any settlement agreement before signing it. For a couple hundred dollars, you could save thousands of dollars. If you have contested issues, you must consider having an attorney. If any of the following issues are contested in your case, it is essential to have an attorney:

> Custody
> Pension division
> Real estate
> Medical insurance
> Spousal maintenance
> Domestic abuse
> Business valuation
> Nonmarital property claims

This book cannot begin to address the additional, often subtle, aspects of a case that an experienced family law attorney must consider. These include the background of the assigned judge, the background of opposing counsel, the issues in the case, the level of emotion involved in the case, and how objectively you are able to understand your case. In addition, there are considerations about how the court processes the cases, which will vary considerably county-to-county and even judge-to-judge.

There are considerations of how a mediator handles cases and your ability to stand up for yourself and successfully mediate, if that is an option. This is only a part of what you and your lawyer must consider in handling your case.

SURVIVING THE PROCESS

The stress of the divorce process can be overwhelming. Many people going through a divorce experience some level of depression or other mental health problem. It is essential that you seek support. Perhaps seek the assistance of a therapist or support group. Some people have the support of family or friends to sustain them. Your attorney is not trained to deal with the psychological issues. You are much better off seeking the advice of a trained therapist (who may be covered by your insurance).

SELECTING AND WORKING WITH AN ATTORNEY

Selecting an attorney can be one of the most important decisions of your life. Your attorney will be involved with you in intimate details during each step of your proceedings.

SOURCES   **Minnesota State Bar Association.** A majority of the attorneys in Minnesota belong to the Minnesota State Bar Association (MSBA) making it the largest professional association for lawyers in Minnesota. The MSBA maintains a referral service for greater Minnesota. They can also provide information on the referral services of your local county bar associations in the Twin Cities area. Their website is

http://www.mnbar.org/attref.htm

American Academy of Matrimonial Lawyers. The Minnesota Chapter of the American Academy of Matrimonial Lawyers (AAML) is a professional organization of family law attorneys. The members are carefully screened and usually have ten or more years of experience in practice. With that level of experience comes a much higher price tag on their hourly rates. Their website is:

http://www.wizmo.com/_public/website/Generalasp?pageID=5666

Collaborative Law Institute. Collaborative Law Institute (CLI) is a professional organization of attorneys. If both parties hire a collaborative attorney, they will agree to settle the matter without going to court. Issues are generally resolved through four-way conferences between the parties and attorneys. Issues that cannot be resolved may be submitted to a neutral expert. In a traditional case, the attorneys are preparing to prove their case to a judge. In a collaborative case, the attorneys focus on preparing for settlement. Collaborative cases tend to be less contentious and less expensive. Their website is:

http://www.collaborativelaw.org

Union. AFL-CIO affiliated unions may participate in a program called "Union Privilege" under which attorneys will work on cases for a discount in fees.

Insurance Program. There are a number of prepaid legal plans. Often they are a benefit of employment. Attorneys screened through such a program must meet qualifications of the plan. The plan may not cover the attorney you want.

OTHER CONSIDERATIONS

You may want to check into an attorney's qualifications. You can contact the Lawyer's Professional Responsibility Board to determine whether there has been public discipline. You should also find out whether your attorney maintains malpractice insurance. In the event of a missed deadline or overlooked document, you want to know that you are protected. You can also ask for references. However, most family law clients will not want to discuss their marital history with a stranger. Speaking with family or friends who have been through the process is a good way to screen attorneys. Also, there are a number of support organizations, such as Chrysalis (A Center for Women). Their phone number is: (612) 871-0118

FEES AND
RETAINERS

There is a tremendous range in the hourly rates attorneys charge. It depends on a number of factors including the years of experience of the attorney, the size of the firm, or the complexity of the case. A down-town firm may charge more than a suburban or neighborhood attorney due to differences in overhead. An attorney in a large metro area may charge more than an attorney in a smaller town. An attorney who focuses on family law may charge more than a general practitioner.

Family law attorneys require an initial payment to cover the work on the case called a *retainer*. The size of the retainers varies dramatically. It will depend in part on the hourly rate and the complexity of the case. It may be a few hundred dollars or several thousand dollars.

It is virtually impossible to anticipate the costs of attorney fees in a family law case. If both parties agree and simply have the attorney draft the papers and little else, the cost can be as little as a few hundred dollars. At the other end of the spectrum it is not unusual for a contested custody case to cost tens of thousands of dollars.

It is possible to seek an award of attorney fees from the opposing party. However, an award of attorney fees is by no means guaranteed. In addition, it is rare that the award of fees meets the need of the party seeking fees.

If you are unable to afford an attorney there are legal aid programs available throughout the State. Most people do not qualify for such programs. Legal aid agencies have guidelines as to the kinds of cases they take. Their services are reserved for those unable to afford an attorney. Cases involving children or domestic abuse take priority. Non-domestic abuse cases may be placed on a waiting list for six months or more. You may be assigned to a staff attorney who knows family law or a volunteer attorney who may or may not normally handle family matters.

RETAINER
AGREEMENTS

Though not technically required, virtually all family law attorneys will ask you to sign a written agreement concerning the financial arrangements between you and the attorney. At the very least you can expect a letter confirming the terms of representation. Generally agreements will lay out hourly rates and costs of a case at the very least. It is essential that you read this agreement. You will be bound by the terms of the agreement. Some agreements provide for non-refundable retainers. (If it is in the agreement, it is permitted.)

ETHICAL RULES

Your attorney is governed by certain ethical rules that limit how he or she can conduct your case, but also require him or her to do certain things to further your cause. The following is a summary of the rules most relevant to family law matters:

At a fundamental level, the lawyer must be competent in his or her representation. (Minnesota Rules of Professional Conduct (Minn. R. of Prof. Con.), 1.1.) The lawyer must pursue your case with promptness and diligence. (Minn. R. of Prof. Con., 1.3.) The lawyer must keep you informed about the progress of your case and promptly comply with requests for information. (Minn. R. of Prof. Con., 1.4(a).) Further, the lawyer must explain matters to you to an extent sufficient to permit you to make informed decisions. (Minn. R. of Prof. Con., 1.4(b).) The lawyer's fees must be reasonable in light of the time and effort the case requires; the customary fees; the experience of the attorney; and a number of other factors. (Minn. R. of Prof. Con., 1.5.) The lawyer should, but is not required, to have a fee agreement in writing. (Minn. R. of Prof. Con., 1.5(b).) A fee arrangement in a family law matter cannot be *contingent* on the outcome (i.e. a lawyer cannot take a percentage of an award of property, child support, or maintenance.) (Minn. R. of Prof. Con., 1.5(d).)

Confidentiality. One of the basics of the attorney-client relationship is the *confidentiality*. A lawyer may not reveal client information, use a client's information to the disadvantage of a client, or use information for the advantage of the lawyer or a third party without the consent of the client. (Minn. R. of Prof. Con., 1.6(a).) However a lawyer may reveal a client's information if: it evidences an intent to commit a crime; a court order requires it; it is necessary to rectify the consequences of a client's criminal or fraudulent act in which the lawyer's services were used; or a lawyer needs to collect a fee or defend against an allegation of improper conduct. (Minn. R. of Prof. Con., 1.6(b).)

Scope of Representation*.* An ethics issue most relevant to family law is determining the scope of representation. It is not unusual for someone to go to a family law attorney for the limited purpose of reviewing documents drafted by the other spouse's attorney. At the other end of the spectrum it is not unusual for someone to hire a family law attorney to handle a divorce and the attorney ends up handling an Order for Protection and a criminal domestic abuse charge as well. You and your lawyer must be clear on the scope of representation and whether your lawyer will handle other matters as well. (Minn. R. of Prof. Con., 1.2(a).) However, a lawyer cannot counsel a client to or assist a client in conduct that the lawyer knows is criminal or fraudulent. (Minn. R. of Prof. Con., 1.2(c).)

Loyalty*.* A lawyer owes a duty of loyalty to a client. A lawyer must avoid *conflict of interest*. (Minn. R. of Prof. Con., 1.7.) For example, it is not unusual for both sides of a case to coincidentally call one attorney. On some occasions the lawyer may represent a party to a dissolution and then represent that party's boyfriend or girlfriend at the same time. There may be some conflicts of interest in such representation.

Your lawyer may not enter into any business transactions with you unless he has notified you in writing that independent counsel should be considered. (Minn. R. of Prof. Con., 1.8(a).) Most recently, a rule prohibiting sexual relations between a lawyer and a client has been added. (Minn. R. of Prof. Con., 1.8(k).)

Family lawyers are frequently asked to represent both sides in a case. The short answer is that it can be done with the permission of both clients. (Minn. R. of Prof. Con., 2.2.) However, such representation is fraught with pitfalls. You cannot ask even the most simple of questions without the attorney being obliged to provide the information to your spouse.

Retainer*.* In most cases, when you retain a lawyer, you will be charged a *retainer* (fee for services). Unless otherwise agreed to, the attorney must deposit the money into a trust account. In addition, there may be circumstances under which your lawyer holds on to some other funds. This could be from a tax return or the equity from the sale of a home. The lawyer is the *trustee* of such account. However, trust accounts are monitored through the Minnesota Supreme Court to ensure that the funds are properly protected. (Minn. R. of Prof. Con., 1.15(a).) In addition, Minnesota attorneys pay into a fund to pay for any improperly used trust funds.

Duty to the Court and Opposing Party. A lawyer has a duty of *candor* toward the court. (Minn. R. of Prof. Con., 3.3.) This issue most often arises when the client offers testimony the lawyer knows to be false. The lawyer must rectify the situation or face discipline. The lawyer also has a duty of fairness to an opposing counsel and opposing party. (Minn. R. of Prof. Con., 3.4.) The lawyer may not obstruct the other party's access to documents; may not alter or destroy documents; make a frivolous discovery request; or request a third party to refrain from voluntarily giving evidence.

A lawyer is limited in dealing with third parties. (Minn. R. of Prof. Con., 4.1.) A lawyer may not communicate directly with an opposing party who is represented by counsel. Clients frequently ask their attorney to call the other side to arrange visitation or deal with a small issue. The attorney must go through the other side's attorney resulting in both sides paying fees. Usually it is best for the parties to work out these issues themselves or use some other intermediary. In dealing with an unrepresented opposing party, an attorney cannot give legal advice.

A lawyer violating these rules is subject to discipline. Depending on the severity of the violation, the lawyer may be privately or publicly admonished, suspended from practice, or disbarred from practice. A complaint of unethical conduct is something the lawyer takes very seriously as his or her reputation and livelihood can be placed in jeopardy. If you believe there has been unethical conduct, you should contact the Lawyer's Professional Responsibility Board at:

http://www.courts.state.mn.us/lprb/olprbroch.html

(651)296-3952; or (800) 657-3601

RESOURCES

There are a number of books used by lawyers to research specific issues. Often the first reference is *Minnesota Statutes Annotated* (Minn. Stat.) by West Publishing. The relevant volume contains section 518--the portion of the statute that deals with divorce proceedings. In addition, at the end of each section of the statute, there are *annotations* that include brief summaries of relevant cases and articles. However, it appears West is no longer updating the article annotations. *Minnesota Statutes Annotated* is found in many public libraries and all law libraries in Minnesota.

CASE
REPORTERS

Other important resources for attorneys are the *Northwestern Case Reporters* (N.W. or N.W. 2d). This publication includes the published decisions of the Minnesota Court of Appeals and all of the decisions of the Minnesota Supreme Court. It also contains cases from other neighboring states. These decisions come from cases of people who have not agreed with the decision of the trial court judge and have sought review by the Minnesota Court of Appeals and, in some cases, the Minnesota Supreme Court. While these cases are helpful in telling us how to interpret the laws, these people may have spent tens of thousands of dollars to get to that point. You do not want to be one of those people whose name is in these volumes.

It is relatively easy to find the case you want in the West Reporters. For example, if you wish to find *Ayers v. Ayers*, 508 N.W.2d 515 (Minn. 1993) you simply have to find the *Northwestern Case Reporter* second series. (N.W. 2d.) Of this set you must find volume 508 (the first number). Turn to page 515 (the last number). It is as simple as that.

ONLINE
RESOURCES

A leading Internet portal is found at **http://www.lawnmouse.com**. It provides cases, attorney websites, referral sources, and a variety of other helpful information.

ALTERNATIVE DISPUTE RESOLUTION

Alternative Dispute Resolution (ADR) refers to a number of different processes designed to settle a case without the involvement of the court. ADR is required in virtually all cases unless there is a history of domestic abuse. The following are more conducive to family law.

MEDIATION

Mediation is the most frequently used form of ADR. It involves a trained neutral person who meets with the parties to guide them to a settlement. In some counties, the court provides mediators on issues concerning the children at little or no cost. Property and other issues may require a private mediator. Fees charged by the mediator can vary greatly. If the court appoints a mediator, you will be stuck with that individual regardless of the fees charged. Therefore, it is wise to select a mediator before the court decides for you. Generally, the mediator meets only with the parties. In a few cases, the attorneys will also be present. If you do not feel you can successfully negotiate for yourself, you may have your attorney attend mediation or try to get out of mediation entirely.

The actions and concessions of a party during mediation are not *discoverable*, meaning the other party cannot use them in court. (Minn. Stat. Section (Sec.), 518.619, Subdivision (Subd.) 5.) Even if there is a mediated agreement, until it is submitted to the court with the agreement of both parties, it is not binding. (Minn. Stat. Sec., 518.619, Subd. 7.)

The mediator cannot force you into a settlement. The mediator can keep the parties focused and have the parties exchange information. If the parties reach an impasse, the case may have to go to court to resolve any remaining issues.

You can select a mediator by checking the yellow pages of the telephone book. (Some mediation services offer a sliding fee scale.) You can also contact the Family Court Administrator at your county courthouse for a list of mediators.

ARBITRATION

Arbitration occurs when you hire a neutral decision-maker rather than using a judge. The benefit of using an arbitrator is that you can schedule a trial or motion on your own terms rather than waiting in line behind the hundreds of other cases the judge is handling. Arbitration can be very expensive. Not only are you paying your attorney, but you are also paying the arbitrator. The arbitrator will act as a judge, issuing orders that are enforceable like any court order.

You will only use arbitration if you have an attorney. You can work with your attorney to select an arbitrator. Arbitrators are selected from among experienced attorneys and retired judges. The arbitrator will hold a proceeding like a trial, and issue a decision on any contested issues.

Sometimes, you may use a hybrid process in which the neutral person first attempts to settle the dispute, then decides the issues if that does not work. Visitation expeditors, discussed later, resolve child-related disputes in this way.

COLLABORATIVE LAW

Collaborative law is a process under which the parties agree to resolve their disputes without going to court. Though many cases are settled in a collaborative manner, the process has been formalized through the Collaborative Law Institute (CLI).

If both parties hire CLI attorneys and agree to proceed collaboratively the cost of the case will be greatly reduced. Documents are exchanged informally rather than through formal discovery. Unresolved issues are submitted to neutral experts to assist in resolution rather than going through a judge. The attorneys and parties meet together to discuss settlement in four-way conferences rather than going through a mediator.

If the case truly reaches an impasse and the case cannot be resolved, the attorneys withdraw and allow the case to proceed to court. However, the financial and emotional costs of changing attorneys acts as a significant impediment to dropping the collaborative process.

To hire a collaborative attorney check the CLI website at:

http://www Collaborativelaw.org

CUSTODY AND PARENTING TIME 4

Minnesota now gives an option to pursue one of two tracks on issues related to children. There is the longstanding arrangement for custody and *parenting time* (formerly called visitation). Issues related to custody are frequently the most contentious in a case. The battle may be over the label of *custodial parent* with one parent "losing custody". The battle may be over child support as the party losing custody pays support. Emotional issues from the marriage may carry into the divorce as a custody battle as that is the only way to vent some of the history of the marriage. All professionals involved in the process have long recognized that the children are the real losers in this situation. Children see the stress of their parents as the process drags on. They may be coached to see things one parent's way. They play one parent against the other. In addition, many assume blame for the divorce itself.

The alternative to a custody battle is to request a *parenting plan*. Essentially the same things can be accomplished in a parenting plan as can be accomplished with a custody and parenting time schedule. However, it is hoped that by reducing the importance of the custody label, there will be fewer contentious cases brought through the courts. The parenting plan is discussed in Chapter 5.

CUSTODY

PHYSICAL
CUSTODY

The court is required to order custody that is in the *best interests* of the children. (Minn. Stat., Sec., 518.17, Subd. 3(a)(3).) Minnesota law provides thirteen factors for the court to consider. (Minn. Stat., Sec., 518.17, Subd. 1(a).) These factors are not the exclusive criteria the court must use, but failure to consider them may result in a reversal of the court's decision on custody. The thirteen factors, with explanations, are set as follows:

(1) the wishes of the child's parent or parents as to custody;

Obviously, the wishes of parent or parents are extremely important. If the parents are in agreement, there is no custody case.

(2) the reasonable preference of the child, if the court deems the child to be of sufficient age to express preference;

This information is generally provided through the custody investigation report or through testimony of a therapist. It is infrequent that the child testifies.

(3) the child's primary caretaker;

This is often seen as the heart of the matter. The primary caretaker is an important consideration, but not the exclusive consideration. Things to point out to the custody evaluator and the court include preparing meals, laundry, dishes, shopping for the children, taking the children to medical and dental appointments, taking time off from work to care for a sick child, scheduling dental appointments, arranging for and transporting to activities, reading to the children, attending school conferences, etc.

(4) the intimacy of the relationship between each parent and the child;

This includes such things as physical affection, and who the child goes to when hurt, sick, or upset. The custody evaluator looks for displays of physical affection and stories about the involvement of each parent in the children's lives.

(5) the interaction and interrelationship of the child with a parent or parents, siblings, and any other person who may significantly affect the child's best interests;

This factor brings into play the other individuals involved in the child's life such as grandparents, significant others, or family friends. The court may frown upon involving boyfriends or girlfriends with the children.

(6) the child's adjustment to home, school, and community;

This factor focuses on stability of the environment for the children. One important thing the court looks at is who will provide the most stability. If you want custody of the children, you may not want to leave the family home. Ensuring that the children will be able to remain in the same home and school, if possible, is very important. This factor is closely tied to the next two.

(7) the length of time the child has lived in a stable, satisfactory environment and the desirability of maintaining continuity;

If one parent has moved out of the home, that parent is unlikely to go back into the home and thus may have a difficult time getting custody. This is not to say that it does not happen that the children end up with the parent who moved out, but it is more difficult.

(8) the permanence, as a family unit, of the existing or proposed custodial home;

Again, stability for the child is extremely important. It is beneficial to remain in the home with the children. This factor often comes into play when someone is seeking to change a custody determination down the road.

(9) the mental and physical health of all individuals involved; except that a disability, (as defined in Minnesota Statutes, Section 363.01), of a proposed custodian or the child shall not be determinative of the custody of the child, unless the proposed custodial arrangement is not in the best interest of the child;

Mental health problems are frequently a contributing factor in a divorce. A parent with a diagnosed mental illness may still be able to prevail in a custody case if that parent is following the recommendations of a psychiatrist or psychologist in treating the illness. Physical disabilities seem less prevalent. So long as the physical or mental disability does not significantly impair the ability to care for the children, it should not play a great role in the case.

(10) the capacity and disposition of the parties to give the child love, affection, and guidance, and to continue educating and raising the child in the child's culture and religion or creed, if any;

The first part of this factor seems to duplicate factor 5 concerning the interaction with the child. The latter part of this factor addresses the intention of the parties to maintain cultural or religious traditions of the child. Again, this reinforces the importance of stability for the child. This factor comes into play when there is a difference in religion or culture between the parties.

(11) the child's cultural background;

Like factor 10, this addresses cultural issues. If the relationship is not intercultural, this factor is often ignored. If there is an intercultural relationship, the court must consider the traditions the child has followed and which parent is most likely to ensure the child continues to observe those traditions.

(12) the effect on the child of the actions of an abuser, if related to domestic abuse (as defined in Minnesota Statutes, Section 518B.01), that has occurred between the parents or between a parent and another individual, whether or not the individual alleged to have committed domestic abuse is or ever was a family or household member of the parent;

Obviously being a victim of domestic abuse is damaging to a child. Observing domestic abuse or observing the damage caused by domestic abuse can also be harmful to the child. The language is broad and is intended to encompass a situation in which the children may be affected by domestic violence committed by a parent on a third party or by third party on a parent.

(13) except in cases in which a finding of domestic abuse has been made, the disposition of each parent to encourage and permit frequent and continuing contact by the other parent with the child.

One of the most frustrating aspects of a divorce involving children is the action of a parent who attempts to interfere with the relationship between the child and the other parent. The legislature is attempting to address this factor up front by requiring the court to consider which parent is most likely to ensure a continuing relationship with the other parent.

The court must consider all thirteen factors and make specific findings on each of the factors. Though the *primary caretaker* factor has historically been the most important factor, the court is not permitted to consider that factor or any other to the exclusion of the other twelve factors. (Minn. Stat., Sec., 518.17, Subd. 1.)

In addition to the thirteen factors, the court is to consider evidence of false allegations of child abuse in determining the best interests of the child.

(Minn. Stat., Sec., 518.17, Subd.1a.) The court is explicitly directed not to consider conduct of a proposed custodian that does not affect the custodian's relationship to the child. (Minn. Stat., Sec., 518.17, Subd.1(b).)

JOINT PHYSICAL CUSTODY

When either party is seeking joint physical custody, the court must consider the factors listed above in addition to the following:

- the ability of parents to cooperate in the rearing of their children;

- methods for resolving disputes regarding any major decision concerning the life of the child, and the parents' willingness to use those methods;

- whether it would be detrimental to the child if one parent were to have sole authority over the child's upbringing; and

- whether domestic abuse has occurred between the parents.

The statute does not presume that joint physical custody is improper. However, as a practical matter, most judges assume that if the parties cannot get along well enough to agree on joint custody, they will not be able to effectively parent in a joint custody arrangement. Therefore, it is quite unusual to have a court award joint custody after a trial.

LEGAL CUSTODY

Joint legal custody concerns the right to participate in the child's upbringing, including education, health care, and religious training. (Minn. Stat., Sec. 518.003, Subd. 3(a).) This custody is presumed to be joint. (Minnesota Statutes Section 518.17, subd. 2.)

CUSTODIAL RIGHTS

In addition to awarding legal and physical custody, the court must grant the following rights:

- Each party has the right of access to, and to receive copies of, school, medical, dental, religious training, and other important records and information about the minor children.

- Each party has the right of access to information regarding health or dental insurance available to the minor children.

- Each party shall keep the other party informed as to the name and address of the school of attendance of the minor children.

- Each party has the right to be informed by school officials about the children's welfare, educational progress and status, and to attend school and parent-teacher conferences.

- The school is not required to hold a separate conference for each party.

- In case of an accident or serious illness of a minor child, each party shall notify the other party of the accident or illness, and the name of the health care provider and the place of treatment.

- Each party has the right to reasonable access and telephone contact with the minor children.

(Minn. Stat., Sec. 518.17, Subd. 3(b).) The court may waive these rights if it specifically explains why.

If your case proceeds down the custody path, you and your spouse must use the part of the statute concerning parenting time (formerly visitation).

PARENTING TIME

The term *parenting time* and *visitation* are to be used to reflect time with the children. It appears the legislature intended to replace the term visitation, but that will require additional legislation to completely eliminate "visitation" from the statute.

If either parent requests, the court is required to grant parenting time to the noncustodial parent to enable the parent and child to maintain a relationship that will be in the best interests of the child. (Minn. Stat., Sec. 518.175, Subd. 1(a).) However, if the parenting time is likely to endanger the child's physical or emotional health, or impair the child's emotional development, the court may limit or eliminate parenting time entirely. (Minn. Stat., Sec. 518.175, Subd. 1(a).)

The court is to establish a specific schedule if requested by either party. The schedule must address the frequency and duration of parenting time and establish a holiday and vacation schedule. (Minn. Stat., Sec. 518.175, Subd. 1(c).) Among the factors to consider in establishing a parenting time schedule, the court must consider whether there is a history of domestic abuse, the age of the child, and the child's relationship with the noncustodial parent. (Minn. Stat., Sec. 518.175, Subd. 1(a).)

If a child is in daycare, the court may allow additional visitation to the noncustodial parent while the other parent is working, if this is reasonable and in the best interest of the child. To make this determination, the court must consider the best interest factors set forth above in addition to (1) the ability of the parents to cooperate; (2) methods for resolving disputes; and (3) whether domestic abuse has occurred between the parties. (Minn. Stat., Sec. 518.175, Subd. 8.)

Parenting time is an area of frequent post-divorce conflict. It is important to consider how disputes will be resolved. A very common arrangement is to provide that visitation disputes shall be subject to mediation. However, mediation may not result in an agreement in some cases. Often, there is a need for someone to make a decision. The statute provides for a *visitation expeditor*. The expeditor will first attempt to mediate and then will make a decision. (Minn. Stat., Sec. 518.1751.) This is discussed in more detail in Chapter 9.

STATE OF
RESIDENCE OF
THE CHILD

One of the most difficult issues in a divorce (or post-divorce) arises when one parent must move out of state. Often people move to make a new start. Sometimes there is a job offer, a new relationship, or a return to where your family lives. There is never an easy answer. Minnesota Statutes, Section 518.175, Subd. 3 provides:

> The custodial parent shall not move the residence of the child to another state except upon order of the court or with the consent of the noncustodial parent, when the noncustodial parent has been given visitation rights by the decree. If the purpose of the move is to interfere with visitation rights given to the noncustodial parent by the decree, the court shall not permit the child's residence to be moved to another state.

Essentially, the custodial parent may leave the state with court permission if there is good cause for the move. The prime case on this issue provides that there is a presumption that the custodial parent may remove the child to another state unless the noncustodial parent can show that removal would endanger the child's physical or emotional health and is not in the best interests of the child, or that the sole purpose of the move is to interfere with the noncustodial parent's visitation rights. (*Auge v. Auge*, 334 N.W. 2d 393 (Minn. 1983).)

In a joint custody arrangement, the parent seeking to move must prove that it is in the best interests of the children. (*Ayers v. Ayers*, 508 N.W.

2d 515 (Minn. 1993).) This is a considerably more difficult standard for the moving parent to meet than in a sole custody case. In a sole custody case, the noncustodial parent seeking to block the move must prove that a move will endanger the child's emotional or physical health. If moving out of state is an issue, discuss it with your attorney immediately.

Custody Evaluation

In either the custody or parenting plan scheme (discussed in the next chapter), the court or the parties may seek recommendations of a professional—either court personnel or an outside expert. The recommendations are to be in writing and shall be available to all attorneys and parties. The professional may be cross-examined at trial. (Minn. Stat. Sec., 518.166.)

If a *private evaluator* is used (generally a licensed psychologist), he or she will conduct an evaluation using the professional and ethical requirements of his or her profession in addition to the best interests factors discussed in Chapter 3. (See Minn. Stat., Sec. 518.17.)

If a court services officer conducts the evaluation, the officer must follow the guidelines set forth in the statute. (Minn. Stat., Sec. 518.17.) As part of the investigation, any evaluator may consult with anyone who has information about the child and potential custody arrangements (except for a mediator), including medical, mental health, or school personnel. (Minn. Stat. Sec., 518.167, Subd. 2(a).) Any evaluator, if permitted by the court, may refer the child to a professional for diagnosis, such as a psychologist or psychiatrist. (Minn. Stat. Sec., 518.167, Subd. 2(a).)

The evaluator must consider the factors of the custody statutes in Chapter 4 and explain the information considered for each factor. (Minn. Stat. Sec., 518.167, Subd. 2(b).)

The evaluator will look for common history between parent and child. It is important to know the stages of development of the child including ages at which the child first spoke and walked, and any hospitalizations, surgeries, or other medical problems. During the home visit, the evaluator will observe the methods of discipline, displays of physical affection, and the routine of the family. The more knowledgeable a parent is about the children and about parenting, the better the results for that parent.

The evaluator must create a report based on all the gathered information. The report must be mailed to the attorneys for the parties (or a party who's not represented by counsel) at least ten days before the hearing. (Minn. Stat. Sec., 518.167, Subd. 3.) In addition, the evaluator's file must be made available for review by all parties and the judge. (Minn. Stat. Sec., 518.167, Subd. 3.) The evaluator's report is admissible in evidence at trial. (Minn. Stat. Sec., 518.167, Subd. 4.) The evaluator and any party consulted for the report may be called for cross-examination. (Minn. Stat. Sec., 518.167, Subd. 3.)

The court may order the parties to pay all or part of the costs of the investigation. (Minn. Stat. Sec., 518.167, Subd. 5.) A court services evaluation may cost $500 or more. A private evaluation will likely cost $5,000 or more.

GUARDIANS FOR CHILDREN

A court may appoint a guardian to speak on behalf of a child to the court on issues of custody, support, and visitation. (Minn. Stat. Sec., 518.165, Subd. 1.) The procedure for appointing this guardian *ad litem* varies from judicial district to judicial district. Some make frequent use of guardians *ad litem*. If the court has reason to believe the child has been a victim of domestic child abuse or neglect, the court <u>must</u> appoint a guardian *ad litem*. Otherwise, appointment is optional.

The guardian is required to conduct an investigation including interviewing the parties, relatives, friends, teachers, clergy, and any other relevant individuals, reviewing documents, and observing the children in the home setting. The guardian advocates for the child's best interests throughout the case, and presents written reports on the child's best interests with recommendations for solutions during custody and visitation proceedings. (Minn. Stat. Sec., 518.165, Subd. 2a.)

Guardian *ad litem* may be a volunteer or a paid professional. If the guardian *ad litem* is paid, the court is required to enter an order concerning payment of the fees. If a party is unable to pay, the court may order the fees paid out of funds available to the court.

PARENT EDUCATION

Every judicial district is required to establish one or more parent education programs for parents going through a divorce. (Minn. Stat. Sec., 518.157.) In addition, there may be an education program for children. (Minn. Stat. Sec., 518.157, Subd. 1.) The fees for the programs vary and you may qualify to have the fee waived. (Minn. Stat. Sec., 518.157, Subd. 6.) The standards for the program are set by the Minnesota Supreme Court though the programs vary from county to county. The judge can waive the education requirement. If there has been a history of domestic abuse, the court cannot require the parties to attend together. (Minn. Stat. Sec., 518.157, Subd. 3.) The court may impose sanctions for failure to attend. (Minn. Stat. Sec., 518.157, Subd. 4.) Any statements made during the parent education program are inadmissible in court. Further, parent education instructors may not be called as witnesses in custody cases. (Minn. Stat. Sec., 518.157, Subd. 5.)

PARENTS WITH CRIMINAL CONVICTIONS

As already stated, the court makes a parenting time or custody decision with an eye toward the best interests of the children. The parties essentially share the burden of proving what is in the best interests of the children. However, if one of the parties has been convicted of certain crimes, that party bears the burden of proving that visitation with him or her is still in the best interests of the children if:

(1) the conviction occurred within the preceding five years;

(2) the person is currently incarcerated, on probation, or under supervised release for the offense; or

(3) the victim of the crime was a family or household member as defined in Minnesota Statutes, Section 518B.01, Subdivision 2.

NOTE: *If there has been a criminal conviction for one of the crimes listed in Minnesota Statutes, Section 518.179, Subd. 2 and Minnesota Statutes Section 631.52, the court may not award joint custody. The court must also use the judicial process rather than an alternative dispute resolution process, such as mediation. (Minn. Stat. Sec., 518.1705, Subd. 6(b).)*

PARENTING PLAN 5

Effective January 1, 2001, the Legislature established a separate track for handling parenting disputes. The *Parenting Plan* legislation allows parents to craft an arrangement for decisions about and access to the children and minimizes the importance of the custody label.

Parenting plans are required to include only three things:

1. a schedule of the time each parent spends with the child;

2. a designation of decision-making responsibilities regarding the child; and

3. a method of dispute resolution.

(Minn. Stat. Sec., 518.1705, Subd. 2(a).) In addition, if the parenting plan uses some other designation than custody, the parenting plan must include an explanation of the legal and physical custody arrangements. (Minn. Stat. Sec., 518.1705, Subd. 4.) However, the plan may (and should) contain other issues and matters the parents agree to regarding the child. (Minn. Stat. Sec., 518.175, Subd. 2(b).)

A parenting plan allows parents to creatively address their children's issues without being hemmed in by the custody/visitation (now *parenting time*) label. Instead of defaulting to rights and responsibilities established by the statute and interpreted by hundreds of appellate court cases, the parents now have a chance to think about and decide every element of the plan.

If a parenting plan makes sense in your case, your attorney may have to educate your spouse, your spouse's attorney, and the court about the benefits of this option since it is so new. It is likely that some judges and attorneys will embrace the new parenting plan legislation. Some will prefer to stick with the custody scheme. If both parents request a parenting plan, the court is required to create a parenting plan unless the court makes detailed findings that such a plan is not in the best interests of the children. (Minn. Stat. Sec., 518.1705, Subd. 3.(a).) If the parents do not agree to use the parenting plan procedure, the court may create one, unless there has been domestic abuse involving the parties or the children. (Minn. Stat. Sec., 518.1705, Subd. 3.(b).)

If both parents agree to use a parenting plan, but cannot agree on all of the terms, the court may create a parenting plan. (Minn. Stat. Sec., 518.1706, Subd. 5.) To assist in making its decision, the court may require the two parties to submit a proposed parenting plan, order an evaluation, or appoint a guardian *ad litem* as described in Chapter 4, page 53. (Minn. Stat. Sec., 518.105, Subd. 5.)

As mentioned above, the parenting plan must include a designation of custody. This is because there are provisions of federal law that require such a designation. In addition, in the event that one or both parties move to a different state or county, the laws of that state or county may come into play. The custody designation may be helpful in allowing other states to interpret the parenting arrangements. In a parenting plan, the designation of custody has no effect under Minnesota Law nor any state in which the custody designation is not required. (Minn. Stat. Sec., 518.1705, Subd. 4.)

If the parties do not seek a parenting plan and the court does not create a parenting plan on its own, the court is required to enter an order on custody and parenting time as discussed in Chapter 4.

A blank parenting plan is included in Appendix B. (see form 17, p.249.)

A filled-in sample is in Appendix A. Follow the sample closely for the instruction on how to fill out your own. Each case is unique, and the form is self-explanatory.

CHILD SUPPORT AND PARENTING PLAN

There are very specific guidelines for calculating child support set forth below in Chapter 5. Generally, the guidelines are not flexible. The parenting plan statute provides that the parents are subject to the child support guidelines. (Minn. Stat. Sec., 518.1705, Subd. 8(a).) It goes on to provide that the parents may allocate expenses between the parties. (Minn. Stat. Sec., 518.1705, Subd. 8(b).) The statute is unclear on whether this means expenses are apportioned in lieu of child support or in addition to child support. The latter would make the provision worthless as someone is not likely to agree to guidelines plus additional support.

Child support is often the basis for battles over the custody label. Unfortunately, this new statute has provided little help along those lines. Until this provision is sorted out by the legislature or the courts, it appears we must continue to apply the guidelines. If the *noncustodial* parent chooses to pay additional sums (under part b), he or she may choose to do so.

MOVING THE CHILD AND PARENTING PLAN

As discussed in Chapter 4, the present law allows the custodial parent to move the children out of state quite readily. The parenting plan statute suggests that a parenting plan may apply a different legal standard to a move out of state. However, it is a strangely worded statute. It provides that if the parents were represented by counsel, were fully informed of the agreement, the agreement was voluntary, and the parents were aware of its implications, then the parenting plan may provide that a change of state of residence would require the very high legal standard that is required for a change in custody (i.e. *endangerment*). (Minn. Stat. Sec., 518.1705, Subd. 7.)

Domestic Abuse and the Parenting Plan

If domestic abuse is an issue, the court may not order mediation or any other settlement processes (other than the judicial process). (Minn. Stat. Sec., 518.1705, Subd. 6(a).) The court is to consider using a parenting plan evaluator or a guardian ad litem to make recommendations for a parenting plan. (Minn. Stat. Sec., 518.1705, Subd. 6(a).)

The court may *not* establish a parenting plan that provides for joint legal custody if either parent has engaged in:

- domestic abuse,

- threats,

- criminal sexual conduct,

- a pattern of emotional abuse of a child,

- willful extended abandonment, or

- substantial refusal to perform parenting functions.

The court must use the judicial process, and no other dispute resolution process, in these cases.

CHILD SUPPORT 6

Child support includes those funds paid or transferred from one parent to the other for the benefit of the child. The court may order either or both parents to pay child support. This award is to be without regard to marital misconduct. (Minn. Stat. Sec., 518.551, Subd. 5(a).) The court may set child support as a percentage or a fixed amount of the obligor's base pay. The court may set child support as a percentage of the obligor's net bonus, commission, or other income. This may be in addition to or in lieu of an award of a fixed amount of child support. The parent paying support is the obligor. The parent receiving support is the obligee.

For purposes of addressing child support, a *child* means an individual under 18 years of age, an individual under age 20 who is still attending secondary school, or an individual who, by reason of physical or mental condition, is incapable of self-support. (Minn. Stat. Sec., 518.54, Subd. 2.)

There is a strong presumption that child support is to be withheld directly from the obligor's wages through Automatic Income Withholding (AIW). If either party applies for collection, the funds must be withheld. If the parent receiving child support is also receiving public assistance, the payments must be made through the **Minnesota Support Payment Center**. (Minn. Stat. Sec., 518.551(b).) The address is:

P.O. Box 64326
St. Paul, MN 55164-0326

If either party is receiving public assistance, the petitioner must notify the public authority of the pending divorce proceeding. (Minn. Stat. Sec., 518.551, Subd. 5(a)). This is so the county attorney can appear to represent the public's interest. It is important to let your attorney know if you or your spouse are receiving public assistance in any form.

CALCULATING CHILD SUPPORT

The calculation of child support can be one of the more straightforward determinations made in family law. Frequently there are issues that can complicate the situation or justify deviation from the guidelines. For example, if both spouses have the children approximately equal amounts of time, the court may make a different calculation. If one spouse's income comes from ownership of a small business, net income may be far more difficult to calculate. There are frequent allegations that the business-owning spouse is putting too much money into the business or even hiding cash to avoid paying more child support. The child support issue can be further complicated if the obligor is a student, disabled or otherwise minimally employed. These circumstances should be discussed with your attorney to determine how to handle the child support calculation.

GUIDELINES Child support is calculated using the Minnesota Child Support Guidelines. Initially these guidelines were used for cases in which the custodial parent was receiving public assistance. Now, the guidelines are used in all cases. (Minn. Stat. Sec., 518.551, Subd. 5(I).) The statute indicates that the Minnesota Child Support Guideline calculations are the presumed method for calculating child support. This would suggest that there are deviations from the Guidelines. In practice, deviations are the unusual exception to the rule.

Regular Income. In order to calculate child support, you must first determine the net income of the obligor of both parties. The obligor's income determines the amount of child support. In addition, the recipient's income must be calculated as it is relevant to the payment of day-care costs. There is also a cap on the statutory child support. This cap is adjusted as of July 1 of every even-numbered year. Through June 30, 2002, the cap is $6,280. (Minn. Stat. Sec., 518.551, Subd. 5(k).) If a child is receiving Social Security benefits as a result of the obligor's old age or disability benefits, the amount of child support ordered shall be offset by the amount of the benefit the child receives. (Minn. Stat. Sec., 518.551, Subd. 5(l).)

However, if a party receives *in-kind contributions* from an employer such as a company car, meals, memberships, etc. that can be included. The statute specifically excludes the income of a parties' new spouse. (Minn. Stat. Sec., 518.551, Subd. 5(b)(1).)

Self-Employed Income. The income of a self-employed person can be difficult to calculate. A self-employed person is to be determined by taking the gross income less ordinary and necessary business expenses.

Overtime. Overtime income is generally included to arrive at net income if it has been a regular part of the parties' income for two years preceding commencement of the divorce. (Minn. Stat. Sec., 518.551, Subd. 5(b).) If it did not begin until after filing for divorce, it need not be included so long as (1) it is an increase in the work schedule over the two years before filing the petition; (2) it is voluntary and not a condition of employment; (3) it is compensable by the hour or fraction of the hour; and (4) the compensation structure has not been changed for purposes of affecting the support or maintenance obligation. (Minn. Stat. Sec., 518.551, Subd. 5(b)(2)(ii)(A)-(E).)

DEVIATING
FROM CHILD
SUPPORT
GUIDELINES

While the Minnesota Child Support Guidelines are presumed to be the correct calculation, the court does have some discretion to deviate upward or downward from the guideline calculation. When setting, modifying, or determining whether to deviate from the guideline amount the court is to consider:

- all earnings, income, and resources of the parties;

- the financial needs and resources, physical and emotional condition, and educational needs of the child or children to be supported;

- the standard of living the child would have enjoyed had the marriage not been dissolved, but recognizing that the parents now have separate households;

- which parent receives the income tax dependency deduction, and the benefit the parent receives from it;

- the parent's debt, especially if related to the support of the child; and

- the obligor's receipt of public assistance. (Minn. Stat. Sec., 518.551, Subd. 5(c).)

CHILD SUPPORT CALCULATION

There is a calculation worksheet for child support in Appendix B. (see form 1, p.189.) Fill it in as directed below for both the Payor and Recipient sections.

☛ *Gross Monthly Income*. The best method to calculate child support is to convert the income figures to monthly amounts. For example, if the pay is bi-weekly, multiply the income on the paycheck by twenty-six weeks. This gives you the annual figure. Then, you must divide by twelve to arrive at the monthly figure. Use one of the following calculations to determine gross monthly income:

Hourly Wage _____ x 2080 = _____

Weekly Wage _____ x 52 ÷ 12 = _____

Twice Monthly Wage _____ x 2 = _____

Every Two Weeks Wage _____ x 26 ÷ 12 = _____

One of the above lines gives you the gross monthly income calculation. If there is bonus, commission, or other income received on a consistent basis, figure that in as well. If it is received annually divide by twelve to arrive at the monthly amount. Insert the gross monthly figure on the "Gross Monthly Income" line.

☛ *Federal Income Tax*. The statute requires that you use the tax tables to determine the proper deductions from net monthly income. These are available in Internal Revenue Service Publication 15 Circular E, Employer's Tax Guide. They are also available on the Internet at **http://www.irs.ustreas.gov**. Use the monthly tables for single individuals. You may elect to use the married tables in some circumstances. Discuss this with your attorney. If you are using the monthly single table go down to the gross income figure you just calculated. Very likely, the party whose net income is being determined will be able to claim himself or herself—use the column for one exemption. If the party whose income you are calculating will be claiming an exemption for one or more of the children, move over to the next column(s) as appropriate. For example, if the party will be claiming himself and two children, use the column for three exemptions. Write the number of the end result on the "Federal Income Tax" line.

☞ ***State Income Tax***. The state income tax must be calculated using tables in Minnesota Department of Revenue Publication Minnesota Income Tax Withholding. You can obtain this publication through: **http://www.state.mn.us/ebranch/mdor/withhold/ form/2000/withhold.html** or by telephone: (651) 289-9999 or (800) 657 3394. Again, turn to the monthly tables for single (or married) and use the same procedure as outlined above. Write the number of the state income tax result on the "State Income Tax" line.

☞ ***Social Security/Deduction***. The total deducted from the wages for Social Security and Medicare is 7.65% of net wages. Simply multiply the Gross Monthly Income by .0765 to arrive at the deduction. The Social Security portion is eliminated for higher earners. Put your calculation on the "Social Security/Medicare" line.

☞ ***Pension Deduction***. The Statute allows a reasonable pension deduction. (Minn. Stat. Sec., 518.551, Subd. 5(b).) A pension deduction of six percent is generally acceptable. However, in many cases a higher deduction is allowed. It is an issue subject to negotiation. If there is a long history of a ten percent deduction, it is possible the court would accept it. However, anything higher is the exception rather than the norm. The court is more concerned with ensuring the well-being of the children at present than the comfort of the parent in retirement. Put the monthly pension deduction on the "Pension Deduction" line.

NOTE: *If the child support recipient is receiving public assistance, the county attorney will be involved in the case. In such a situation, it is not unusual for the county attorney to insist on a cap of six percent as a pension deduction.*

☛ **Union Dues**. Union dues are deductible. In determining union dues it can be important to review several paystubs. (It is possible that the dues are taken out only monthly or on every paycheck.) Make sure to figure the monthly amount and write it on the "Union Dues" line.

☛ **Dependent Health Insurance**. In the line entitled "Dependent Health Insurance," you place the cost of medical insurance for any dependent children. You may need to contact the employer or insurer directly to determine what portion of insurance is for the party and which portion is for the children.

☛ **Dental Insurance**. This is not explicitly addressed in the statute. However, it is generally accepted as it is important for the children to have such coverage. Put this figure on the "Dental Insurance" line.

☛ **Individual Health Insurance**. This refers to coverage paid for by the individual for himself or herself. In many cases, the employer pays all insurance costs for the employee. If there is no such insurance, you are allowed to deduct an amount equal to the "actual medical expenses." Write the monthly amount on the "Individual Health Insurance" line.

☛ **Other Child Support or Maintenance**. If either party has an existing child support or spousal maintenance order, that amount is deducted from the gross income as well and inserted on the "Other Child Support" line.

☛ **Total Deductions**. Add up all of the deductions and write that on this line.

☞ **Net Monthly Income**. Subtract the "Total Deductions" line from the "Gross Monthly Income" line to arrive at the net monthly income. Write this amount on the "Net Monthly Income" line.

☞ **Child Support Multiplier**. The Minnesota Legislature has created a table of child support multipliers to multiply by net income to arrive at the child support amount. The table is based upon the net income and the number of children. (see the chart on this page.) If the net income is greater than $1,000 per month and there is one child the obligor must pay 25% so you multiply the net income by .25. If there are two children, use 30%. If the net income is under $1,000, apply the child support multiplier as indicated in the Child Support Multiplier table below. Write this amount on the "Child Support Multiplier" line. (This figure will only appear in the payor's section and not the recipient's.)

CHILD SUPPORT MULTIPLIER

Net Income Per Month of Obligor	Number of Children						
	1	2	3	4	5	6	7 or more
$551 - 600	16%	19%	22%	25%	28%	30%	32%
$601 - 650	17%	21%	24%	27%	29%	32%	34%
$651 - 700	18%	22%	25%	28%	31%	34%	36%
$701 - 750	19%	23%	27%	30%	33%	36%	38%
$751 - 800	20%	24%	28%	31%	35%	38%	40%
$801 - 850	21%	25%	29%	33%	36%	40%	42%
$851 - 900	22%	27%	31%	34%	38%	41%	44%
$901 - 950	23%	28%	32%	36%	40%	43%	46%
$951 - 1000	24%	29%	34%	38%	41%	45%	48%
$1001- 5000	25%	30%	35%	39%	43%	47%	50%

CALCULATING CHILDCARE COSTS

Once you have determined the net income of both parties, you can calculate the apportionment of work or education related childcare costs using another worksheet. (see form 2, p.190.)

☛ For the obligor (payor), take net income and subtract child support. (See child support calculations to determine net income.) Write this number on the "Obligor's Total" line.

☛ For the obligee (recipient) take net income and add child support. Put this total on the "Obligee's Total" line. This shows each party's available cash after transfer of child support.

☛ Add the two totals together to determine the total household income. Write this amount on the "Total Income" line.

☛ Divide the obligor's income by the total income to determine the obligor's percentage of the total. Write this amount on the "Obligor's Percentage" line.

☛ Finally, multiply the obligor's percentage by .75. This last calculation is based upon the Minnesota Legislature's determination that the "custodial" parent has a tax benefit of approximately twenty-five percent of the total childcare cost. The amount transferred to the other parent should reflect this. This percentage goes on the "Childcare Percentage" line."

Childcare costs must be related to time the parent spends in work or at school. The court is to require verification of work or school attendance. (Minn. Stat. Sec., 518.551, Subd. 5(b).)

Often, childcare expenses fluctuate due to differences between summer and school year costs and due to time the noncustodial parent has with the child. The court is to determine the average in making the calculation.

NOTE: *Under the present tax code, the deductions related to childcare costs are tied to the exemption. If the exemptions are not awarded to the* *"custodial" parent, then the twenty-five percent credit should be reconsidered. This is an issue to discuss with your attorney.*

There are additional child support issues that are beyond the scope of this book including allegations of voluntary underemployment; decreased income due to a change in employment; issues of additional children; notice to the public authority if public assistance is at issue, etc. These issues must be discussed with your attorney if relevant to your case.

AUTOMATIC INCOME WITHHOLDING

If either party requests it, child support is to be withheld through Automatic Income Withholding (AIW). You can obtain AIW by going to the office of child support and collections, which may be within the county attorney's office. You will have to fill out an application and provide a copy of the order setting child support.

Except in cases of public assistance, the person applying for child support collection services must pay a twenty-five dollar fee. (Minn. Stat. Sec., 518.551, Subd. 7.) The withholding agency may charge a fee to the child support payor who is not current in child support payments. (Minn. Stat. Sec., 518.551, Subd. 7.) At present, some counties charge for collecting spousal maintenance, but not child support.

Every support order must address AIW, either ordering it or waiving it. (Minn. Stat. Sec., 518.6111, Subd. 3.) Upon receipt of an order for or notice of withholding, an employer or other payor of funds is required to implement income withholding. The employer is required to begin withholding within a short time after receiving notice. (Minn. Stat. Sec., 518.6111, Subd. 5(a).) Thereafter, the employer must forward to the payment center the funds withheld within seven days of withholding. (Minn. Stat. Sec., 518.6111, Subd. 5(b).) The employer is prohibited from terminating an employee for wage withholding. (Minn. Stat. Sec., 518.6111, Subd. 5(c).)

If the obligor is self-employed, funds can be withheld from bank accounts. (Minn. Stat. Sec., 518.6111, Subd. 6.)

There are some limitations on what can be withheld. In some cases, the obligor has a previous child support obligation and the subsequent order will result in withholding that exceeds the limits of the Consumer Credit Protection Act. (United States Code, Title 15, Section 1673(b).) This can also happen when a party is ordered to pay child support and spousal maintenance, which result in withholding that exceeds the limits of the Act.

Sometimes the order does not come out until well after papers are served or until ninety days after the hearing. On top of that, very often, by the time support is withheld, a few weeks or even months have passed. It would be preferable that the obligor begins paying upon notice of the order. Due to the delay, whatever the cause, the obligor may be two or more months in arrears in payments by the time withholding starts. In order to collect these arrearages the public authority may withhold an additional twenty percent of the award to the amount withheld by the employer to collect arrearages. (Minn. Stat. Sec., 518.6111, Subd. 10.) As a practical matter, for every month someone is in arrears, it takes five months of extra withholding to catch up.

> **Example**: The custodial parent serves motion papers on February 1. There is a hearing March 15. The court's order comes out May 15 setting child support at $500 per month, making child support retroactive to the date of service of the motion papers (February 1). The custodial parent applies for AIW on May 30. It takes four weeks for the agency to get notices out to the employer to withhold. By that time the obligor has changed employers. It takes another two weeks to learn of the change and get notices to the new employer. The new employer starts withholding July 1. At that point, the obligor is five months in arrears ($2,500). He will pay $600 for two years and one month to make up the arrears.

The custodial parent has called her attorney several times because she cannot pay rent without that support. About June 15, she decides to go forward with a motion for contempt. The attorney drafts the papers at a cost of about $750. However, she starts receiving checks two weeks later and has a legal bill for motion papers she will not use. The delay is very frustrating. However, once the system starts withholding, the vast majority of people find it very effective.

NOTE: *If arrearages exist after the child is emancipated and no longer entitled to child support, the agency is to continue collecting support at the guideline amount plus twenty percent until the outstanding balance is paid. (Minn. Stat. Secs., 518.6111, Subd. 10 (c) and 518.6195.)*

If an employee is to receive a lump sum payment over $500, such as a bonus, severance, etc., the employer is required to hold the bonus for thirty days and notify the agency that a lump sum payment is pending. The limits of the Consumer Credit Protection Act do not apply to lump sum payments. (Minn. Stat. Sec., 518.6111, Subd. 11.)

There are still many other ways to collect child support using the procedures available for collecting on any judgment.

WAIVING AUTOMATIC INCOME WITHHOLDING (AIW)

There is a strong preference for AIW. It helps avoid conflict between parties and keeps an accounting of the child support paid. Even if the parties agree, it is possible the court will not approve the waiver. However, if there are no arrearages, the parties are in agreement, and the court finds that a waiver is likely to result in timely and regular payments, and withholding would not be in the best interests of the child, the court may order the waiver. (Minn. Stat. Sec., 518.6111, Subd. 16.) If the court waives withholding, the obligee may request withholding at any time. (Minn. Stat. Sec., 518.6111, Subd. 16(b).)

COST OF LIVING ADJUSTMENTS

An order for child support or maintenance must provide for a biennial cost of living adjustment to an award of child support. (Minn. Stat. Sec., 518.641, Subd. 1.) This adjustment becomes effective on May first every other year when child support is paid through AIW. If there is no

69

AIW, the recipient may apply for a cost-of-living adjustment every two years in any month. The cost of living adjustment may be waived if the court finds that there is no cost-of-living wage increase to the obligor.

The procedure for seeking this adjustment is to serve notice on the obligor at least twenty days before the adjustment will go into effect. If the obligor fails to request a hearing, the increase goes into effect. If the obligor so requests, the matter can be set for hearing. Minnesota Statutes Section 518.641, subd. 2. The obligor must attempt to show that he has not experienced a sufficient increase in income to meet the increased child support obligation.

JOINT/SPLIT CUSTODY CALCULATION

In a joint custody case each parent pays for the time when the other has the child. Using the following example:

Example: If Petitioner earns $2,000 per month and Respondent earns $1,000 per month, Petitioner would pay $500 (twenty-five percent of his net income) for the support of one child.

If the parties have joint custody and an equal time split petitioner would pay one-half of the $500.00 for a total of $250.00. Respondent would pay $1,000.00 x .25 = $250.00 x .5 = $125.00. Respondent would receive a net $125.00 per month. This represents a significant reduction in support from a sole custody case.

This calculation method works even if the percentage is not equal. If husband has the child 40% of the time, the calculation is as follows:

Husband would pay $2,000.00 x .25 = $500.00 x .6 = $300.00. The .6 reflects the fact that the wife has the child 60% of the time. Wife would pay $1,000.00 x .25 = $250.00

x .4 = $100.00. Wife receives $200.00 net.

Split custody is a bit more straight-forward. *Split custody* occurs when each party assumes custody of at least one child. If the above parties had custody of one child each, support would be calculated as follows:

The husband pays $2,000.00 x .25 = $500.00 for the child in wife's care. Wife pays $1,000.00 x .25 = $250.00 for the child in husband's care. Wife receives $250.00 net per month.

NOTE: *There are powerful statutory provisions for enforcement of child support. These issues are discussed in more detail in Chapter 9, Post-Divorce Issues.*

MEDICAL SUPPORT

Minnesota Statutes, Section 518.171 requires every support order (a divorce decree is a support order if it orders child support) to:

- assign or reserve the responsibility for maintaining medical support;

- determine the division of uninsured medical and dental costs. If the custodial parent is not receiving public assistance and has the ability, the expenses are to be apportioned between the parties based upon their incomes. (Minn. Stat. Sec., 518.171, Subd. 1(d));

- contain the name and address of the parents and the children. In the alternative the court may order the information be provided to the health plan administrator and not included in the addresses and social security numbers in the orders;

- require the parent with the better group health and dental insurance coverage to name the child as beneficiary; and

- if no group plan is available, the noncustodial parent may be ordered to obtain coverage, be liable for the reasonable and necessary medical or dental expenses of the child, or pay at least $50 per month toward the costs of coverage or medical and dental expenses of the children.

As with child support, an individual is required to disclose, at the time of hiring, whether medical support is required. (Minn. Stat. Sec., 518.171, Subd. 2a.) Enrollment is not dependent on enrollment periods. (Minn. Stat. Sec., 518.171, Subd. 4(b).)

There are a number of other provisions in Minnesota Statutes, Section 518.171 designed to ensure coverage for the children, including:

- The child may not be disenrolled without notice to the custodial parent.

- The custodial parent may sign for reimbursement payments even if coverage is not through that parent. The payment may be made to the provider of services or the custodial parent if that parent has paid for the medical services.

- The employer or union must provide the names of the insurance carrier.

- The employer, union, or insurer must provide identification cards and any other necessary information to enable the custodial parent to utilize coverage for the children.

- If the obligor fails to maintain medical or dental support, the obligor is liable for any costs incurred.

The medical support provision of the divorce statute is likely to change. The legislature has directed the commissioner of human services to recommend changes to the statute in light of regulations from the federal government.

SPOUSAL MAINTENANCE 7

If spousal maintenance is an issue in your case, it is essential that you have an experienced family law attorney. Unlike child support, there are no clear guidelines in spousal maintenance. There is only a vague statute and case law interpreting that statute that is sometimes inconsistent from case to case. As a general matter, maintenance is based upon the ability of one party to pay balanced against the needs of the other party.

Specifically, the court may grant maintenance if it finds that a party lacks sufficient property to provide for his or her reasonable needs after considering the standard of living established during the marriage. The court is to consider awarding maintenance for a period to allow the spouse to engage in some training or education. (Minn. Stat. Sec., 518.552, Subd. 1(a).) The court may also award spousal maintenance if a spouse is unable to provide self-support (based upon the standard of living enjoyed during the marriage) through employment, or is limited due to the need to care for a child whose circumstances are such that the custodian should not be required to seek work outside the home. (Minn. Stat. Sec., 518.552, Subd. 1(b).) If neither of these qualifications are met, the court may not award maintenance.

Once the court has made the above determination that maintenance should be awarded, it must next determine the amount and duration. The court may make maintenance temporary or permanent.

NOTE: *Neither temporary nor permanent are absolute terms in this context. Temporary maintenance can end up lasting indefinitely. Permanent maintenance can prove to be short lived in certain circumstances.*

In determining the amount of maintenance, the court must consider the following:

- the financial resources of the party seeking maintenance including property and the party's ability to meet his or her needs without the assistance of the other party. Again the court must consider the impact of being a custodial parent on the ability to meet one's needs;

- the time necessary to acquire sufficient training or education to enable the party seeking maintenance to find appropriate employment. In addition, the court must consider, in light of the age and skills of the party, the probability of the party completing her education or training and becoming fully or partially self-supporting;

- the standard of living enjoyed during the marriage;

- the duration of the marriage;

- in the case of a homemaker, the length of absence from employment and the extent to which his or her education, skills, or training have become outmoded and the earning capacity has been permanently diminished;

- the loss of earnings, seniority, retirement benefits, and other employment opportunities of the spouse seeking maintenance;

- the age, physical, and emotional condition of the spouse seeking maintenance;

- the ability of the paying spouse to meet his or her needs and the needs of the other spouse; and

- the contribution of each party in building the marital estate as well as the contribution of a spouse as a homemaker or in support of the other party's employment or business. (Minn. Stat. Sec., 518.552, Subd. 2.)

Judges use different methods of calculating the amount of maintenance in light of the above factors. Some judges take the total net income and divide it in half so that each party has an equal share of the income. This often makes sense in light of the fact that a married couple should have approximately the same standard of living and the same needs. However, appellate cases have suggested that this simplistic analysis is insufficient. Another method of calculating the award of maintenance is to take the two parties' reasonable budgets, and then leave each side with the same deficiency.

Example: The parties have equal expenses except that the wife will stay in the home. The parties have owned the home for twenty years and pay mortgage of $750 per month, which the wife will assume. The wife's remaining expenses including food, clothing, utilities, entertainment, etc. are $750 and she pays $300 to lease a 2000 Saturn. The wife's budget is $1,800. Wife's net income is $1,000 per month.

Husband must rent a modest apartment for $950. He drives a 2001 Cadillac for which he is paying $800 per month plus food, clothing, utilities, entertainment, etc. of $750 per month. His monthly budget is $2,500. His net income is $2,500 per month.

The court determines that the husband's apartment cost is reasonable in light of the market. However, the court may determine that he does not need such an expensive car. The court determines his reasonable budget to be $2,000 per month. The parties' combined incomes are $3,500 per month. This is not sufficient to meet their combined budget of $3,800.

The court awards spousal maintenance to the wife of $650 per month. This leaves the wife with $1,650—$150 short of her monthly budget. This also leaves the husband with $1,850—$150 short of his monthly budget. Again, this is only one of the many possible methods of calculation used by different judges. However, this method would very likely survive review by an appellate court.

TEMPORARY VS. PERMANENT MAINTENANCE

There is no preference for a temporary award. In fact, when there is uncertainty as to whether an award should be permanent, the court is required to make the award permanent subject to later modification. (Minn. Stat. Sec., 518.552, Subd. 3.)

The distinction between temporary and permanent maintenance is very important. If a party is awarded temporary maintenance, that party has to attempt to *rehabilitate* so as to need no spousal maintenance in the future. If a party is awarded permanent maintenance, that award may go on indefinitely.

The obligation is presumably terminated on the death of either party or the remarriage of the party receiving maintenance. (Minn. Stat. Sec., 518.552, Subd. 3.) However, a party can attempt to negotiate a different arrangement.

WAIVING MAINTENANCE

Maintenance, like most other issues in a divorce is negotiable. In fact, the uncertainty surrounding an award of maintenance makes it important that the parties seriously consider a negotiated settlement on this issue. In many cases neither party will ever pay the other maintenance. For example, if both parties have comparable incomes and employment prospects, an award of maintenance is unlikely. However, in the event one of these spouses faces a disability or loss of employment, it is possible to seek an award of maintenance in the future. In order to avoid this possibility, the parties may want to negotiate an arrangement by which neither party will ever pay maintenance to the other.

In some cases you want to enter into an arrangement whereby spousal maintenance is paid for a period of time and in an amount that is acceptable to both parties. In the settlement agreement you can provide that neither party may seek to change the award of maintenance in the future.

It is important to discuss this issue with your attorney. Taking the issue of maintenance out of the hands of the court requires great precision in drafting. Any mistakes can leave maintenance open to modification either up or down in the future.

TAXES

One important thing to keep in mind is that spousal maintenance is taxable to the recipient and a deduction for the payor. This can be used to transfer income from one spouse to another and reduce the tax bill. However, careful drafting and knowledge of tax law is important to avoid running afoul of the IRS.

AUTOMATIC INCOME WITHHOLDING

There is a strong presumption that spousal maintenance is to be withheld directly from an obligor's wages. If either party requests this method, the funds must be withheld. Counties generally charge a collection fee of approximately fifteen dollars to withhold spousal maintenance. This fee is charged to the payor. If spousal maintenance and child support are both being withheld, the fee is not imposed in most cases. See Chapter 6, p.67 for more information on Automatic Income Withholding.

SPOUSAL MAINTENANCE CALCULATOR

The Minnesota State Bar Association, Family Law Section has prepared a computer program to calculate spousal maintenance. While this is not entirely consistent with the statute, it is the result of input from dozens of family law attorneys who have handled thousands of cases. The calculator may not convince a judge, but it can be helpful in discussing settlement.

You may ask your attorney whether he or she has the software. The new version may be available in some law libraries.

PROPERTY 8

All property acquired during the marriage is marital property except for a few, limited exceptions. The court is to make a just and equitable division of property. (Minn. Stat. Sec., 518.58, Subd. 1.) The court considers "all relevant factors" including:

- length of the marriage;

- any prior marriage of a party;

- the age, health, station, and occupation of the party;

- vocational skills and employability;

- estate worth;

- liabilities and needs;

- opportunity for future acquisition of capital assets;

- income of each party; and

- the contribution of each in the acquisition, preservation, depreciation, or appreciation in the amount or value of the marital property, and the contribution of a spouse as a homemaker.

Generally, the property division is *equal* (50/50) as that is equitable in most cases. However, there are frequent deviations from that arrangement for any number of reasons. For example, the spouse with the primary care of the children will require the bulk of the children's property or the higher earning spouse may be in a better position to replace furnishings and other household goods. Again, the statute requires an equitable division of property, not necessarily equal.

VALUATION DATE

One important aspect of a case is the *valuation date* of assets. With things like the stock market fluctuating and real estate values increasing significantly, a time must be set for valuation. The statute provides that the valuation date should be "the day of the initially scheduled pre-hearing settlement conference, unless a different date is agreed upon by the parties, or unless the court makes specific findings that another date of valuation is fair and equitable." (Minn. Stat. Sec., 518.58, Subd. 1.) The court frequently finds that the date of separation is a "fair and equitable" date as that is the time when many parties separate their finances and divide assets and debts.

There are a number of considerations that go into setting the valuation date. If one spouse is making significant payments to a pension plan, he may want the valuation date to be sooner rather than later. The other spouse would want the opposite. You also have to consider practical issues in setting a valuation date. For example, many retirement plans and some other accounts may only produce statements at the end of a calendar quarter, so it may make sense to use the end of a quarter for that reason. These are only a few of the many considerations that enter into a decision on valuation date. Discuss it with your attorney as it may alter the value of the marital estate by thousands of dollars.

There are statutory provisions to protect against a change in value. If there is a substantial change in value of an asset between the date of valuation and the final distribution, the court may adjust the valuation of that asset as necessary to make an equitable distribution. (Minn. Stat. Sec., 518.58, Subd. 1.)

DISPOSING OF MARITAL PROPERTY

The SUMMONS that is served with the PETITION FOR DISSOLUTION OF MARRIAGE explicitly prohibits the parties from disposing of assets except to provide for necessities. The statute suggests that even before a divorce proceeding is actually commenced by service of the SUMMONS and PETITION FOR DISSOLUTION OF MARRIAGE documents, each spouse owes a fiduciary duty to the other for any loss or gain in marital assets. (Minn. Stat. Sec., 518.58, Subd. 1a.) If a party has disposed of marital property, without the consent of the other, the court is to make the party whole by adjusting the property division to reflect the lost asset or make a remedy to rectify the situation. There is an exception for property used to provide for the necessities of life or for use in the usual course of business.

One of the more difficult issues to deal with is when a party disposes of marital assets. It is often very difficult to prove. It makes sense to conduct an inventory of the home and record it in photographs or videotape. If the court believes that property has been concealed or destroyed, there will likely be sanctions which can include the court imputing the value of the asset.

NONMARITAL PROPERTY

Nonmarital property is property owned before the marriage, gifts inherited, or personal injury settlements received during the marriage. Generally, nonmarital property is awarded to the party who owns it. However, if there is insufficient marital property and there would be an unfair hardship on one of the parties, the court may apportion up to one-half of the nonmarital property to prevent the unfair hardship. (Minn. Stat. Sec., 518.58, Subd. 2.)

Frequently, a spouse brings a nonmarital interest into a marriage. One way is for one party to own the home before the marriage. The other is for a party to use nonmarital assets to purchase the home. As the home appreciates in value, the nonmarital portion is to increase as well.

Example: Wife's parents give her $10,000.00, which is used as the down payment on the parties' $100,000.00 home. This represents ten percent of the market value. If the home if worth $200,0000.00 at the time of divorce, wife's nonmarital claim is worth $20,000.00 (ten percent of the "divorce" market value).

NOTE: *If nonmarital property is cash, it must be traceable to its nonmarital source.*

EMPLOYEE BENEFITS

There are a number of employee benefits that may qualify as marital assets. The most common type is retirement plans. However, stock options, unused vacation or sick leave, and other benefits may be considered additional marital assets. Your attorney may request employee benefit information from your spouse's employer through the discovery process.

RETIREMENT PLANS

Retirement plans are marital assets to the extent that they were earned during the marriage. In many cases, retirement plans are the largest assets of the marital estate. They are subject to division in the dissolution proceeding. How the division is handled depends upon the type of plan and the specific language of each individual plan. There are special considerations in deciding whether or how to divide certain plans. Some are quite simple and require only a copy of the JUDGMENT AND DECREE. Often IRAs and 401(k)s are handled this way. These types of plans are known as *defined contribution plans*.

Some plans are more complex and require a qualified domestic relations order (QDRO) to transfer the assets. (Minn. Stat. Sec., 518.581, Subd. 1.) Some such plans like traditional union retirement plans are a form of annuity. They pay an amount for the life of the beneficiary (and spouse in some cases). Depending on the plan, the benefit may increase or decrease due to fluctuations in the stock market or with inflation. These are called *defined benefit plans*.

Valuing the defined contribution plans is as simple as looking at the most recent statement. However, it is important for your attorney to review the plan or at least the plan summary to determine whether there is any other benefit available under the plan.

Valuing the defined benefit plan (*annuitized* plan) can be more complex. Generally, the employee benefits department or plan administrator provides a document indicating how much the plan would pay in the event of retirement. Generally, the longer you are with the employer and the higher your wages, the higher the payment. The plan may report that you will receive $1,400.00 per month if you retire at age 55 or $1,800.00 per month if you retire at age 62. Sometimes the parties will simply agree to divide the plan equally. Sometimes, the parties will want to know the present value of the plan so it can be offset against the homestead or other marital assets.

Many attorneys have a computer program that can convert the information into a present value. Of course, the result depends upon the assumptions you use. It is common practice to forward the information to an *actuary* who determines the present value of the plans. The court may appoint a neutral actuary to value the plan. (Minn. Stat. Sec., 518.582.) Issues of valuation and division of retirement plans should be discussed with your attorney.

TYPES OF RETIREMENT PLANS

There are many different sections of the tax code that provide for retirement plans. Within each type of plan there are many variations depending on the needs of the employer. You may have heard of 401(k)s, profit sharing plans, stock bonus plans, money purchase pension plan, employee stock ownership plan (ESOP), defined benefit plans, Keogh plans, individual retirement accounts (IRAs), simplified employee pensions (SEP IRAs), Simplified Incentive Match Plan for Employees (SIMPLE IRAs), Roth IRAs, qualified annuity plans (403(a)s), tax-deferred annuities (TDAs or 403(b)s), and others. These plans have different requirements for division incident to a divorce. In addition, there is considerable variation in the flexibility of the plans. If you want to cash in a plan to buy a house, you may or may not be able to do so. Some plans prohibit a party from drawing any benefit until the plan participant retires. You must discuss this with your attorney to determine what your needs are and the tax implications upon withdrawal.

NOTE: *Drafting documents used to divide a retirement plan can be extremely difficult and it often can happen that a scenario is not addressed. For example, if your spouse dies before he or she starts receiving benefits, the Plan Administrator is going to have to deal with the benefits available to you. If the QDRO does not address pre-retirement survivor benefits, you may be hard pressed to get anything out of the plan. This area of law is a significant malpractice trap for attorneys. You should never draft a domestic relations order; too much is at stake. Many family law attorneys have an expert handle these types of plans. You should do so as well.*

INSURANCE

An often overlooked asset is insurance. The cash value of an insurance policy is an asset that should be considered in the division of property. Insurance is used for a number of tax-related purposes other than simply providing a benefit to the family that is left behind. Sometimes, it is an investment vehicle with an insurance component and an investment component. You should be able to obtain a statement from the insurance agent or company providing a present cash balance. However, term life insurance should not have a cash value.

REAL ESTATE

Real property includes land and all fixtures to the land such as a home, garage, fence, etc. It is important to clear title to real property as part of a divorce. Real estate is unique in that if either party owns any real estate during the marriage, the other party gains an interest in that property. That interest may be worth nothing because it is entirely non-marital; it may be entirely marital and subject to equitable division principles; or it may be some combination of marital and nonmarital. Any real property owned by either or both parties during a divorce must be addressed. Even if your spouse is not on the title, you must have that property transferred in the divorce decree so there is not a problem with the title when you want to sell it in the future.

Real property is frequently transferred as part of a divorce. Often it is awarded subject to a *lien* (an interest in the property). The arrangements vary dramatically. For example, a custodial parent may be awarded the home until such time as the children are done with high school. One party may be granted the use of the home until it is sold or for a period of years. The other party may have a lien for a fixed amount; a fixed amount plus interest; a percentage of the sale price; a percentage of sale price less the costs of sale; or any number of other arrangements depending upon the circumstances.

NOTE: *Real estate transfers must be recorded.*

The transfer document can be the JUDGMENT AND DECREE that dissolves the marriage; a quit claim deed; or a summary real estate disposition judgment. First, the parties may file the JUDGMENT AND DECREE. (see form 18, p.258.) The JUDGMENT AND DECREE must provide for the disposition of any real estate owned by either party. It is standard practice to provide within the text of the divorce decree that a certified copy of that decree is filed with the county recorder or the registrar of titles (as appropriate), and that will be sufficient to transfer title. For obvious reasons, a party may not want their entire divorce decree filed on the property records.

The second option is to transfer the property by deed. If the terms of the lien are fairly brief, they can be incorporated into the basic deed form. You can obtain a deed at a stationary store. A deed is not provided in this book because they are to be on legal-sized paper.

A third option is the Summary Real Estate Disposition Judgment. The Summary Real Estate Disposition Judgment is an abbreviated judgment and decree that addresses only the real estate issues. If you want to fill one of these out, it would be best to see a real estate attorney. This form can get extremely complex.

Domestic Abuse 9

Domestic abuse is frequently a cause of dissolution of a marriage. The issue may be dealt with in a criminal or a civil proceeding, or both. For example, a domestic abuse victim may file a police report, which may lead to charges of *fifth degree domestic assault*, which is intentionally causing fear of physical harm or actually physically harming a family or household member. The court may establish a *no-contact order* that prohibits the other abuser from having any contact with the victim.

Order for Protection

The victim may also seek a domestic abuse order for protection, in which the court will order the spouse to keep away. It may also establish custody and child support, which are not dealt with in the no-contact order. It is very important to discuss this domestic abuse with your attorney early in the representation. If it is not raised early in the proceedings, the court may be suspicious of your motives in raising the issue. However, if domestic abuse occurs during the divorce proceeding, you can still seek an order for protection and criminal charges.

While a great many people exiting marriages believe they have been a victim of domestic abuse, the legal definition of domestic abuse is quite specific. When directed against a spouse or child, *domestic abuse* includes the following:

- physical harm, bodily injury, or assault;

- the infliction of fear of imminent physical harm, bodily injury, or assault;

- terroristic threats (threats of a crime of violence); or

- criminal sexual conduct (first, second, third, or fourth degree).

(Minn. Stat., Sec., 518B, Subd. 2(a).)

The action for an order for protection may be brought in the county in which either party resides, the county in which there is a pending or completed dissolution proceeding, or in the county in which the abuse occurred. (Minn. Stat., Sec., 518 B, Subd. 3.) There is no filing fee to commence an order for protection. (Minn. Stat. Sec., 518B, Subd. 3a.) In addition, there is no fee for having the sheriff serve the order for protection papers.

PETITION   An action for an order for protection is commenced by service of a petition and supporting documents. A party may bring an action on behalf of him or herself, on behalf of the children, or both. (Minn. Stat., Sec., 518B, Subd. 4(a). The *petitioner* (the person filing the petition) must allege the existence of domestic abuse and must attach an affidavit stating the specific facts of the abuse. (Minn. Stat., Sec., 518B, Subd. 4(b).) The court is required to provide assistance in writing and filing the necessary documents. (Minn. Stat., Sec., 518 B, Subd. 4(e).)

NOTE: *The court is required to hold a hearing on the petition within fourteen days. (Minn. Stat., Sec. 518B, Subd. 5(a).) If the hearing is continued beyond the fourteen-day period due to inability to retain counsel or some other reason, the matter may be dismissed. It is important for a petitioner to ensure that the matter is heard within the fourteen days to avoid losing the case. This "fourteen-day rule" is the result of a Court of Appeals decision. This restrictive interpretation of the statute may be reversed by the legislature. Discuss this with your attorney.*

EX PARTE
ORDER

If the petition alleges an immediate and present danger of domestic abuse, the court may grant an *ex parte order*. The ex parte order may grant some emergency relief including: restraining the other party from committing further abuse; excluding the other party from the residence; excluding the other party from the victim's place of employment; and continuing all insurance coverage. (Minn. Stat., Sec., 518B, Subd. 7(a).) The petitioner may opt for no hearing. However, if the petitioner requests a hearing, it must be held within seven days. If the *respondent* (the person responding to petitions) wants a hearing, it is to be held eight to ten days from the date the respondent requests the hearing. (Minn. Stat., Sec., 518B, Subd. 7(c).)

NOTE: *There may be some conflict with the fourteen-day rule.*

RELIEF

The court may grant the following relief in the order for protection:

- restrain the abusing party from committing acts of domestic abuse;

- exclude the abusing party from the dwelling that the parties share or from the residence of the petitioner;

- exclude the abusing party from a reasonable area surrounding the dwelling or residence, and describe the area specifically in the order;

- award temporary custody or establish temporary parenting time with regard to minor children of the parties on a basis that gives primary consideration to the safety of the victim and the children. If custody is contested, the court must make findings under the custody factors. The court may require supervised or limited parenting time, if necessary;

- establish temporary support for minor children or spouse, and order Automatic Income Withholding (explained later);

- provide upon request of the petitioner counseling or other social services for the parties or minor children;

- order the abusing party to participate in treatment or counseling services;

- award temporary use and possession of property and restrain one or both parties from transferring, encumbering, concealing, or disposing of property except in the usual course of business or for the necessities of life, and to account to the court for all such transfers, encumbrances, dispositions, and expenditures made after the order is served or communicated to the party restrained in open court;

- exclude the abusing party from the place of employment of the petitioner;

- order the abusing party to pay restitution to the petitioner (this is enforceable as a civil judgment.) (Minn. Stat., Sec., 518 B, Subd. 6(f));

- order the continuance of all currently available insurance coverage without change in coverage or beneficiary designation; and

- such other relief as the court deems necessary.

(Minn. Stat., Sec., 518B, Subd. 6.) The order shall be in effect for one year unless the court deems a different period is necessary. (Minn. Stat., Sec., 518 B, Subd. 6(b).) In some circumstances, the order may be extended. (Minn. Stat., Sec., 518 B, Subd. 6a.)

The respondent may be prohibited from possessing, transporting, or accepting a firearm under the 1994 amendment to the Gun Control Act, United States Code, Title 18, Section 922(g)(8). (Minn. Stat., Sec., 518B, Subd. 18(4).)

VIOLATION   A peace officer must arrest someone when there is reason to believe that the person has violated an order for protection. (Minn. Stat., Sec., 518 B, Subd. 14(e).) Violation of an order for protection is a criminal offense. If convicted, the person must be sentenced to three days in jail and counseling. The jail time may be waived if the person complies with the counseling requirement. (Minn. Stat., Sec., 518B, Subd. 14(b).) The violator may also be found in contempt of court for violation though this remedy is rarely used since the criminal process is so much more powerful and free of charge since the prosecutor handles it.

HARASSMENT RESTRAINING ORDER

In certain cases there is not sufficient evidence for an order for protection. When the other party's actions do not rise to the level of abuse, but that party makes repeated unwanted contact through telephone calls, letters, or just showing up unwanted, a harassment restraining order is an alternative.

Harassment for this purpose is defined as a single incident of physical or sexual assault or repeated incidents of intrusive or unwanted acts, words, or gestures that have a substantial adverse effect or are intended to have a substantial adverse effect on the safety, security, or privacy of another. (Minn. Stat., Sec., 609.748, Subd. 1(a)(1).) The victim of harassment or the parent of a juvenile victim may seek a restraining order. (Minn. Stat., Sec., 609.748, Subd. 2.)

PETITION The process is quite similar to seeking an order for protection. The petition must include only the names of the parties and allege that the respondent has engaged in abuse. (Minn. Stat., Sec., 518.609, Subd. 3.) The petition must be accompanied by an affidavit stating the specific facts of the harassment. The court is to provide assistance in completing the forms. The court must set a hearing within fourteen days. Unlike an order for protection, the petitioner must pay filing fees and service fees unless the harasser has engaged in the most egregious behavior like stalking or race-based harassment. (Minn. Stat., Sec., 609.748, Subd. 3a.)

EX PARTE As with an order for protection, there is a procedure for an *ex parte* harassment restraining order. If the petition alleges "an immediate and present danger or harassment" the court may issue a temporary restraining order. (Minn. Stat., Sec., 609.748, Subd. 4(a).) The temporary restraining order will remain in effect until the hearing.

At the hearing, if the court finds that there are reasonable grounds to believe that the respondent has engaged in harassment, the court may order the respondent to cease or avoid the harassment, or to have no contact with that person. (Minn. Stat., Sec., 609.748, Subd. 5.)

VIOLATION

A violation of the order is a misdemeanor. If there is another violation within five years of this or a similar restraining order, violation is a *gross misdemeanor*, which is more severe than a misdemeanor. Violation is a *felony* if any of the following occur:

- if there have been two previous violations of this or a similar order within five years;

- the violation is based on race, color, religion, gender, sexual orientation, or disability;

- false impersonation of another;

- violation while possessing a dangerous weapon;

- tampering with a jury or in retaliation against a judicial officer; or

- actions against a victim under age 8.

A peace officer may arrest a violator upon probable cause of violation without a warrant. (Minn. Stat., Sec., 609.748, Subd. 6.)

OBTAINING AN
ORDER

To obtain a restraining order under either the domestic abuse or harassment statues you should contact your attorney or domestic abuse officer at your county court house. Every county is required to have people available to assist you in preparing the petition and affidavit.

Post-Divorce Issues 10

Once your divorce is completed, you will have to ensure that the terms are carried out. It is hoped that both sides will agree to abide by the terms of the decree. However, if a spouse does not cooperate, you may need to seek the assistance of the court in enforcing the divorce decree.

Enforcement of the Divorce Decree

CHILD SUPPORT
If you apply for Automatic Income Withholding (AIW) for child support, the county attorney is to assist you in collection efforts. As a practical matter, if you are not receiving public assistance, you may be down the list of those receiving services from the limited resources of the county attorney's office. It may take many months for your case to be addressed. You can check with the child support officer or county attorney to determine whether you may need to seek the assistance of a private attorney. You should keep in mind that the county attorney is not technically representing you. The county attorney is working to ensure enforcement of the court order. There are circumstances in which the county attorney's obligations in the matter are not consistent with your interests.

In addition to contempt discussed below, a party in need of child support may seek to have a number of sanctions imposed. You should discuss with your attorney the process and which sanctions to seek. Among your choices are:

- sequestration of personal or other property;

- occupational license suspension;

- driver's license suspension;

- lien against a motor vehicle;

- bar access to recreational licenses (e.g. hunting and fishing);

- seizure of tax refunds;

- liens and garnishment against accounts;

- seek employment orders;

- seizure of unemployment and workers' compensation benefits; or

- subpoena of employers.

AUTOMATIC INCOME WITHHOLDING
If there are child support arrearages, an additional twenty percent of the ongoing amount can be collected through AIW. (Minn. Stat., Sec. 518.5513, Subd. 5(a)(7).) This is the most common and can be the most effective means of collection.

CONTEMPT
If a person is at least three months in arrears on child support or maintenance payments, the party may be cited for contempt. (Minn. Stat., Sec. 518.617, Subd. 1 and Minn. Stat., Sec. 518.64.)

As a defense to the contempt, the obligor must prove to the court that he is unable to work. An obligor is presumed to be able to work full time.

NOTE: *In a contempt proceeding, the court may determine that a party is only able to pay an amount less than the court ordered child support to avoid having contempt sanctions imposed. For example, if someone is ordered to pay $500 per month, but the court finds that he is only able to pay $400 that is all he must pay to avoid going to jail or having some other sanction imposed. In that case, he will continue to incur an additional $100 in monthly arrearages. If the obligor is indeed able to pay only $400, he must bring a motion to modify child support.*

ATTORNEY FEES

Often the cost of hiring a private attorney to aggressively pursue collection of past due support make it impossible or impractical for the party due to the cost of attorney fees. If the child support is in arrears in the amount of at least $500, 90 days past due, and docketed as a judgment, the child support recipient is entitled to an award of attorney fees and collection costs. (Minn. Stat., Sec. 518.14, Subd. 2(a).) Attorney fees awarded in this way may be collected using the same procedures as collecting child support. (Minn. Stat., Sec. 518.14, Subd. 2(b).) If you are receiving child support collection services or any other form of public assistance from the child support agency, you or your attorney must provide written notice to the agency within five days of your retaining the attorney. You must also notify the public authority within five days of receipt of any funds collected by a private attorney. (Minn. Stat., Sec. 518.14, Subd. 2(b).) This is to avoid duplicating collection efforts.

If you seek collection of attorney fees under this provision, your attorney must serve notice of intent to collect attorney fees. The notice must include an itemization of the attorney fees and costs and indicate that the attorney fees will become an additional judgment for child support unless the obligor requests a hearing within twenty days of mailing the notice. The only issues the obligor can contest are the reasonableness of the fees or that there is a mistake of fact (e.g. he paid, but has not been credited for the payments). (Minn. Stat., Sec. 518.14, Subd. 2(c).) The attorney fees and costs may not exceed thirty percent of the arrearages. (Minn. Stat., Sec. 518.14, Subd. 2(d).)

If the obligor does not request a hearing within twenty days of mailing of the notice, the fees and costs become an additional judgment for child support. (Minn. Stat., Sec. 518.14, Subd. 2(e).)

VISITATION EXPEDITORS

Minnesota law provides for the appointment of a *visitation expeditor* upon the request of either or both parties or upon the court's own motion. (Minn. Stat., Sec. 518.1751, Subd. 1.) The expeditor is to resolve visitation disputes by enforcing, interpreting, clarifying, and addressing circumstances not specifically addressed by an existing order and determine whether there has been a violation of an order. The expeditor may be appointed to resolve a one-time problem or to provide ongoing visitation dispute resolution services. (Minn. Stat., Sec. 518.1751, Subd. 1b(a).)

The expeditor is to attempt to mediate any dispute by facilitating discussions between the parties. (Minn. Stat., Sec. 518.1751, Subd. 1b(c).) If the parties are unable to reach an agreement with the assistance of the expeditor (as mediator), the expeditor is to decide the issue. (Minn. Stat., Sec. 518.1751, Subd. 1b(c).) See Chapter 3 for a discussion on mediation and arbitration.

SELECTING AN
EXPEDITOR

The statute provides a mechanism for appointing an expeditor. The easiest method is for the parties to reach an agreement on the expeditor and submit it to the court. (Minn. Stat., Sec. 518.1751, Subd. 2(a).)

If the parties are unable to agree, the court is to provide the court administrator's roster of expeditors. The parties are to select three names each from the roster and exchange their lists. (Minn. Stat., Sec. 518.175, Subd. 2(b).) Unfortunately, not all court administrators maintain such rosters. In addition, there is no explanation as to the purpose of exchanging the lists of three expeditors. Apparently, the legislature believed that there would be some overlap thus resolving the dispute as to selection of the expeditor.

If exchanging the lists of expeditors does not result in selection of an expeditor, the court is to appoint one. (Minn. Stat., Sec. 518.1751, Subds. 2(b) and 2b.) The court is to consider the financial circumstances of the parties in apportioning fees. (Minn. Stat., Sec. 518.1751, Subd. 2(b).)

An order appointing an expeditor must provide the following:

- the name of the expeditor;

- the nature of the dispute;

- the responsibilities of the expeditor;

- whether the expeditor is appointed for one issue or on an ongoing basis;

- the term of the appointment;

- the apportionment of fees; and

- notice that the expeditor is authorized to make a decision resolving the dispute if the parties are unable to agree.

Within five days of the dispute being submitted, the expeditor is to meet with the parties either together or separately. (Minn. Stat., Sec. 518.1751, Subd. 3(a).) The expeditor must make a diligent effort to facilitate an agreement. If the matter requires immediate attention, the expeditor is to consult via telephone or otherwise use the most expedient means. In certain circumstances, the expeditor may make a decision without conferring with a party, if the expeditor made a good faith effort to contact the other party and that party chose not to participate in resolving the dispute.

Within five days of receiving the information necessary to make a decision, the expeditor must issue a decision. The decision may include compensatory visitation, and may recommend the payment of attorney fees, court costs, and other costs. (Minn. Stat., Sec. 518.1751, Subd. 3(b).) The decision must be within the bounds of the existing order, but may clarify or interpret the order, unless the parties agree otherwise. (Minn. Stat., Sec. 518.1751, Subd. 3(c).)

The expeditor is required to put the agreement or decision in writing. The expeditor may provide reasons for the decision, but is not required to do so. (Minn. Stat., Sec. 518.1751, Subd. 3(d).) The agreement or decision is binding on the parties unless or until vacated by the court. If a party does not comply with a decision, there can be a motion to the court to seek enforcement. (Minn. Stat., Sec. 518.1751, Subd. 3(a).)

CONFIDENTIALITY

Statements or documents provided as part of the visitation expeditor process are not discoverable unless they are otherwise subject to discovery. Further, they are not admissible at trial. (Minn. Stat., Sec. 518.1751, Subd. 4(a).)

REMOVAL OF EXPEDITOR

A party may seek the removal of an expeditor who has been appointed on a long-term basis for good cause only. Minn. Stat., Sec. 518.1751, Subd. 5a.)

DOMESTIC ABUSE AND THE EXPEDITOR

As with many provisions, the visitation expeditor statute does not apply if either party claims to be the victim of domestic abuse, the child or one of the parties has been physically abused, or the party is unable to pay the costs of the visitation expeditor. (Minn. Stat., Sec. 518.1751, Subd. 1a.) If the parties have been advised by counsel, have agreed to use an expeditor, and there is no requirement of face-to-face meetings, they may use an expeditor.

MODIFYING CUSTODY, VISITATION, SUPPORT, AND MAINTENANCE 11

Custody, visitation, child support, and spousal maintenance are issues that may be modified after the divorce is over. The court must apply the relevant legal standard (discussed below) to determine whether modification is in order.

CUSTODY

It is essential that custody be set properly in the initial proceeding. The initial custody determination is made using the thirteen factors discussed in Chapter 4 to determine the best interests of the child. However, if you later wish to change custody and your spouse does not agree, you must prove that the child is endangered in your ex-spouse's care.

In general, a motion to modify custody may not be brought until a year has passed since the initial custody determination. (Minn. Stat., Sec. 518.18 (a).) If there has been a motion to change custody, the parties must wait two years before filing another motion to modify custody, whether or not the change in custody was granted. (Minn. Stat., Sec. 518.18 (b).) This is to prevent frequent and harassing filings for custody. Neither of the above restrictions on filing motions applies if the court finds that there has been interference with visitation, or has reason to believe that the child's present environment may endanger the child. (Minn. Stat., Sec. 518.18(c).)

If the above qualifications are met, the court may not modify the custody arrangement unless it finds, based on facts that were not known or not available at the time of the previous custody determination, that a change has occurred in the circumstances of the parties or the child. Furthermore, modification must be necessary to serve the best interests of the child. (Minn. Stat., Sec.518.18(d).) The statute goes on to provide that the court will retain the old custody arrangement unless it finds:

- both parties agree to the modification;

- the child has been integrated into the family of the petitioner with the consent of the other party; or

- the child's present environment endangers the child's physical or emotional health or impairs the child's emotional development and the harm likely to be caused by a change of environment is outweighed by the advantage of a change to the child.

NOTE: *If you are seeking to change custody, it is essential that you hire an attorney.*

MODIFYING JOINT CUSTODY

If you are seeking to change a joint custody arrangement the same requirements apply unless the parties agree in writing to applying a different standard or if a party is seeking to move the child out of state.

NOTE: *The statute provides nothing beyond that as far as what standard to apply if a party is seeking to move the child out of state. (Minn. Stat., Sec. 518.18(e).)*

The Minnesota Supreme Court filled the gap and provided that, in order to move a child out of state under a joint custody arrangement, the parent seeking to move must prove that it is in the best interests of the child to move out of state. This is a considerably more difficult burden to meet than if the parent seeking to move has sole physical custody.

PARENTING TIME

The court shall modify an order granting or denying parenting time rights whenever modification would serve the best interests of the child. (Minn. Stat., Sec. 518.175, Subd. 5.) The court may not restrict parenting time unless it finds that parenting time is likely to endanger the child's physical or emotional health or impair the child's emotional development or the noncustodial parent has chronically and unreasonably failed to comply with court ordered parenting time. (Minn. Stat., Sec. 518.175, Subd. 5(1) and (2).)

If a party has been denied parenting time, the court may impose a variety of sanctions:

- compensatory visitation of the same type and duration as the deprived parenting time;

- civil penalty of up to $500;

- require the depriving party to post a bond;

- award attorney fees and costs;

- require reimbursement of costs incurred due to loss of parenting time;

- any other remedy the court finds to be in the best interests of the child involved; or

- in egregious cases, the court may reverse custody.

Child Support

If you believe that circumstances justify a change in child support there are a number of ways in which you can proceed. Most people enlist the assistance of the child support officer. The *child support officer* can provide the forms or information necessary to schedule a motion. If you have complex issues or time pressure you may want to hire a private attorney.

If you use a child support officer, the child support officer can compel the parties to disclose information necessary to determine whether a modification of child support is permissible. In addition, parties are required to disclose tax returns every two years, if so requested by the other party. Once the information is obtained the child support officer prepares financial worksheets. Sometimes this is not done until the hearing. Once all the information is provided, it is time to run the child support calculation from Chapter 6. If there is an agreement, the child support officer can prepare an agreement for the parties and the court to sign.

The terms of an order respecting maintenance or support may be modified upon a showing of one or more of the following:

- substantially increased or decreased earnings of a party;

- substantially increased or decreased needs of a party or the child or children that are the subject of these proceedings;

- receipt of assistance under the MFIP;

- a change in the cost of living for either party as measured by the Federal Bureau of Statistics, any of which makes the terms unreasonable and unfair;

- extraordinary medical expenses of the child not provided for under section 518.171; or

- the addition of work-related or education-related child care expenses of the obligee or a substantial increase or decrease in existing work-related or education-related child care expenses. (Minn. Stat., Sec. 518.64, Subd. 2(a).)

In modifying support, the court must consider any needs of the child.

It is presumed that there has been a substantial change in circumstances as discussed above and the terms of a current support order shall be rebuttably presumed to be unreasonable and unfair if:

- the application of the child support guidelines in the statute, to the current circumstances of the parties results in a calculated court order that is at least 20 percent and at least $50 per month higher or lower than the current support order;

- the medical support provisions of the order are not enforceable by the public authority or the custodial parent;

- health coverage ordered is not available to the child for whom the order is established by the parent ordered to provide; or

- the existing support obligation is in the form of a statement of percentage and not a specific dollar amount. (Minn. Stat., Sec. 518.64, Subd. 2(b).)

If the court determines that modification is necessary, the court is to apply the guidelines of Minnesota Statutes, Section 518.551, subd. 5. The income of a new spouse is not to be considered. In addition, if the obligor has started to work additional overtime, that is not to be considered in most cases. (Minn. Stat., Sec. 518.64, Subd. 2(c).) However, if the obligor is in arrears, all of the net income from the additional employment must be used to satisfy arrearages until the arrearages are paid in full. (Minn. Stat., Sec. 518.64, Subd. 2(c)(2)(vi).)

Motions for modification of child support are only retroactive to the date a motion is served, except in extraordinary circumstances. (Minn. Stat., Sec. 518.64, Subd. 2(d).)

A child support order terminates automatically upon the *emancipation* of a child. (Minn. Stat., Sec. 518.64, Subd. 4a.) However, if there are two or more children, the award must be terminated explicitly in the order or by motion. (Minn. Stat., Sec. 518.64, Subd. 4a(b).) The child support obligation does not terminate upon the death of the obligor. (Minn. Stat., Sec. 518.64, Subd. 4.)

Child support modification proceedings are generally handled by a magistrate under the Expedited Child Support Process. This process is intended to speed up child support procedures. However, the rules have been modified several times over the past few years. The final rules of the process are not yet available at this writing. The process involving magistrates is more friendly to the unrepresented party, and the traditional rules of evidence do not apply.

CHILDCARE COSTS

Though childcare is deemed child support, it is not subject to cost-of-living adjustments. If there has been a substantial change in childcare costs, either party may seek modification of the order. If either parent reports that there are no more childcare costs, the public authority is to verify the information and terminate child support as of the date of the request.

MODIFYING SPOUSAL MAINTENANCE

Once spousal maintenance has been set, it can be modified in certain circumstances. Except in certain unique situations, modification is only retroactive to the date of service of a motion to modify. (Minn. Stat., Sec. 518.552, Subd 2(d).) If you need additional support or need to reduce the amount you are paying, it is important to move quickly and have motion papers served to preserve the effective date of modification.

In order to even consider modifying maintenance, a party must show one of the following:

- substantially increased or decreased earnings of a party;

- substantially increased or decreased need of a party or the child or children that are the subject of these proceedings;

- receipt of public assistance;

- a change in the cost of living for either party as measured by the federal bureau of statistics, any of which makes the terms unreasonable and unfair; or

- extraordinary medical expenses of the child not provided for under other terms of the divorce.

In addition, the court is to consider the factors for establishing spousal maintenance as set forth in Minnesota Statutes Section 518.552 as discussed in Chapter 6. The court may require an evidentiary hearing (trial) to modify spousal maintenance. However, such a hearing is not necessary. (Minn. Stat., Sec. 518.552, Subd. 2(f).) The court may simply take the information on written affidavits and other documentary evidence rather than testimony.

Motions for modification of maintenance are only retroactive to the date a motion is served, except in extraordinary circumstances. (Minn. Stat., Sec. 518.64, Subd. 2(d).)

Unless otherwise agreed, spousal maintenance terminates upon the death of either party or the remarriage of the recipient. (Minn. Stat., Sec. 518.64, Subd. 3.) Death can be dealt with through insurance on the life of the payor.

RETIREMENT

Many divorce decrees provide for a permanent award of spousal maintenance without any consideration for what will happen upon retirement. For more information on this issue see Chapter 10 Post Divorce Issues. One issue is when a party retires. There is a question as to when a party is retiring to avoid continued payments of spousal maintenance in bad faith and when a party is retiring in the normal course of business.

If the payor's retirement plan has been divided as part of a divorce, that marital portion generally may not be considered as income. It is property that has already been divided. If the payor's sole income upon retirement is from a retirement plan that was divided in the marriage, his effective income for spousal maintenance purposes is nothing. There are a number of subtle distinctions in the case law on this issue that you should discuss with your attorney.

Glossary

A

affidavit. A sworn written statement.

alternative dispute resolution. Any of a number of methods for resolving the issues in a divorce without using the courts. Alternatives include mediation, arbitration, collaborative law, and a number of others.

annulment. A determination that a marriage never existed as opposed to a divorce that terminates a marriage.

arbitration. A method of dispute resolution in which a neutral party decides a dispute after a hearing.

B

Best Interests Standard. The thirteen factors concerning custody addressed in Chapter 4 make up the Best Interests Standard.

C

collaborative law. A method of dispute resolution in which the parties and their attorneys agree to resolve their divorce without going to court.

conflict of interest. This refers to a situation in which an attorney cannot fully represent a client due to a prior relationship or other interest in a case. For example, an attorney may have represented the opposing party in a previous divorce or other case and cannot now represent you against that former client. Another example occurs when your attorney asks for a lien in your home to cover your legal bill. Since homes are protected to some extent, your attorney is asking you to give up something significant to secure your bill. He must advise you to consult with another attorney on that issue.

custody. Decision-making rights and duty to care for children. There are two types of custody—legal custody and physical custody. Either may be joint or sole.

custodial parent or custodian. The person who has the physical custody of the child at any particular time.

D

defined benefit plan. An annuity type of retirement plan that provides a certain amount upon retirement, usually a monthly payment. The amount depends upon the type of plan. Often, it is based on years of service and salary.

defined contribution plan. A family of plans including IRAs and 401(k)s in which the party or employer (or both) contribute a sum which is known. The plan grows through investment growth in addition to the contribution.

deposition. A discovery process in which the party to be deposed is asked questions by the opposing party (or attorney) in front of a court reporter. The testimony is sworn and often used in court.

dissolution of marriage. *See* **divorce.**

divorce. The termination of the marital relationship.

E

emancipation. When a child becomes independent of a parent either upon reaching age 18 or earlier by virtue of having a child, entering the military, marrying, living independently of the parent, or by some other act evidencing independence.

endangerment standard. In order to change custody of a child, the party seeking the change must show that the emotional or physical health of the child is endangered under the existing custody arrangement.

ex parte. A request for relief to the court without the other party being present. It is used in limited circumstances as it is contrary to notions of the adversarial process.

F

filing. When documents are delivered to the court administrator to be placed in the court's file on a case.

I

interrogatories. A list of questions submitted as part of the discovery process.

J

joint legal custody. Both parents have equal rights and responsibilities, including the right to participate in major decisions determining the child's upbringing, including education, health care, and religious training.

joint physical custody. The routine daily care and control and the residence of the child is structured between the parties.

L

legal custody.   The right to participate in the child's upbringing, including education, health care, and religious training. There is a presumption the custody will be joint.

legal separation.   A court determination of the rights and responsibilities of a husband and wife arising out of the marriage relationship. A decree of legal separation does not terminate the marriage.

M

maintenance.   An award made in a dissolution or legal separation proceeding of payments from the future income or earnings of one spouse for the support and maintenance of the other. This was once called alimony and is also referred to as spousal maintenance.

marital property.   Property acquired during the marriage. May include the increase in value.

marital termination agreement.   The settlement agreement. Sometimes referred to as the "contract" between the parties that dissolves the marriage.

mediation.   A process in which an impartial third party facilitates an agreement between two or more parties in a proceeding.

O

obligor.   The party paying child support.

obligee.   The party receiving child support.

P

parenting time. The time a parent spends with a child regardless of the custodial designation regarding the child.

personal service. When documents are delivered to a party to the case rather than mailed. Generally, personal service is only required when the Summons and Petition for Dissolution of Marriage must be served at the beginning of the divorce. After that, documents may be served by mail.

petition for dissolution of marriage. Document commencing a divorce action upon service to responding spouse..

petitioner. The party initiating the divorce proceeding.

physical custody. The routine daily care and control of the child.

R

referee. A judicial officer who is not a judge, but may hear a case and issue orders like a judge. These officials are heavily used in Ramsey and Hennepin Counties.

residence. The place where a party has established a permanent home from which the party has no present intention of moving.

respondent. The party responding to the divorce proceeding.

S

service. Delivery or mailing of documents to the opposing party.

T

temporary relief. An expedited process allowing for a hearing before a judicial officer for determining issues such as child support, custody, property division, etc. pending final resolution of the case.

tracing. The party claiming that an asset is non-marital must trace the asset back to its nonmarital origin. For example, if you claim that your parents made the down payment on your home as a gift to you alone, you must try to produce the check and any other documents supporting this claim.

V

venue. The county courthouse in which the case is heard. The case may be venued in the county in which either party resides.

vesting. Indicates when the employee has the right to an employment benefit, usually a retirement plan. For example, if a plan vests after three years of service, the employee must work there for three years before he may be entitled to any benefit.

visitation. *See* **parenting time**.

visitation expeditor. A neutral person authorized to use a mediation-arbitration process to resolve visitation disputes. A visitation expeditor shall attempt to resolve a visitation dispute by facilitating negotiations between the parties to promote settlement and, if it becomes apparent that the dispute cannot be resolved by an agreement of the parties, the visitation expeditor shall make a decision resolving the dispute.

Appendix A
Sample Filled-in Forms

Completing Forms

The following section is an example situation and a set of completed forms for a fairly simple case. After this appendix, there is an Appendix B of blank forms that can be completed for your case. Not all forms in this appendix can be found blank in Appendix B. Some forms must be obtained at the court house where your case will be heard.

Hypothetical Case

Jane Smith is seeking a divorce from her husband John. She is thirty-three years old, and he is thirty-five. They married June 8, 1978. They have been separated since April 2, 2001, and John is living with a friend from work until the divorce is final. Jane believes John is procrastinating in discussing the divorce and drafts the **Summons** and **Petition for Dissolution of Marriage**. She provides the **Summons** and the **Petition for Dissolution of Marriage** to the sheriff for service upon John. She could hire a private process server or other person to deliver the papers, but it is more convenient for her to hire the sheriff. The sheriff serves the papers on June 1, 2001. Jane also files the documents with the required **Certificate of Representation and Parties** and the required filing fee. John hopes for reconciliation, but recognizes that Jane does not agree. He is not surprised to receive the papers. He serves an **Answer** and files that with the court.

The couple has two daughters Amber Lynn (age 12) and Barbara Ann (age 10). The couple wants to resolve the case amicably with both parties being involved in the children's lives. They want to enter into a parenting plan that provides frequent access for one another. (If they would have decided on traditional custody with support, the calculation forms (1 and 2) are filled in the way they would have done them.)

They own a home at 1417 Main Street in Saint Paul, which they bought on June 1, 1990. The legal description is: Lot 7, Block 2 Dayton's Addition, County of Ramsey, State of Minnesota. The home is worth $250,000 and they owe $125,000 on the mortgage. They bought the house for $100,000 shortly after they married using John's veteran's benefits. They have made significant improvements to the home. Jane's parents gave the couple $10,000 to help with the down payment on the house.

They own a 1999 Oldsmobile Silhouette minivan that Jane drives. The fair market value of the vehicle is $18,000, and they owe $10,000 on it. John drives a leased 1999 Ford Taurus. In addition, John owned a 1955 Chevrolet before the marriage. The parties also own a boat, which they use for water-skiing and fishing.

They have $10,000 in Series EE U.S. Savings for the kids' college education. They have nominal bank account balances. They have a MasterCard that Jane uses with a balance of $4,000, which includes Christmas gifts, a family trip, and clothing for her. They have a Visa account with a balance of $2,000 that John uses mostly for things related to his car and car club activities. They have a Sears card that has a balance of $2,500 for a stove, refrigerator, washer and drier. They each have a universal life insurance policy with a face value of $250,000. The policy on Jane's life has a cash value of $12,000. John's has a cash value of $10,000.

Jane is employed as an engineer at 3M. She earns $50,000 per year. John is employed as a personal banker at U.S. Bank and earns $40,000 per year. She provides medical insurance for the family through her employment at $250 per month. He provides dental insurance for the family at a cost of $30.00 per month. Both contribute five percent of their salaries to their retirement plans. Jane's various profit sharing and retirement plans are worth $65,000. John's plans are worth $75,000 since he has contributed to them longer and used more aggressive investment options. Jane travels for work about every six weeks for up to a week at a time. She needs John to take the kids since her family does not live in Minnesota.

The couple cannot agree on a mediator or make any further progress. Jane serves and files with the court a SCHEDULING INFORMATION STATEMENT. The court issues a scheduling order based upon this document requiring, among other things, mediation and setting a pretrial hearing.

Though both parents recognize that each should have significant access to the children, they anticipate difficulties with access for holidays and cannot agree on financial arrangements. John is trying to set up a new household and must buy all new items, as Jane claims she needs virtually all of the household goods to provide for the kids, especially the kitchen items. In addition, Jane is the higher earner and John feels she can make due for the time being. Jane wants John to pay some support for the kids since she provides most of their meals and buys their clothing and other needs. John points out that the girls eat breakfast at daycare, lunch at school and he has them as much after school as she does. He is splitting daycare costs. John believes rent for an apartment big enough for himself and the girls is too expensive if he has to pay support. Finally, Jane is only cooperative in giving him the girls in periods leading up to her business trips when she expects him to take care of them. However, when she returns she tries to monopolize the girls' time. John decides it is time for the court to assist, and he schedules a temporary relief hearing.

John prepares a NOTICE OF MOTION AND MOTION; an APPLICATION FOR TEMPORARY RELIEF; and an AFFIDAVIT for the hearing. He calls the court to schedule the hearing and learns that Referee Anderson has been assigned to the case. He has someone serve the papers at least fourteen days before the hearing (seventeen days if by U.S. Mail). The person serving completes an AFFIDAVIT OF PERSONAL SERVICE which is filed with the court along with the motion documents.

At the hearing in late July, the court immediately makes an order for a parenting plan evaluation. However, the remaining issues are taken under advisement. The court takes the full ninety days to render a decision on the remaining issues of child support, a temporary parenting plan, division of household goods, etc.

The parties start to make progress in mediation while awaiting the temporary order. However, they are unable to reach a final agreement. They must prepare Prehearing Statements for the scheduled pretrial conference. Attached is Respondent's PREHEARING STATEMENT. He has someone serve and file it ten days before the pretrial (thirteen days if by U.S. Mail). In addition, because the case is in Ramsey County, the Ramsey County Court Administrator sends a form called a JOINT DISPOSITIONAL CONFERENCE REPORT to fill out which requires the parties to meet and discuss the issues to be presented to the court. This form too must be completed and returned to the court at least ten days before the pre-trial. Only Ramsey County requires this form.

At the pretrial in November, the parties explain to the court the issues on which they were stuck. John wanted Jane to refinance since she was tying up his share of the equity and his VA housing benefit. John's share of the equity in the home would be $50,000. Jane did not believe she could afford the new mortgage payment though she wanted to keep the house. Referee Anderson suggested the parties consider an arrangement whereby Jane would refinance and give John $30,000. He would have a lien for the balance payable in five years. In addition, since Jane was receiving the vehicle with $8,000 more in equity and the insurance policy with $2,000 more in equity, John would be awarded an additional $5,000 in the lien to equalize the property division. The lien would be for $25,000.

A few weeks later they did reach an agreement on all the issues. The agreement included a PARENTING PLAN which provided for the children to reside primarily with their father during the school year and their mother during the summer. John will have the children every weekend in the summer so that they can be at his parent's cabin--something they had done for the past several years. Jane will provide all of the clothing for the children and pay for their activities and will pay the medical insurance premium. They will each pay for copayments and deductibles. Since the children will be in the care of both parents nearly equally during the year, they agreed that no other cash payments would change hands. Another consideration for John was that he got to keep the entire value of his pension plan which was worth $10,000 more than Jane's. Jane also assumed the Sears debt since she was keeping the appliances purchased on the card. John would pay $1,000 from his Visa card toward Jane's MasterCard to equalize the division of debt. These terms are included in the MARITAL TERMINATION AGREEMENT.

Jane drafts the FINDINGS OF FACT, CONCLUSIONS OF LAW, ORDER FOR JUDGMENT AND JUDGMENT AND DECREE (JUDGMENT AND DECREE) and the DEFAULT SCHEDULING REQUEST. Since they do not have attorneys and there are children involved, she must appear before the court for a brief hearing. The court will inquire as to whether this arrangement is best for the children. If all goes smoothly, the court will sign the JUDGMENT AND DECREE and the divorce will be granted.

TABLE OF FORMS

Child Support Calculation Worksheet

Obligor/Payor Calculation

Gross Monthly Income		$3,333
Federal Income Tax (M-2)	348	
State Income Tax (M-2)	166	
Social Security/Medicare (.0765)	255	
Pension Deduction	166.65	
Union Dues		
Dependent Health Insurance		
Dental Insurance	30	
Individual Health Insurance		
Other Child Support		
Total Deductions		965.65
Net Monthly Income		$2,367.35
Child support multiplier (.30___)		710.24

Obligee/Recipient Calculation

Gross Monthly Income		$4,167
Federal Income Tax (M-2)	474	
State Income Tax(M-2)	225	
FICA (.0765)	318.78	
Pension Deduction	208.35	
Union Dues		
Dependent Health Insurance	250	
Dental Insurance		
Individual Health Insurance		
Other Child Support		
Total Deductions		$1,476.13
Net Monthly Income		$2,690.87

Child Care Calculation Proportion

<u>Obligor</u>

Net income   2,367.35

Support Paid (710.21   )

Total   1,657.14

<u>Obligee</u>

Net income   2,690.87

Support Rec'd   710.21

Total   3,401.08

Obligor's Total   1,657.14

Obligee's Total +   3,401.08

Total Income   5,058.22

Obligor's Total   1,657.14

Total Income   ÷   5,058.22

Obligor's Percentage   .3276

Childcare Benefit   x   .75

Childcare Percentage: 24.51%

NOTE: *The above child support calculation would apply if Jane was awarded sole custody and John was paying full child support. This does not fit with the settlement in the hypothetical case.*

DISSOLUTION WITH CHILDREN - 4

~~DISSOLUTION WITHOUT CHILDREN - 5~~

STATE OF MINNESOTA

COUNTY OF <u>RAMSEY</u>

In Re the Marriage of:

DISTRICT COURT

<u>SECOND</u> JUDICIAL DISTRICT

FAMILY COURT DIVISION

<u>Jane Smith   </u>,

        Petitioner,

and

SUMMONS

Court File No. <u>F4-01-3737   </u>

Judicial Officer _____

<u>John Smith   </u>,

        Respondent.

_____

THE STATE OF MINNESOTA TO THE ABOVE-NAMED RESPONDENT.

You are hereby summoned and required to serve upon the Petitioner's attorney an Answer to the Petition which is herewith served upon you within thirty (30) days, exclusive of the date of service. If you fail to do so, judgment by default will be taken against you for the relief demanded in the Petition.

This proceeding involves, affects, or brings into question real property situated in the County of <u>Ramsey</u> and legally described as:

Lot 7, Block 2 Dayton's Addition, County of Ramsey, State of Minnesota

NOTICE OF TEMPORARY RESTRAINING PROVISIONS

UNDER MINNESOTA LAW, SERVICE OF THIS SUMMONS MAKES THE FOLLOWING REQUIREMENTS APPLY TO BOTH PARTIES TO THIS ACTION, UNLESS THEY ARE MODIFIED BY THE COURT OR THE PROCEEDING DISMISSED;

(1) NEITHER PARTY MAY DISPOSE OF ANY ASSETS EXCEPT (i) FOR THE NECESSITIES OF LIFE OR FOR THE NECESSARY GENERATION OF INCOME OR PRESERVATION OF ASSETS, (ii) BY AN AGREEMENT IN WRITING, OR (iii) FOR RETAINING COUNSEL TO CARRY ON OR TO CONTEST THIS PROCEEDING.

(2) NEITHER PARTY MAY HARASS THE OTHER PARTY; AND

(3) ALL CURRENTLY AVAILABLE INSURANCE COVERAGE MUST BE MAINTAINED AND CONTINUED WITHOUT CHANGE IN COVERAGE OR BENEFICIARY DESIGNATION.

(4) PARTIES TO A MARRIAGE DISSOLUTION PROCEEDING ARE ENCOURAGED TO ATTEMPT ALTERNATIVE DISPUTE RESOLUTION PURSUANT TO MINNESOTA LAW. ALTERNATIVE DISPUTE RESOLUTION INCLUDES MEDIATION, ARBITRATION, AND OTHER PROCESSES AS SET FORTH IN THE DISTRICT COURT RULES. YOU MAY CONTACT THE COURT ADMINISTRATOR ABOUT RESOURCES IN YOUR AREA. IF YOU CANNOT PAY FOR MEDIATION OR ALTERNATIVE DISPUTE RESOLUTION, IN SOME COUNTIES, ASSISTANCE MAY BE AVAILABLE TO YOU THROUGH A NONPROFIT PROVIDER OR A COURT PROGRAM. IF YOU ARE A VICTIM OF DOMESTIC ABUSE OR THREATS OF ABUSE AS DEFINED IN MINNESOTA STATUTES, CHAPTER 518B, YOU ARE NOT REQUIRED TO TRY MEDIATION AND YOU WILL NOT BE PENALIZED BY THE COURT IN LATER PROCEEDINGS.

IF YOU VIOLATE ANY OF THESE PROVISIONS, YOU WILL BE SUBJECT TO SANCTIONS BY THE COURT.

Dated:_____   By: _____
                                          Name: Jane Smith_____
                                          Petitioner *Pro Se*
                                          Address: 1417 Main Street____
                                          Saint Paul, Minnesota 55106__
                                          Telephone No. (651) 771-0050

DISSOLUTION WITH CHILDREN - 4

~~DISSOLUTION WITHOUT CHILDREN - 5~~

STATE OF MINNESOTA	DISTRICT COURT
COUNTY OF <u>RAMSEY</u>	<u>SECOND</u> JUDICIAL DISTRICT
In Re the Marriage of:	FAMILY COURT DIVISION

<u>Jane Smith   </u>,

          Petitioner,

and

<u>John Smith   </u>,

          Respondent.

**PETITION FOR DISSOLUTION
OF MARRIAGE**

Court File No. <u>F4-01-3737</u>

Judicial Officer _____

_____

Petitioner for her Petition for Dissolution of Marriage, against the above-named Respondent alleges that:

I.

The name, address, date of birth, age, and Social Security Number of Petitioner are as follows:

        Name: <u>Jane A. Smith   </u>
        Address: <u>1417 Main Street.   </u>
                 <u>Saint Paul, Minnesota 55106   </u>
        County: <u>Ramsey County   </u>
        Born: <u>April 15, 1968   </u>
        Age: <u>33   </u>
        Social Security Number: <u>Confidential Information Form </u>

The Petitioner has formerly been known by the following name(s):

<u>Jane A. Jones. She is proceeding *pro se*.   </u>

II.

The name, address, date of birth, age, and Social Security Number of Respondent are as follows:

        Name: <u>John B. Smith   </u>

Address: <u>1966 Oak Street.</u>

<u>Minneapolis, Minnesota 55424</u>

County: <u>Hennepin County</u>

Born: <u>June 30, 1966</u>

Age: <u>35</u>

Social Security Number: <u>Confidential Information Form</u>

Respondent has formerly been known by the following name(s):

<u>none. It is not known whether Respondent has an attorney.</u>

III.

The parties were married to each other on (date) <u>June 8, 1978</u> in the City of <u>Stillwater</u>, County of <u>Washington</u>, State of <u>Minnesota</u>, and ever since have been and are now husband and wife.

IV.

The parties have the following minor children, including date of birth, age, and social security number.

Name: <u>Amber Lynn Smith</u>

Born: <u>December 3, 1989</u>

Age: <u>12</u>

Social Security No. <u>Confidential Information Form</u>

Name: <u>Barbara Ann Smith</u>

Born: <u>September 5, 1991</u>

Age: <u>9</u>

Social Security No. <u>Confidential Information Form</u>

The minor children of the parties are now in the care of (Petitioner/~~Respondent/both parties~~). The minor children of the parties are not subject to the jurisdiction of any juvenile court.

_____ Custody of the minor children should be awarded to (Petitioner/Respondent/both parties)

__X__ The parties should enter into a parenting plan regarding the care of the minor children.

V.

(~~Petitioner~~/Respondent) should pay temporary and permanent support for the care of

121

the minor child of the parties.

VI.

(~~Petitioner/Respondent/~~Neither party) should pay temporary or permanent spousal maintenance for the support of the other.

VII.

Petitioner/~~Respondent~~ provides medical insurance for the benefit of Petitioner.

~~Petitioner/~~Respondent provides medical insurance for the benefit of Respondent

Petitioner/~~Respondent~~ provides medical insurance for the benefit of the minor children.

VIII.

The parties own various items of personal property.

IX.

Petitioner/~~Respondent~~ has resided within the State of Minnesota for more than 180 days immediately preceding commencement of this proceeding. Petitioner presently resides in __Ramsey__ County.

X.

The wife is not presently pregnant.

XI.

No separate proceedings for dissolution of marriage or legal separation have been commenced or are pending in any court in the State of Minnesota or elsewhere.

XII.

There has been an irretrievable breakdown of the marriage relationship pursuant to Minn. Stat. § 518.06, as amended, so as to constitute grounds for dissolution of the marriage.

XIII.

Neither party hereto is in the military service of the United States Government so, accordingly, the Soldiers' and Sailors' Relief Act of 1940, as amended, is not applicable in this proceeding.

XIV.

The parties have been separated since April 2, 2001.

XV.

Petitioner is employed as an engineer _____ by Minnesota Mining and Manufacturing. Petitioner has a net monthly income of approximately $2,691.

XVI.

Respondent is employed as a personal banker by U.S. Bank Corporation. Respondent has a net monthly income of approximately $2,367.

XVII.

The parties own the following real property:

a home at 1417 Main Street in Saint Paul with a fair market value of $250,000 and a mortgage of $125,000. Petitioner has a non-marital interest in said property. The property is located in the County of Ramsey, State of Minnesota and is legally described as follows:

Lot 7, Block 2 Dayton's Addition, County of Ramsey, State of Minnesota

~~The parties own no real estate.~~

XVIII.

The parties own the following motor vehicles:

Year	Make	Model	VIN	Value	Debt
1999	Oldsmobile	Silhouette minivan			$10,000
1999	Ford	Taurus			None
1955	Chevrolet				None

XIX.

The parties are the owners of cash, savings, and checking accounts.

XX.

The parties have incurred miscellaneous debts and obligations during their marriage.

The parties have incurred various individual debts since their separation on April 2, 2001 for which each party should be responsible.

XXI.

_____ There is an order for protection presently in effect.

_X_ There is no order for protection presently in effect.

XXII.

This Petition has been filed in good faith and for the purposes set forth herein.

WHEREFORE, Petitioner prays for the Judgment and Decree of the Court as follows:

_X_ 1. Granting a dissolution of the marriage of Petitioner and Respondent.

_____ 2. Awarding to (Petitioner/Respondent/the parties jointly) the physical custody of the children. Awarding to (Petitioner/Respondent/the parties jointly) the legal custody of the children.

_X_ 3. Ordering a parenting plan for the care of the minor children of the parties.

_X_ 4. Ordering (Petitioner/Respondent/neither party) to pay child support for the minor child of the parties, as is consistent with Minnesota Child Support Guidelines.

_X_ 5. Granting to (Petitioner/Respondent/neither party) an award of spousal maintenance.

_X_ 6. Ordering (Petitioner/Respondent) to keep in full force and effect medical, health, and hospitalization insurance for the benefit of the minor child of the parties. Further ordering that the (Petitioner/Respondent/both parties) parties pay the cost of any premiums, co-payments, or deductibles for the above mentioned medical, health, and hospitalization insurance.

_X_ 7. Ordering that each party be responsible for their own individual debts incurred or assets purchased since their separation on _____. Further ordering an equitable division of the debts existing prior to the date of separation.

_X_ 8. Awarding to (Petitioner/Respondent) exclusive right, title, and interest in the homestead of the parties.

_____ 9. Order the homestead sold.

_X_ 10. Awarding to the parties exclusive use and possession of the motor vehicles in his or her individual possession.

~~_____ 11. Awarding to Petitioner the following motor vehicles:~~

~~Awarding to Respondent the following motor vehicles:~~

  X 12.   Awarding an equitable division of the personal property of the parties.

  X 13.   Granting such other and further relief as may be just and equitable.

By: _____

Name: Jane Smith

Petitioner *Pro Se*

Address: 1417 Main Street

Saint Paul, Minnesota 55106

Telephone No. (651) 771-0050

Attorney Reg.: *Pro Se*

ACKNOWLEDGMENT

The undersigned hereby acknowledges that costs, disbursements, and reasonable attorney and witness fees may be awarded pursuant to Minn. Stat. § 549.21, subd. 2 to the party against whom the allegations in this pleading are asserted.

Dated:_____   By: _____

                                                Name: Jane Smith

                                                Petitioner *Pro Se*

                                                Address: 1417 Main Street

                                                Saint Paul, Minnesota 55106

                                                Telephone No. (651) 771-0050

                                                Attorney Reg.: *Pro Se*

VERIFICATION

STATE OF MINNESOTA)

)ss.

COUNTY OF <u>RAMSEY</u>)

     <u>Jane A. Smith</u>, being first duly sworn upon oath, deposes and states that she is the Petitioner in the above-entitled proceeding; that she has read the foregoing Petition for Dissolution of Marriage and knows the contents thereof; that the same is true to her knowledge except as to those matters therein stated on information and belief, and to those matters she believes them to be true.

                                        _____

                                        Petitioner

Subscribed and sworn to before me

this _____ day of _____, 20___.

_____

Notary Public

FORM 104. CERTIFICATE OF REPRESENTATION AND PARTIES

STATE OF MINNESOTA   DISTRICT COURT

COUNTY OF <u>RAMSEY</u>   <u>SECOND</u> JUDICIAL DISTRICT

<u>CERTIFICATE OF REPRESENTATION AND PARTIES</u>

(ONLY THE INITIAL FILING LAWYER NEEDS TO COMPLETE THIS FORM)

Date Case Filed: <u>June 1, 2001</u>

<u>In Re the Marriage of: Jane A. Smith and John B. Smith</u>

      This certificate must be filed pursuant to Rule 104 of the General Rules of Practice for the District Courts, which states: "A party filing a civil case shall, at the time of filing, notify the court administrator in writing of the name, address, and telephone number of all counsel and unrepresented parties, if known (see form 104 appended to these rules). If that information is not then known to the filing party, it shall be provided to the court administrator in writing by the filing party within seven days of learning it. Any party impleading additional parties shall provide the same information to the court administrator. The court administrator shall, upon receipt of the completed certificate, notify all parties or their lawyers, if represented by counsel, of the date of filing the action and the file number assigned."

LIST ALL LAWYERS/PRO SE PARTIES INVOLVED IN THIS CASE.

<u>LAWYER FOR PETITIONER</u>	<u>LAWYER FOR RESPONDENT</u>
	(If not known, name party and address)
<u>Jane A. Smith</u>	<u>John B. Smith</u>
Name of Party	Name of Party
Pro Se	*Pro Se*
Atty Name	Atty Name
<u>1417 Main Street</u>	<u>1966 Oak Street</u>
<u>Saint Paul, Minnesota 55106</u>	<u>Minneapolis, Minnesota 55424</u>
Address	Address
<u>(651) 771-0050</u>	<u>(612) 555-5555</u>
Phone Number	Phone Number
N/A	N/A
MN Atty ID No.	MN Atty ID No.

DISSOLUTION WITH CHILDREN - 4

~~DISSOLUTION WITHOUT CHILDREN - 5~~

STATE OF MINNESOTA	DISTRICT COURT
COUNTY OF <u>RAMSEY</u>	<u>SECOND</u> JUDICIAL DISTRICT
In Re the Marriage of:	FAMILY COURT DIVISION

<u>Jane Smith   </u>,

ANSWER

Petitioner,

Court File No. <u>F4-01-3737</u>

and

Judicial Officer _____

<u>John Smith   </u>,

Respondent.

_____

TO: <u>JANE SMITH</u>, THE ABOVE-NAMED PETITIONER:

1.   That except as expressly admitted or otherwise qualified each and every allegation of the Petition is denied.

2.   Respondent admits the allegations of paragraphs <u>I, II, III, IV, VI, VII, IX, XI, XII, XIII, XIV, XVI, XVII, XVIII, XIX, XX, XXI, XXII, XXIII</u>.

3.   Respondent is without sufficient knowledge to admit or deny the allegations of paragraph(s) <u>X and XV</u>.

4.   Respondent denies the allegations of paragraph(s) <u>V</u>.

Dated:_____

By: _____

Name: <u>John Smith   </u>

Respondent *Pro Se*

Address: <u>1966 Oak Street   </u>

<u>Minneapolis, Minnesota 55424</u>

Telephone No. <u>(612) 555-5555</u>

DISSOLUTION WITH CHILDREN - 4

~~DISSOLUTION WITHOUT CHILDREN - 5~~

STATE OF MINNESOTA

COUNTY OF <u>RAMSEY</u>

In Re the Marriage of:

DISTRICT COURT

<u>SECOND</u> JUDICIAL DISTRICT

FAMILY COURT DIVISION

<u>Jane Smith</u>   ,

Petitioner,

and

<u>John Smith</u>   ,

Respondent.

SCHEDULING   INFORMATION
STATEMENT

Court File No. <u>F4-01-3737</u>

Judicial Officer _____

_____

1.   All parties have/~~have not~~ been served with process.

2.   All parties ~~have~~/have not joined in the filing of this form.

3.   The parties are in agreement on all matters and this case will proceed by default.

      Yes _____   No __X__

      ___   Default hearing by General Rules of Practice, Rule 306

             ___   Marriage includes minor children

      ___   Approval without a hearing pursuant to M.S.A. 518.13, subd. 5.

             ___   The marriage includes minor children, each party is represented by a lawyer and each party has signed a stipulation.

             ___   The marriage does not include minor children, at least 50 days has elapsed since service of the Summons and Petition, and the respondent has not appeared in the action.

4.   The case involves the following (check all that apply and supply estimates where indicated):

      a. minor children   No ____   Yes __X__   number: __2__

b. custody dispute   No _____   Yes _X_

Specify: <u>Both parties wish to have custody of the children. However, they are willing to try to work out a parenting plan.</u>

c. parenting time dispute   No _____   Yes _X_

Specify: <u>Both parties wish to have custody of the children. However, they are willing to try to work out a parenting plan.</u>

Each party will submit a proposal outlining custody and visitation proposals for each child.

d. marital property   No _____   Yes _X_

Identify the asset and requested disposition: <u>Petitioner believes the parties have fairly divided their property. However, Respondent indicates that he wants some additional property. At this time he has not identified the specific items.</u>

e. non-marital property   No ___   Yes _X_

Each party shall identify any non-marital claims, their respective positions for the basis for the claim, the method(s) used to arrive at the claimed amount or trace the claim and requested disposition:

<u>Petitioner's parents gave her a gift of $10,000 to assist in the purchase of the home. She should be reimbursed for this money. Respondent has owned a 1955 Chevrolet since before the parties were married. It should be awarded to him.</u>

f. complex evaluation issues   No _X_   Yes _____

5.   It is estimated that discovery specified below can be completed within _3_ months from the date of this form. (Check all that apply and supply estimates where indicated.)

a.   Factual Depositions   No _X_   Yes _____

Identify the person who will be deposed by either party:

_____

_____

_____

b.   Medical/Vocational Evaluations   No _X_   Yes _____

Identify the person who will conduct such evaluations for either party:

_____

_____

_____

c.   Experts   No _____   Yes __X__

Identify experts for either party.

The party's retirement plans must be valued.

6.   The dates and deadlines specified below are suggested.

    a. __8/21/01__ Deadline for motion regarding: temporary relief.

    b. __10/21/01__ Deadline for completion and review of property evaluation

    c. __10/21/01__ Deadline for completion and review of custody/visitation mediation

    d. __N/A__ Deadline for completion and review of custody/visitation evaluation.

    e. __N/A__ Deadline for submitting _____ to the court.

    f. __11/21/01__ Date for prehearing conference.

    g. __12/15/01__ Date for trial or final hearing.

7.   Estimated trial or final hearing time: __3 days__ ~~hours~~ (estimates less than a day must be stated in hours).

8.   Alternative dispute resolution is/is not recommended in the form of: Mediation (specify, e.g., arbitration, mediation, or other means).

    __8/21/01__ Date for completion of mediation/alternative dispute resolution expected to extend over a period of __4__ ~~days~~/weeks.

9.   Please list any additional information which might be helpful to the court when scheduling this matter, including, e.g., facts which will affect readiness for trial and any issues that significantly affect the welfare of the children.

_____
_____
_____

Dated:_____   By: _____

                                          Name: Jane Smith

                                          Petitioner *Pro Se*

                                          Address: 1417 Main Street

                                          Saint Paul, Minnesota 55106

                                          Telephone No. (651) 771-0050

                                          Attorney Reg.: *Pro Se*

DISSOLUTION WITH CHILDREN - 4

~~DISSOLUTION WITHOUT CHILDREN - 5~~

STATE OF MINNESOTA

COUNTY OF <u>RAMSEY</u>

In Re the Marriage of:

DISTRICT COURT

<u>SECOND</u> JUDICIAL DISTRICT

FAMILY COURT DIVISION

<u>Jane Smith   </u>,

            Petitioner,

and

NOTICE OF MOTION AND MOTION

Court File No. <u>F4-01-3737   </u>

Judicial Officer: <u>Referee Anderson</u>

<u>John Smith   </u>,

            Respondent.

TO: <u>JANE SMITH</u>, THE ABOVE NAMED PETITIONER, <u>1417 MAIN STREET, SAINT PAUL, MINNESOTA 55106</u>

PLEASE TAKE NOTICE that on <u>July 6, 2001</u> at <u>9:00</u> a.m.<del>/p.m.</del> or as soon thereafter as counsel can be heard before <u>Referee Anderson</u> at <u>760 Government Center West, 50 West Kellogg Boulevard, Saint Paul, Minnesota</u> the undersigned counsel will move the court for the following relief:

1.   Ordering the Ramsey County Department of Court Services to conduct an evaluation and recommend a parenting plan.

2.   Ordering a temporary parenting plan.

3.   Awarding to Respondent temporary child support childcare costs consistent with the parenting plan and the Minnesota Child Support Guidelines.

4.   Awarding to Petitioner temporary occupancy of the homestead.

5.   Awarding to the parties the temporary, exclusive use of the motor vehicle in his or her possession. Further, awarding to Respondent the exclusive use and possession of the Chevrolet.

6.   Further awarding to the parties an equitable share of the household goods, specifically sufficient kitchen items.

7.   For such other relief as the court deems just and equitable.

This motion is based upon the attached Affidavit of Respondent and upon all the files and records in the above-entitled action.

PLEASE TAKE FURTHER NOTICE that all responsive pleadings shall be served and mailed to or filed with the court administrator no later than five days prior to the scheduled hearing. The court may, in its discretion, disregard any responsive pleadings served or filed with the court administrator less than five days prior to such hearing in ruling on the motion or matter in question.

Dated:_____

By: _____

Name: <u>John Smith</u>
~~Petitioner~~/Respondent *Pro Se*
Address: <u>1966 Oak Street</u>
<u>Minneapolis, Minnesota 55424</u>
Telephone No. <u>(612) 555-5555</u>

ACKNOWLEDGMENT

The undersigned hereby acknowledges that costs, disbursements, and reasonable attorney and witness fees may be awarded pursuant to Minn. Stat. § 549.21, subd. 2 to the party against whom the allegations in this pleading are asserted.

Dated:_____

By: _____

Name: <u>John Smith</u>
~~Petitioner~~/Respondent *Pro Se*
Address: <u>1966 Oak Street</u>
<u>Minneapolis, Minnesota 55424</u>
Telephone No. <u>(612) 555-5555</u>

DISSOLUTION WITH CHILDREN - 4

~~DISSOLUTION WITHOUT CHILDREN - 5~~

STATE OF MINNESOTA

COUNTY OF <u>RAMSEY</u>

DISTRICT COURT

<u>SECOND</u> JUDICIAL DISTRICT

FAMILY COURT DIVISION

_____

In Re the Marriage of:

<u>Jane Smith</u>   ,

**APPLICATION FOR
TEMPORARY RELIEF**

Court File No. <u>F4-01-3737</u>

Petitioner,

and

Judicial Officer _____

<u>John Smith</u>   ,

Respondent.

_____

STATE OF MINNESOTA   )

)SS

COUNTY OF <u>RAMSEY</u>   )

    <u>John Smith</u>, the Respondent, hereinafter called ~~Wife/~~Husband being first duly sworn, upon oath, respectfully represents to the Court that:

1.   The parties were married on <u>June 8, 1978</u>; the Wife's age is <u>33</u>; the Husband's age is <u>35.</u>

2.   That parties have been separated <u>two</u> months during which the Husband/Wife has paid $<u>0.00</u> to the Wife/Husband.

3.   (a) There are <u>two</u> children of the parties, aged <u>10</u> and <u>12</u> now in the care of ~~Wife/Husband/~~both at <u>1966 Oak Street</u>   .

    (b) The family home is owned/~~rented~~ by the parties and is now occupied by the Wife/~~Husband/both parties~~.

    (c) For the best interests of the minor children, they should be in the temporary custody of the ~~Husband/Wife/~~both.

(d) The Wife has __0__ children of a prior marriage. The amount of support received, paid is $ _N/A_ per month.

(e) The Husband has __0__ children of a prior marriage. The amount of support received, paid is $ _N/A_ per month.

4.   The assets of the parties include:

APPROXIMATE VALUE AND ENCUMBRANCE

Item	Wife	Husband	Joint Tenancy	Encumbrances
Cars	$18,000			$10,000
(Year, make)	1999 Oldsmobile	1955 Chevrolet	1999 Ford Taurus (leased)	
Stocks, bonds, notes	$	$	$	$
Cash and Savings	$	$	Nominal	$
Claims	$	$	$	$
Accounts Receivable	$	$	$	$
Homestead	$	$	$250,000	$125,000

5.   Secured Debts, not listed above (excluding homestead):

(a) Creditor	1._____	2._____	3._____	4._____
(b) Total Out	$_____	$_____	$_____	$_____
(c) Monthly Payment	$_____	$_____	$_____	$_____
(d) Party Obligated	_____	_____	_____	_____
(e) Security Pledged	_____	_____	_____	_____

6.   Necessary Monthly Expenses:

	Husband	Child(ren) (if separate)
(a) Rent	$600	$
(b) Mortgage Payment	$	$
(c) Contract for Deed Payment	$	$
(d) Homeowner's Insurance	$	$
(e) Real Estate Taxes	$	$
(f) Utilities	$ 60	$
(g) Heat	$	$

(h) Food	$150	$150
(i) Clothing	$100	$
(j) Laundry and Dry Cleaning	$ 20	$
(k) Medical and Dental	$ 20	$
(l) Transportation (includes car payment)	$360	$
(m) Car Insurance	$100	$
(n) Life Insurance	$100	$
(o) Recreation, Entertainment, Travel	$100	$
(p) Newspapers and Magazines	$ 20	$
(q) Social and Church Obligations	$ 20	$
(r) Personal Allowance and Incidentals	$100	$
(s) Babysitting and Child Care	$100	$
(t) Home Maintenance	$ 0	$
(u) Children School Needs and Allowances	$	$40
(v) Additional Information_____	$	$
re: Debts and Expenses _____	$80	$
TOTAL:	$1930	$190

7. Employment Data: Provide the following data for each employer. Attach prior month's paycheck stub(s) as Exhibit.

	Husband	Wife
(a) Name of Employer	U.S. Bank	$50,000
Type of Employment	Banker	Engineer
(b) Income:		
(1) Gross Income per month	$ 3,333	$4,167
(2) Statutory Deductions:		
Federal Income Tax	$348	$474
State Withholding	$166	$225
Social Security (FICA)	$255	$318.78
Pension Deduction	$166.65	$208.35
Union Dues	$	$
Dependent Health/Hospitalization	$	$250
Dental Coverage	$30	$
(3) Subtotal of Statutory Deductions	$965.65	$1,476.13
(4) Net Income (line 1-line 3)	$2,367.35	$2,690.87

(5) Other Paycheck Deductions

Specify _____

_____ $_____ $_____

(6) Subtotal (Other Deductions) $_____ $_____

(7) NET TAKE HOME PAY (Line 4-Line 6) $2367.35 $2690.87

(c) Tax withholding figures above are based on Married
of Single taxpayer with # of deductions
(Example: M-4 or S-2) M-2_____ M-2_____

(d) Employer reimbursed expenses $_____ $_____

Specify _____ $_____ $_____

_____ $_____ $_____

(e) Other Income:

(1) Public Assistance (AFDC/GA) $_____ $_____

(2) Social Security benefits for party or

child(ren) $_____ $_____

(3) Unemployment/Worker's Compensation $_____ $_____

(4) Interest income per _____ $_____ $_____

(5) Dividend income per _____ $_____ $_____

(6) Gross Rental Income $_____ $_____

(7) Other Income _____ $_____ $_____

*Monthly income is to be calculated using 4.3.

8.   (a) $0.00 is a reasonable amount for temporary support for ___ children per month.

(b) $0.00 is a reasonable amount for temporary maintenance per month.

(c) Payment should be made on N/A.

9.   (a) $ 0.00 has been paid on the wife's attorney fees and costs.

(b) $ 0.00 has been paid on the Husband's attorney fees and costs.

(c) $ 0.00 is reasonable for Wife/Husband's attorney fees and costs.

10.   Additional material facts:

WHEREFORE, Respondent prays for an order granting such relief prior to trial as may be just and lawful.

_____

~~Petitioner~~/Respondent

Subscribed and sworn to before me

this ____ day of _____, 20___.

_____

Notary Public

DISSOLUTION WITH CHILDREN - 4

~~DISSOLUTION WITHOUT CHILDREN - 5~~

STATE OF MINNESOTA

COUNTY OF <u>RAMSEY</u>

DISTRICT COURT

<u>SECOND</u> JUDICIAL DISTRICT

FAMILY COURT DIVISION

In Re the Marriage of:

<u>Jane Smith</u>,

         Petitioner,

and

<u>John Smith</u>,

         Respondent.

PREHEARING STATEMENT

Court File No. <u>F4-01-3737</u>

Judicial Officer: <u>Referee Anderson</u>

---

1.   PERSONAL INFORMATION

	HUSBAND	WIFE
Full Name	John B. Smith	Jane A. Smith
Present Mailing Address	1966 Oak Street	1417 Main Street
	Minneapolis, MN 55454	St. Paul, MN 55106
Employer	U.S. Bank	3M
Street Address	1111 Energy Park Drive	2222 Century Avenue
City, State, ZIP	St. Paul, MN 55108	Maplewood, MN 55119
Birthdate	6/30/66 Age: 35	4/15/68 Age: 33
Marriage Date	June 8, 1966	
Separation Date (Different Residences)	April 2, 2001	
Date of Temporary Order(s), if any	November 3, 2001	

Minor children born to this marriage or who will be affected by this legal action:

FULL NAME	BIRTHDATE	AGE	LIVING WITH:
Amber Lynn Smith	12/3/89	13	Both parents
Barbara Ann Smith	9/5/91	10	Both parents

Is the wife pregnant now? __X__ no _____ yes-due date _____

Is the issue of custody contested? __X__ yes _____ no

If custody is disputed, each party shall submit proposals for custody and visitation for each child as Exhibit 1A.

2.   **EMPLOYMENT**: Provide the following data for each employer.

	HUSBAND	WIFE
a) Name of Employer	U.S. Bank	3M
Length of Employment	11 years	8 years
Income:		
(1) Gross income per month	$3,333	$4,167
Statutory Deductions		
Federal Income Tax	$348	$474
State Withholding	$166	$225
Social Security (FICA)	$255	$318.78
Pension Deduction	$166.65	$208.35
Union Dues	$	$
Dependent Health/Hospitalization Coverage	$	$250
Dental Coverage	$30	$
(2) Subtotal of statutory deductions	$	$
(3) Net income (line 1-Line2)	$2,367.35	$2690.87
Other paycheck deductions:	$	$
Specify: _____	$	$
_____	$	$
(4) Subtotal of Other Deductions	$	$
(5) NET TAKE HOME PAY PER MONTH		
(line 3-line 4)	$2,367.35	$2690.87

Tax withholding figures above are based upon Married or Single taxpayer with # of exemptions   M-2   M-2
(example M-4 or S-2)

Attach prior month's paycheck stub(s) as Exhibit 2A

(b)   Employment benefits: identify all benefits in addition to wages including bonus paid or due, automobile or travel expense reimbursement, other per diem compensation, memberships paid by the employer.

_____   _____

_____   _____

_____   _____

Will medical and dental insurance coverage be available for your spouse after the dissolution?

__X__ yes _____ no

(c) Other income   _____   _____

   (1) Public assistance (AFDC/GA) $_____ $_____

   (2) Social Security benefits for party of child (ren) $_____ $_____

   (3) Unemployment/Workers Comp. $_____ $_____

   (4) Interest income per month $_____ $_____

   (5) Dividend income per month $_____ $_____

   (6) Other income: _____ $_____ $_____

   (7) Last Year's Tax Refunds   Federal 700   Federal _____

                                         State 130   State _____

3.   CHILD SUPPORT/SPOUSAL MAINTENANCE

(a)   Does either party receive child support or spousal maintenance from a separate proceeding? ____ yes __X__ no

    If yes, specify the $ _____ received each month for child support/alimony for _____ by the order of _____, County dated _____.

(b)   Child Support or Spousal Maintenance established by court order for person(s) not included in this proceeding currently being paid:

_____   _____

_____   _____

    To whom is this obligation owed? _____

142

(c)   Current Monthly Child Support or Spousal Maintenance Order established by temporary order for either party and minor children in this proceeding:

Child Support: $ _____ Spousal Maintenance $ _____

Any claim or arrearages claimed under existing court order(s): ____ yes _____ no

If yes, specify the amount(s) claimed: Child Support $ _____

Spousal Maintenance $ _____

4.   LIVING EXPENSES

Your estimated monthly expenses: $ 2,120

(Attach an itemization as Exhibit 4A)

5.   REAL PROPERTY

	HOMESTEAD	OTHER*
(a) Date Acquired	June 1, 1980	_____
(b) Purchase Price	$100,000	$_____
(c) Present Fair Market Value	$250,000	$_____
(d) First Mortgage Balance	$125,000	$_____
(e) Second Mortgage Balance or Home Improvement Loan	$_____	$_____
(f) Net Value	$125,000	$_____
(g) Monthly Payment (PITI)	$1207	$_____
(h) Rental Income, if any	$_____	$_____

* Other Real Estate: Provide the same information for other real property such as rental property, lake cabin, etc. as Exhibit 5C.

6.   PERSONAL PROPERTY: Fair Market Value

In possession of:

	Husband	Wife	Joint
(a) Household Contents	_____	_____	_____
(b) Stocks, bonds, etc._____	$_____	$_____	$10,000
_____	$_____	$_____	$_____
(c) Checking Accounts	$_____	$_____	$Nominal
Savings Accounts	$_____	$_____	$Nominal
(d) Receivables and Claims	$_____	$_____	$_____
_____	$_____	$_____	$_____

(e) Motor Vehicles: year/make/model

	(1) Silhouette	(2) 1999 Ford Taurus	(3) 1955 Chevrolet
Market Value	$18,000		
Encumbrance	$10,000		
Net Value	$8,000	leased	Husband's nonmarital
Monthly Payment	$450		
In Possession of :	Wife	Husband	Wife

(f) Boats, Motors, Campers, Snowmobiles, Trailers, etc.:

	(1)	(2)	(3)
Market Value	$	$	$
Encumbrance	$	$	$
Net Value	$	$	$
Monthly Payment	$	$	$
In Possession of :			$

(g)   Other: (such as power equipment, tools, guns, valuable animals, etc.)

Description: _____   Fair Market Value: $_____

Encumbrance: $_____

Net Value: $_____

7.   NON-MARITAL CLAIMS:

(a)   Description: (1) 1955 Chevrolet   (2) Down payment on home

(b)   Amount claimed: $6,000 $

Set forth the basis for and method used to arrive at your claims to be attached as Exhibit 7A.

8.   LIFE INSURANCE:

	a) Husband	b) Wife	c)
Company	AAL	AAL	
Policy Number	00-8675309	00-62000	
Type of Insurance	Universal Life	Universal Life	
Face Amount	$250,000	$250,000	$
Cash Value	$10,000	$12,000	$
Loans	$	$	$
Insured	Husband	Wife	
Beneficiary	Wife	Husband	
Owner	Husband	Wife	

9.   PENSION PLAN AND/OR PROFIT SHARING PLAN:

	HUSBAND	WIFE
a) Through Employment		
1) Present Cash Value	$75,000	$65,000
2) Vested or Nonvested	Vested	Vested
(b) Private Plans (IRA, Keogh, SEP, etc.)	None	None
Present cash value	_____	_____
(c) Deferred Compensation	_____	_____
(d) Military Pension or Disability	Yes ____ No ____	Yes ____ No ____

10.   DEBTS: (Not listed in 4 or 5 above)

(a)   All secured debts:

Creditor	1)_____	2)_____	3)_____
Total Amount Owing	$_____	$_____	$_____
Total Monthly Payment	$_____	$_____	$_____
When Incurred	_____	_____	_____
Party Obligated (H, W, J)	_____	_____	_____
Reason for debt	_____	_____	_____
Totals	H:_____	W:_____	J:_____

(b)   Unsecured Debts: Attach a separate schedule showing the creditor, balance, owed, monthly payment, etc. to be attached as Exhibit 9B. Include attorney fees and costs.

Total   Husband: $_____ Wife: $_____ Joint: $8,500

Dated: _____ The statements contained herein are true and complete to the best of my knowledge.

_____

~~Petitioner~~/Respondent

EXHIBIT 1A

RESPONDENT'S CUSTODY/PARENT ACCESS SCHEDULE PROPOSAL

I would like to have the girls most of the time during the school-year. Petitioner travels for work and is not there enough to help the kids with their schoolwork and get them to activities. I agree that she should have the children frequently and most of the summer.

EXHIBIT 4A
RESPONDENT'S MONTHLY LIVING EXPENSES

	Husband	Child(ren) (if separate)
(a) Rent	$600	$
(b) Mortgage Payment	$	$
(c) Contract for Deed Payment	$	$
(d) Homeowner's Insurance	$	$
(e) Real Estate Taxes	$	$
(f) Utilities	$ 60	$
(g) Heat	$	$
(h) Food	$150	$150
(i) Clothing	$100	$
(j) Laundry and Dry Cleaning	$ 20	$
(k) Medical and Dental	$ 20	$
(l) Transportation (includes car payment)	$360	$
(m) Car Insurance	$100	$
(n) Life Insurance	$100	$
(o) Recreation, Entertainment, Travel	$100	$
(p) Newspapers and Magazines	$ 20	$
(q) Social and Church Obligations	$ 20	$
(r) Personal Allowance and Incidentals	$100	$
(s) Babysitting and Child Care	$100	$
(t) Home Maintenance	$ 0	$
(u) Children School Needs and Allowances	$	$40
(v) Additional Information_____	$	$
re: Debts and Expenses _____	$80	$
TOTAL:	$1930	$190

EXHIBIT 7A

NON-MARITAL CLAIMS

I owned a 1955 Chevrolet before the marriage. Petitioner's parents gave us $10,000 to buy a house. She claims it was a gift to her.

EXHIBIT 9B
UNSECURED DEBTS OF PARTIES

Debt	Monthly Payment	Amount Owing	Party Obligated
MasterCard	$ 120	$4,000	Both
Visa	$ 80	$2,000	Both
Sears	$ 40	$2,500	Both
	$	$	
	$	$	
	$	$	
	$	$	
	$	$	
	$	$	
	$	$	
	$	$	
	$	$	
TOTALS:	$240	$8,500	

DISSOLUTION WITH CHILDREN - 4

~~DISSOLUTION WITHOUT CHILDREN - 5~~

STATE OF MINNESOTA

COUNTY OF <u>RAMSEY</u>

DISTRICT COURT

<u>SECOND</u> JUDICIAL DISTRICT

FAMILY COURT DIVISION

_____

In Re the Marriage of:

<u>Jane A. Smith</u>   ,

               Petitioner,

and

<u>John B. Smith</u>   ,

               Respondent.

MARITAL   TERMINATION AGREEMENT

Court File No. <u>F4-01-3737</u>

Judicial Officer: <u>Referee Anderson</u>

_____

WHEREAS, Petitioner has commenced the above-entitled proceeding for dissolution of the marriage relationship with Respondent; and

WHEREAS, on <u>June 1, 2001</u> a copy of the Summons and Petition for Dissolution of Marriage were served upon Respondent; and

WHEREAS, it appears to both parties hereto that efforts toward reconciliation would not be fruitful; and

WHEREAS, the parties desire to settle their differences amicably with regard to the issues between them; and

WHEREAS, with full knowledge of their right to be represented by counsel of their choice and with full disclosure of all facts, matters, and things, each has chosen to represent himself or herself for purposes of this agreement; and

WHEREAS each party has fully disclosed to the other party all of his or her income, including any and all income which he or she has in the name of a third person, but which is under his or her control; and

WHEREAS each party has fully disclosed to the other party all of his or her assets, both real and personal, including any and all assets which he or she has in the name of a third person, but which are under his or her control; and

NOW, THEREFORE, IT IS HEREBY STIPULATED AND AGREED by and between the parties to the above-entitled proceeding as follows:

1.   MARITAL STATUS. The bonds of matrimony heretofore existing between the parties shall be dissolved.

2   MILITARY SERVICE. Neither party is entitled to the protections of the Soldier's and Sailor's Civil Relief Act of 1940 as amended.

3.   COMPLETE AGREEMENT. The parties have made this agreement intending that it be a full, complete, and final settlement and satisfaction of any and all claims of any kind, nature, or description which involve issues addressed in the marital termination agreement to which either party may be entitled or may claim to be entitled, now or in the future, against the other. Except as is expressly provided herein to the contrary, each is released from any and all further liability whatsoever to the other.

4.   M.T.A. AS EVIDENCE. Respondent will not appear in these proceedings, save and except through this Marital Termination Agreement. Petitioner may proceed with said dissolution as by default. As a part of these proceedings, Petitioner will submit this agreement to the above-entitled court. If said dissolution is not granted, the terms of this agreement shall be of no effect. If this agreement is not approved by the court, Respondent shall be advised and shall be given the opportunity to appear and present his arguments, witnesses, and testimony. If this agreement is approved by the court and if the court grants a dissolution to the Petitioner herein, the terms of this agreement shall be made by reference a part of any decree issued, whether or not each and every portion of this agreement is literally set forth in said decree.

5.   UNIFORM CHILD CUSTODY JURISDICTION. Minnesota is the proper jurisdiction within the contemplation of the Uniform Child Custody Jurisdiction and Enforcement Act, Minnesota Statutes Section 518D to enter an order regarding the custody, care, and control of the minor child[ren].

6.   CUSTODY. The Parenting Plan attached as Appendix B shall be incorporated into any Judgment and Decree and shall control all issues related to access to the children.

7.   PARENTING PLAN. The parties have entered into a parenting plan which is attached as Appendix B.

8.   UNDERSTANDING AS TO DECISIONS AFFECTING THE CHILDREN. We agree that the actual residence of the children may be changed at any time as the parties mutually agree or as allowed by order of the Court.

We further agree that all decisions pertaining to the education, discipline, health, extracurricular or summer activities, religious training, medical and dental care will be decided by both of us after reasonable and adequate discussion. We also agree that the parent with actual physical custody shall make day-to-day decisions affecting the children, including any medical or dental emergencies. We agree that if we are unable to reach agreement on any decisions affecting our children, we will use the services of a mediator (as discussed below) to resolve our differences.

We further agree that each parent has the right to know of any circumstances or decisions that affect the children and that each of us has the right to any medical, dental, or school records of our children. Neither of us will knowingly do anything to hamper or interfere with the natural and continuing relationship between our children and the other parent, nor will we allow others to interfere.

Further, we recognize that the well-being of our children is of paramount importance, and, therefore, we agree that our children should have as much contact as possible with the parent that does not have physical custody and our children may visit the non-custodial parent as often as may be agreed upon.

9. <u>MEDIATION</u>. Any claim or controversy involving parenting time or any other issue involving the children (other than child support) which cannot be resolved by the parties through direct communication without mediation, shall be promptly submitted to mediation.

    a. <u>Definition of Mediation</u>. Mediation is a voluntary process entered into by the parties. In this process, the parties continue direct communication with each other, but with the assistance of a neutral person who is the mediator. The mediator has no authority to require any concession or agreement. A good faith effort shall be made between the parties to resolve any claim or controversy.

    b. <u>Selection of Mediator</u>. The mediator shall be named by mutual agreement of the parties or by obtaining a list of five qualified persons from the Court and by alternately striking names.

    c. <u>Duties and Responsibilities of Mediator</u>. The mediator shall have the duty to assist the parties in resolving visitation issues.

    d. <u>Duty to Cooperate and Complete</u>. Both parties agree to cooperate and act in good faith to resolve the disputes with the assistance of the mediator.

    e. <u>Payment of Costs.</u> The parties shall share the costs of mediation equally unless they mutually agree otherwise.

  f. <u>Exhaustion of Remedies</u>. The above procedure shall be followed before either party may apply to the Court for relief.

10. <u>CHILD SUPPORT</u>. Neither party shall pay child support to the other. The parties shall have joint legal and physical custody of the child with each sharing equally in the time of custody and support of the minor child pursuant to a Parenting Plan. In light of the relative incomes of the parties, such an arrangement is in the best interests of the children. Petitioner shall pay for the clothing and activities for the children.

11. <u>INSURANCE FOR CHILD SUPPORT</u>. In order to insure that funds are available for the support of minor children of the parties, for so long as there exists an obligation of support the parties shall maintain life insurance in the amount of $50,000 and each shall name the other party as beneficiary thereof.

12. <u>MEDICAL COVERAGE FOR CHILD</u>. As additional child support, during the time that the child of the parties is a minor, Petitioner/~~Respondent~~ maintain in full force and effect and pay the premium cost for all medical insurance available to her through his employer she shall be responsible for notifying her employer. ~~Petitioner/~~Respondent shall be responsible for dental coverage.

13. <u>UNINSURED MEDICAL AND DENTAL FOR CHILD</u>. To the extent not covered by insurance, all deductibles, all medical and dental expenses, including but not limited to necessary orthodontia, eye care (including prescription lenses), psychological care and psychiatric care, shall be shared equally by the parties.

14. <u>SPOUSAL MAINTENANCE</u>. Neither party shall pay temporary or permanent maintenance to the other, and the parties hereby waive the right to have the other pay temporary or permanent maintenance.

By presently waiving their right to receive maintenance, the parties intend to immediately divest the court of jurisdiction to order maintenance in the future. Consideration for this agreement is the parties' mutual waiver of past, present, and future maintenance.

15. <u>INSURANCE FOR SPOUSE</u>. Any insurance conversion rights granted under the Judgment and Decree or state or federal law shall be construed so as to afford to the other party the greatest coverage available to a former spouse under state and federal law or rule.

The parties shall be entitled to medical coverage through the other parties' employer for any period of time for which he or she requests eligibility and is eligible under the state or federal law or insurer's rules, but he or she shall be responsible for paying any premium for said insurance relating to said coverage.

16. <u>HOMESTEAD</u>.

a. Petitioner/~~Respondent~~ shall have all the parties' right, title, interest, and equity in the real property located at <u>1417 Main Street, Saint Paul,</u> Minnesota, <u>Ramsey</u> County

Legal Description: Lot 7, Block 2 Dayton's Addition, County of Ramsey, State of Minnesota

subject to all encumbrances presently against said homestead including mortgages and real estate taxes. ~~He/~~She shall pay to ~~Petitioner/~~Respondent the sum of <u>$30,000</u> within thirty days of entry of this judgment and decree dissolving the marriage. ~~Petitioner/~~Respondent shall hold a lien against the property for the remaining balance of his/~~her~~ marital interest of <u>$25,000</u>. Said lien shall accrue interest at a rate of six percent per annum.

The parties' previous rights in said homestead are extinguished as of the date of the decree herein, and Petitioner/~~Respondent~~ shall become owner in fee simple simultaneously with the attachment of ~~Petitioner's/~~Respondent's equitable lien.

b. Petitioner/~~Respondent~~ shall be solely liable for the normal maintenance and all monthly payments of principal, interest, taxes and insurance on said homestead, and ~~he/~~she shall indemnify and hold ~~Petitioner/~~Respondent harmless from any liability or obligation to make any payment whatsoever regarding said homestead.

c. Upon the happening of any events hereinafter enumerated in Paragraph d herein, said homestead shall be placed on the market for sale (at a price and upon terms to be mutually agreed upon by the parties), and the "net proceeds" from said sale shall be paid to Petitioner/~~Respondent~~ after satisfying any liens or mortgage of the parties in full.

d. The conditions on which said sale shall occur shall be as follows:

(1) Petitioner's/~~Respondent's~~ remarriage, at which time she will have the option of refinancing the home and satisfying the lien owed to ~~Petitioner/~~Respondent;

(2) Petitioner's/~~Respondent's~~ moving from the premises;

(3) Petitioner's/~~Respondent's~~ death;

(4) Petitioner/~~Respondent~~ becoming more than three (3) months in arrears in any twelve (12) month period on the monthly payment of principal, interest, taxes or insurance for said homestead.

e.   The filing of either a certified copy of the Judgment and Decree or a certified copy of a Summary Real Estate Disposition Judgment or a Quit Claim Deed with the Ramsey County Recorder's Office shall operate as a conveyance of ~~Petitioner's~~/Respondent's entire interest in said property to Petitioner/~~Respondent~~. If said real property is Torrens or registered property, then the Ramsey County Registrar of Titles is hereby directed, upon filing such Judgment and Decree, Summary Real Estate Disposition Judgment or Quit Claim Deed, to cancel any Certificate of Title showing both parties herein as registered owners and to issue a new Certificate of Title covering such real property in the sole name of Petitioner/~~Respondent~~ subject to ~~Petitioner's~~/Respondent's lien interest.

f.   Immediately upon entry of the Judgment and Decree herein, ~~Petitioner~~/Respondent shall execute a Quit Claim Deed conveying ~~Petitioner's~~/Respondent's interest in the homestead to Petitioner/~~Respondent~~ subject to his lien interest.

g.   As between the parties, Petitioner/~~Respondent~~ shall be entitled, if she chooses, to claim all income tax deductions relating to said property for the year 2001 and all years thereafter.

h.   Said transfer to Petitioner/~~Respondent~~ is a transfer of property incident to dissolution of marriage and is therefore not a realization event for income tax purposes.

17.   ERROR IN LEGAL DESCRIPTION. In the event there is any technical error or omission made in describing the legal title or description to any of the real property referenced herein, the parties are required to make, execute, and deliver to each other any and all documents necessary to correct any such error or omission.

18.   PERSONAL PROPERTY. The parties have divided the personal property between them except as otherwise set forth herein.

19.   MOTOR VEHICLES. Petitioner shall have all right, title, interest, and equity, free and clear of any claim on the part of Respondent to the 1999 Oldsmobile Silhouette

automobiles of the parties. Respondent shall, upon entry of judgment, or sooner if he desires, execute all necessary documents to effect transfer of title.

Respondent shall have all right, title, interest, and equity, free and clear of any claim on the part of Petitioner to the leased 1999 Ford Taurus and the 1955 Chevrolet automobiles of the parties. Petitioner shall, upon entry of judgment, or sooner if he/she desires, execute all necessary documents to effect transfer of title.

20. BANK ACCOUNTS. The parties have divided their bank accounts and cash assets in a manner agreeable to both parties.

21. STOCK, BOND, AND INVESTMENT ACCOUNTS. The parties have no stock account. They have equitably divided their bonds between themselves.

22. RETIREMENT PLANS. Petitioner is awarded the entire right, title, interest, and equity, free and clear of any claim of Respondent in and to any retirement, pension, profit-sharing, 401(k), Keogh and IRA accounts or plans in her own name

Respondent is awarded the entire right, title, interest, and equity, free and clear of any claim of Petitioner in and to any retirement, pension, profit-sharing, 401(k), Keogh and IRA accounts or plans in his own name.

23. INCOME TAX EXEMPTIONS. The parties shall each be entitled to one of the income tax exemptions for the children. At such time as there is only one exemption available to the parties, they shall alternate the exemption with Petitioner claiming the exemption in even-numbered years and Respondent in odd-numbered years.

24. CURRENT INCOME TAXES. Any refund or payment due to the state or federal government for the filing of the parties joint federal and state income tax returns shall be equally divided between the parties.

25. WAIVER OF AUTOMATIC STAY. The automatic stay provision of Rule 125 of the General Rules of Practice is hereby waived and the District Court Administrator is hereby ordered to immediately enter Judgment and Decree in this matter.

26. CAPITAL GAINS TAXES. Each of the parties shall be responsible for their own capital gains taxes.

27. DEBTS. The parties have satisfied all bills and obligations of the parties incurred during the marriage, not otherwise specified herein which constitute a joint obligation of the parties except the following:

a. Petitioner shall assume and pay the above stated debts to MasterCard and Sears, and ~~he/~~she shall indemnify and hold the Respondent harmless from any obligation to make payment of the same.

b. Respondent shall assume and pay the above stated debts to <u>Visa</u>, and he~~/she~~ shall indemnify and hold the Petitioner harmless from any obligation to make payment of the same. He~~/She~~ shall pay $1,000 to Petitioner's MasterCard account to equalize the debts of the parties.

c. Both of the parties shall assume and pay the debts which each has incurred since their separation.

d. Any undisclosed debts shall become sole responsibility of the party that incurred it.

28. <u>FORMER NAME RESTORED</u>. Petitioner~~/Respondent~~ does not seek to change ~~his/~~her name.

29. <u>ATTORNEY FEES</u>. The parties shall each pay their own attorney fees, if any.

30. <u>APPENDIX A</u>. The attached Appendix A is incorporated and made a part of any Judgment and Decree entered based upon this Marital Termination Agreement.

31. <u>SERVICE</u>. Service of a copy of the final Judgment and Decree entered herein may be made by U.S. Mail on each party named herein, in lieu of personal service.

32. <u>EXECUTION OF DOCUMENTS REQUIRED</u>. Within twenty (20) days each party hereto shall execute any and all documents necessary to transfer real and personal property in the manner described herein without further order of the court. Should either party fail to comply with this provision, the filing with the agency of a certified copy of the judgment and decree shall have the same effect as if the party had executed the necessary documents.

33. <u>RELEASE</u>. Except as hereinbefore provided, each party hereto releases and waives any claim in and to the property of the other, provided the existence of that property was fully disclosed in this proceeding.

34. <u>DISCLOSURE</u>. Each party warrants to the other that there has been an accurate, complete, and current disclosure of all income, assets, debts, and liabilities. Both parties understand and agree that the deliberate failure to provide complete disclosure constitutes perjury. The property referred to in this agreement represents all the property which either party has any interest in full or in part by either party, separately or jointly.

This agreement is founded upon the complete financial disclosure by each party.

35. <u>UNDERSTANDING</u>. The parties have read this agreement and understand its contents. This agreement was signed by the parties after they had given it serious thought and consideration. This agreement is fair, just, and equitable under the circumstances. This agreement was signed by the parties after it was definitely understood between them that there could be no reconciliation. This agreement was made in aid of an orderly and just termination of property settlement in this matter satisfactory to the parties, with the further mutual understanding and agreement between the parties that this agreement shall be made a part of any judgment and decree of dissolution to be entered in this matter if Petitioner is granted a decree of dissolution as prayed for in ~~his/~~her petition.

IT IS FURTHER STIPULATED AND AGREED that the signing of this agreement shall not be construed as an appearance by Respondent and that Petitioner may proceed to place this matter upon the default calendar and try this matter as by default.

IT IS FURTHER STIPULATED AND AGREED that this agreement may be approved by the court without notice to the parties.

Dated: Dated:

_____

Petitioner   Respondent

Subscribed and sworn before me,

this ___ day of _____, 20___.

Subscribed and sworn before me,

this ___ day of _____, 20___.

_____

Notary Public   Notary Public

WAIVER OF COUNSEL

I, <u>Jane Smith</u>, acknowledge that I have been told that I have a right to be represented by counsel of my choice, and that I state that I am of sound mind and that I have freely and voluntarily chosen to waive my right to be represented by counsel for the purpose of this agreement.

_____
Petitioner

Subscribed and sworn to before me

this _____ day of _____, 20____

_____
Notary Public

I, <u>John Smith</u>, acknowledge that I have been told that I have a right to be represented by counsel of my choice, and that I state that I am of sound mind and that I have freely and voluntarily chosen to waive my right to be represented by counsel for the purpose of this agreement.

_____
Respondent

Subscribed and sworn to before me

this _____ day of _____, 20____

_____
Notary Public

DISSOLUTION WITH CHILDREN - 4

~~DISSOLUTION WITHOUT CHILDREN - 5~~

STATE OF MINNESOTA

COUNTY OF <u>RAMSEY</u>

DISTRICT COURT

<u>SECOND</u> JUDICIAL DISTRICT

FAMILY COURT DIVISION

_____

In Re the Marriage of:

<u>Jane Smith</u>_____,

         Petitioner,

and

<u>John Smith</u>_____,

         Respondent.

_____

PARENTING PLAN

Court File No. <u>F4-01-3737</u>_____

Judicial Officer:_____

This parenting plan applies to the following children:

<u>Name</u>	<u>Birthdate</u>
Amber Lynn Smith	December 13, 1989
Barbara Ann Smith	September 5, 1991

RESIDENTIAL SCHEDULE

Unless the parents agree otherwise, the following provisions set forth where the child(ren) shall reside each day of the year and what contact the child(ren) shall have with each parent:

PRESCHOOL SCHEDULE

  <u>X</u>   There are no children of preschool age

____   Prior to enrollment in school, the children shall reside or be with

      ____   father the following days and times

    from _____ to _____

      ____ every week   ____ every other week

                     and

      ____ from _____ to _____

___ every week   ___ every other week

___ mother the following days and times

     from _____ to _____

___ every week   ___ every other week

     and

___ from _____ to _____

___ every week   ___ every other week

___ other (specify) _____

SCHOOL SCHEDULE

Unless the parents agree otherwise, upon enrollment in school, the child(ren) shall reside or be with the

     _X_ father the following days and times

from ___Sunday at 7:00 p.m.___ to ___Friday at 9:00 a.m.___

     _X_ every week   ___ every other week

     and

___ from _____ to _____

___ every week   ___ every other week

_X_ mother the following days and times

     from ___Friday at 9:00 a.m.___ to ___Sunday at 7:00 p.m.___

     _X_ every week   ___ every other week

     and

___ from _____ to _____

___ every week   ___ every other week

___ other (specify) _____

The school schedule will start when each child begins

     ___ kindergarten   ___ first grade   ___ other (specify)

SCHOOL BREAKS

Unless the parents agree otherwise, the child(ren) shall reside with the parents during winter breaks as follows:

     ___   With father every year

     _X_   With mother every year

     ___   With father alternate   ___ odd   ___ even years

     ___   With mother alternate   ___ odd   ___ even years

     ___   With father the first half   ___ odd   ___ even years

     ___   With mother the second half ___ odd   ___ even years

     ___   Other (specify) _____.

The children shall reside with the parents as follows during the spring break as follows:

     ___   With father every year

     ___   With mother every year

     _X_   With father alternate   _X_ odd   ___ even years

     _X_   With mother alternate   ___ odd   _X_ even years

     ___   With father the first half   ___ odd   ___ even years

     ___   With mother the second half ___ odd   ___ even years

     ___   Other (specify) _____.

SUMMER SCHEDULE

Unless the parents agree otherwise, upon completion of the school year, the child(ren) shall reside with the

     _X_   father the following days and times

from ____Friday at 7:00 p.m.____ to _____Sunday at 7:00 p.m.____

     _X_   every week   ___   every other week

                  and

     ___   from ___day/time_____ to _____day/time_____

___ every week   ___ every other week

_X_ mother the following days and times

from ___Sunday at 7:00 p.m.___ to _____Friday at 7:00 p.m._____

_X_ every week   ___ every other week

and

___ from ___day/time_____ to _____day/time_____

___ every week   ___ every other week

___ same as school year schedule

___ other (specify)_____

VACATION WITH EACH PARENT

___ Does not apply

_X_ Unless the parents agree otherwise, the schedule for vacation with parents is as follows:

___ One week per year

_X_ Two weeks per year

___ Consecutive

___ Non-consecutive

_X_ Summer only

___ Other (specify) _____

SCHEDULE FOR HOLIDAYS

(Parents may include any religious or cultural holidays they wish to observe.) Unless the parents agree otherwise, the residential schedule for the child(ren) for the holidays listed below is as follows:

	With Mother (Specify Year Odd/Even/Every)	With Father (Specify Year Odd/Even/Every)
New Years Day	Even	Odd
Easter	Even	Odd
Memorial Day Weekend	Odd	Even
July 4th	Odd	Even

Labor Day Weekend	Even	Odd
Thanksgiving Day	Odd	Even
Christmas Eve (overnight until 10:00 a.m.)	Even	Odd
Christmas Day	Odd	Even

For purposes of this plan, a holiday shall begin and end as follows (set forth times):

<u>7:00 p.m. the night before the holiday until 7:00 p.m. the night of the holiday. Memorial Day and Labor Day shall include the weekend commencing Friday at 7:00 p.m. - Sunday at 7:00 p.m. Thanksgiving shall commence Wednesday at 7:00 p.m. - Thursday at 7:00 p.m. The other parent will have the children Thursday at 7:00 p.m. - Friday at 7:00 p.m. Christmas Eve will commence at 5:00 p.m. Christmas Day visitation shall end at 7:00 p.m.</u>

___ Holidays which fall on a Friday or Monday shall include Saturday and Sunday

___ Other (specify) _____

SCHEDULE FOR SPECIAL OCCASIONS

Unless the parents agree otherwise, the residential schedule for the child(ren) for the following special occasions is as follows:

	With Mother (Specify Year Odd/Even/Every)	With Father (Specify Year Odd/Even/Every)
Mother's Day	Every	
Father's Day		Every
Child's Birthday (Amber)	Odd	Even
Child's Birthday (Barbara)	Odd	Even
Father's Birthday		Every
Mother's Birthday	Every	
Halloween	Odd	Even

PRIORITIES UNDER THE RESIDENTIAL SCHEDULE

___ Does not apply

_X_ Holidays have priority over vacations

_X_ Special occasions have priority over vacations

_X_ Vacations have priority over regular residential time

___ Other (specify) _____

TRANSPORTATION ARRANGEMENTS

Unless the parents agree otherwise, transportation arrangements for the children between the parents shall be as follows:

___ Father shall pick up as follows: _____

___ Father shall drop off as follows _____

___ Mother shall pick up as follows _____

___ Mother shall drop off as follows: _____

___ Parents will meet at the following location _____

_X_ Other (specify): <u>The parents shall return the children to the other parent at the end of his or her visit.</u>

The parents will share equally in the transportation necessary to effectuate the Parenting Plan.

TELEPHONE CONTACTS

_X_ Reasonable ___ Mother ___ Father

___ Specific ___ Mother ___ Father

Days and times _____

RESTRICTIONS

_X_ Does not apply

___ The ___ Father's ___ Mother's residential time with the child(ren) shall be limited due to the following factor(s): _____

_____

The following restrictions shall apply when the child(ren) spend time with this parent: _____

_____

_____

___ Contact shall be supervised by:

___ A mutually agreed upon third party

___ Specify: _____

DECISION MAKING

Major decisions regarding the child(ren) shall be made as follows:

Health care   ___ father   ___ mother   _X_ joint

Education   ___ father   ___ mother   _X_ joint

Religious Upbringing ___ father   ___ mother   _X_ joint

Extracurricular Act   ___ father   ___ mother   _X_ joint

___ father shall be solely responsible for making decisions in the following specific areas:

_____

___ mother shall be solely responsible for making decisions in the following specific areas: _____

___ father and mother shall share responsibility for making decisions in the following specific areas: _____

ADDITIONAL ARRANGEMENTS

Should any decisions involve additional expenses not covered by child support, we agree to:

_X_ share them equally

___ share them in the following way (specify): _____

___ have father be solely responsible for the following additional expenses: _____

_____

___ have mother be solely responsible for the following additional expenses: _____

_____

OTHER

RIGHT OF FIRST REFUSAL

If a parent named in this parenting plan is unable to care for the children for a period of five (5) hours, the other parent shall have the option of the residential placement of the children. If the non-residential parent is unavailable, the residential parent will make appropriate child care arrangements. The parents agree not to advise the children of any changes or negotiations until the matter is settled. Each parent shall give the other parent at least 24 hours notice if he/she is unable to comply with the regular schedule.

SICK CHILD

When a child is ill

    _X_   the residential schedule shall remain in effect

    ___   the residential schedule shall not remain in effect

___   the child will remain with the residential parent with make-up time for the nonresidential parent

    ___   other (specify) _____

DISPUTE RESOLUTION

Disputes between the parents, other than child support disputes, shall be submitted to:

    ___   Counseling by _____

    _X_   Mediation by _____ Mediation Center _____

    _X_   Arbitration by: _Mediation Center_

There shall be mediation followed by arbitration. It is intended that this persons role is consistent with the role of a "Visitation Expediter".

The cost of this process shall be allocated between the parties as determined in the dispute resolution process.

The dispute resolution process shall be commenced by notifying the other parent by:

    _X_   written request

    ___   certified mail

    ___   other (specify) _____

    ___   No dispute resolution process, except court action, shall be ordered because the following limiting factor applies (specify): _____

_____

In the dispute resolution process:

1. Preference shall be given to carrying out this Parenting Plan.

2. Unless an emergency exists, the parents shall use the designated process to resolve disputes relating to implementation of the plan.

3. A written record of any agreement reached in counseling or mediation and of each arbitration award shall be provided to each party.

4. If the court finds a parent has use or frustrated the dispute resolution process in bad faith, the court may alter the parenting plan and/or award attorney's fees and financial sanctions to the other parent.

OTHER PROVISIONS

___   There are no other provisions

_X_   The following other provisions apply:

Neither parent shall take the children out of the State of Minnesota without notice to the other parent. The other parent will not be able to prohibit travel.

Neither party will take the children out of school without the agreement of the other party except for scheduled appointments.

DESIGNATION OF CUSTODIAN

Solely for the purpose of state and federal statutes which require a designation or determination of custody the ___ father ___ mother _X_ both are designated the custodian of the children.

_____   _____

Jane Smith, Petitioner   John Smith Respondent

Subscribed and sworn to before me,   Subscribed and sworn to before me,
this ____ day of _____, 20___.   this ____ day of _____, 20___.

_____   _____

Notary Public   Notary Public

The foregoing constitutes the Parenting Plan Order of the Court:

RECOMMENDED FOR APPROVAL   APPROVED FOR ENTRY:

Dated: _____   Dated: _____

_____   _____

Referee   Judge of District Court

DISSOLUTION WITH CHILDREN - 4

~~DISSOLUTION WITHOUT CHILDREN - 5~~

STATE OF MINNESOTA

COUNTY OF <u>RAMSEY</u>

DISTRICT COURT

<u>SECOND</u> JUDICIAL DISTRICT

FAMILY COURT DIVISION

In Re the Marriage of:

<u>Jane A. Smith</u>   ,

               Petitioner,

and

<u>John B. Smith</u>   ,

               Respondent.

FINDINGS OF FACT, CONCLUSIONS OF LAW, ORDER FOR JUDGMENT, AND JUDGMENT AND DECREE

Court File No. <u>F4-01-3737</u>

Judicial Officer: <u>Referee Anderson</u>

The above-entitled matter came on for default hearing before the Honorable <u>Joanne Anderson</u>, ~~Judge/~~Referee of <u>Ramsey</u> County District Court, Family Division on <u>January 5, 2002</u>. Petitioner~~/Respondent/Neither party~~ appeared personally.

Based upon the complete file and the written Marital Termination Agreement of the parties, the Court makes the following Findings of Fact, Conclusions of Law, and Order for Judgment:

FINDINGS OF FACT

I.

The name, address, date of birth, age, and Social Security Number of Petitioner are as follows:

        Name: <u>Jane A. Smith</u>

        Address: <u>1417 Main Street</u>

        <u>Saint Paul, Minnesota 55106</u>

        County: <u>Ramsey County</u>

        Born: <u>April 15, 1968</u>

        Age: <u>33</u>

        Social Security Number: <u>Confidential Information Form</u>

The Petitioner has formerly been known by the following name(s):

Jane A. Jones. She is proceeding *pro se*.

II.

The name, address, date of birth, age, and Social Security Number of Respondent are as follows:

Name: John B. Smith
Address: 1966 Oak Street
Minneapolis, Minnesota 55424
County: Hennepin County

Born: June 30, 1966
Age: 35
Social Security Number: Confidential Information Form

Respondent has formerly been know by the following name(s)

None. He is proceeding *pro se*.

III.

The parties were married to each other on (date) June 8, 1978 in the City of Stillwater, County of Washington, State of Minnesota, and ever since have been and are now husband and wife.

IV.

The parties have the following minor children, including date of birth, age, and social security number:

Name: Amber Lynn Smith
Born: December 3, 1989
Age: 12
Social Security No. Confidential Information Form

Name: Barbara Ann Smith
Born: September 5, 1991
Age: 10
Social Security No. Confidential Information Form

The minor children of the parties are now in the care of [~~Petitioner/Respondent/~~both parties]. The minor children of the parties are not subject to the jurisdiction of any juvenile court.

_____ It is in the best interests of the children that custody should be awarded to (Petitioner/Respondent/both parties)

__X__ It is in the best interests of the children that the parties enter into a parenting plan regarding the care of the minor children.

V.

It is in the best interests of the children that neither party pay support to the other as their incomes are comparable and they will have the children approximately equal amounts of time. Each of the parties has sufficient income to allow each to provide for the children while they are in his or her care.

VI.

(~~Petitioner/Respondent/~~Neither party) should pay temporary or permanent spousal maintenance for the support of the other.

VII.

Petitioner~~/Respondent~~ provides medical insurance for the benefit of Petitioner.

~~Petitioner/~~Respondent provides medical insurance for the benefit of Respondent

Petitioner~~/Respondent~~ provides medical insurance for the benefit of the minor children.

VIII.

The parties own various items of personal property which they have divided between themselves.

IX.

Petitioner~~/Respondent~~ has resided within the State of Minnesota for more than 180 days immediately preceding commencement of this proceeding. Petitioner presently resides in Ramsey County.

X.

The wife is not presently pregnant.

XI.

No separate proceedings for dissolution of marriage or legal separation have been commenced or are pending in any court in the State of Minnesota or elsewhere.

XII.

There has been an irretrievable breakdown of the marriage relationship pursuant to Minn. Stat. § 518.06, as amended, so as to constitute grounds for dissolution of the marriage.

XIII.

Neither party hereto is in the military service of the United States Government so, accordingly, the Soldiers' and Sailors' Relief Act of 1940, as amended, is not applicable in this proceeding.

XIV.

The parties have been separated since <u>April 2, 2001.</u>

XV.

Petitioner is employed as a<u>n engineer</u> by <u>Minnesota Mining and Manufacturing.</u> Petitioner has a net monthly income of approximately $<u>2,691.</u>

XVI.

Respondent is employed as a <u>personal banker</u> by <u>U.S. Bank Corporation.</u> Respondent has a net monthly income of approximately $<u>2,367.</u>

XVII.

<u> X </u> The parties own the following real property:

The parties own a home at 1417 Main Street in Saint Paul with a fair market value of $250,000 and a mortgage of $125,000. Petitioner has a nonmarital interest in the property of $25,000. Petitioner's parents gave her $10,000 the home which the parties purchased for $100,000. This represents ten percent of the value of the property. The property is located in the County of Ramsey, State of Minnesota and is legally described as follows:

Lot 7, Block 2 Dayton's Addition, County of Ramsey, State of Minnesota

~~_____ The parties own no real estate.~~

172

XVIII.

The parties own the following motor vehicles:

Year	Make	Model	VIN	Value	Debt
1999	Oldsmobile	Silhouette		$18,000	$10,000
1999	Ford	Taurus		leased	0
1955	Chevrolet			$4,000	0

XIX.

The parties are the owners of the following cash, savings, and checking accounts:

Institution	Type	Account #	Owner	Balance
	Checking		Joint	Nominal
	Savings		Joint	Nominal

The parties are the owners of savings, and checking accounts with nominal balances

XX.

The parties own the following retirement plans:

Institution	Type	Account #	Owner	Value

Petitioner has retirement plans with a value of $65,000.

Respondent has retirement plans with a value of $75,000.

XXI.

The parties have the following marital debts and obligations:

Institution	Type	Account #	Owner	Balance
MasterCard	credit card	4444-5555-6666-7777	Both	$4,000
Visa	credit card	7777-6666-5555-4444	Both	$2,000
Sears	credit card	5555-4444-7777-6666	Both	$2,500

The parties have incurred various individual debts since their separation on April 2, 2001 for which each party should be responsible.

XXII.

_____ There is an order for protection presently in effect.

___X___ There is no order for protection presently in effect.

XXIII.

The Petition was filed in good faith and for the purposes set forth therein.

CONCLUSIONS OF LAW

1. <u>MARITAL STATUS</u>. The bonds of matrimony heretofore existing between the parties are hereby dissolved.

2. <u>MILITARY SERVICE</u>. Neither party is entitled to the protections of the Soldier's and Sailor's Civil Relief Act of 1940 as amended.

3. <u>RELEASE</u>. Except as is expressly provided herein to the contrary, by agreement, each party is released from any and all further liability whatsoever to the other.

4. <u>MARITAL TERMINATION AGREEMENT INCORPORATED</u>. The terms of the Marital Termination Agreement are hereby incorporated into the Judgment and Decree, whether or not each and every portion of this agreement is literally set forth in said decree.

5. <u>UNIFORM CHILD CUSTODY JURISDICTION</u>. Minnesota is the proper jurisdiction within the contemplation of the Uniform Child Custody Jurisdiction and Enforcement Act, Minnesota Statutes Section 518D, to enter an order regarding the custody, care, and control of the minor children.

6. <u>PARENTING PLAN</u>. The Parenting Plan attached as Appendix B shall be incorporated into any Judgment and Decree and shall control all issues related to access to the children.

7. <u>PARENT ACCESS</u>. The Parenting Plan attached as Appendix B shall be incorporated into any Judgment and Decree and shall control all issues related to access to the children.

8. <u>UNDERSTANDING AS TO DECISIONS AFFECTING THE CHILDREN</u>. It is in the best interest of the children that the parties follow the Parenting Plan attached as Appendix B. The actual residence of the children may be changed at any time as the parties mutually agree or as allowed by order of the Court.

    All decisions pertaining to the education, discipline, health, extracurricular or summer activities, religious training, medical and dental care shall be decided by both parties after reasonable and adequate discussion. The parent with actual physical custody shall make day-to-day decisions affecting the children, including any medical or dental emergencies. If the parties are unable to reach agreement on any decision affecting the children, they shall use the services of a mediator to resolve their differences.

Each parent has the right to know of any circumstances or decisions that affect the children and each has the right to any medical, dental, or school records of the children. Neither may knowingly do anything to hamper or interfere with the natural and continuing relationship between the children and the other parent, nor may they allow others to interfere.

9. MEDIATION. Any claim or controversy involving visitation or any other issue involving the children (other than child support) which cannot be resolved by the parties through direct communication without mediation, shall be promptly submitted to mediation.

   a. Definition of Mediation. Mediation is a voluntary process entered into by the parties. In this process, the parties continue direct communication with each other, but with the assistance of a neutral person who is the mediator. The mediator has no authority to require any concession or agreement. A good faith effort shall be made between the parties to resolve any claim or controversy.

   b. Selection of Mediator. The mediator shall be named by mutual agreement of the parties or by obtaining a list of five qualified persons from the Court and by alternately striking names.

   c. Duties and Responsibilities of Mediator. The mediator shall have the duty to assist the parties in resolving visitation issues.

   d. Duty to Cooperate and Complete. Both parties agree to cooperate and act in good faith to resolve the disputes with the assistance of the mediator.

   e. Payment of Costs. The parties shall share the costs of mediation equally unless they mutually agree otherwise.

   f. Exhaustion of Remedies. The above procedure shall be followed before either party may apply to the Court for relief.

10. CHILD SUPPORT. Neither party shall pay child support to the other. The parties shall have joint legal and physical custody of the child with each sharing equally in the time of custody and support of the minor child. In light of the relative incomes of the parties, such an arrangement is in the best interests of the children. Petitioner shall pay for the clothing and activities for the children.

11. INSURANCE FOR CHILD SUPPORT. In order to insure that funds are available for the support of minor children of the parties, for so long as there exists an obligation

of support the parties shall maintain life insurance in the amount of $50,000 and each shall name the other party as beneficiary thereof.

12. MEDICAL COVERAGE FOR CHILD. As additional child support, during the time that the child of the parties is a minor, Petitioner/~~Respondent~~ maintain in full force and effect and pay the premium cost for all medical insurance available to her through his employer she shall be responsible for notifying her employer. ~~Petitioner/~~Respondent shall be responsible for dental coverage.

13. UNINSURED MEDICAL AND DENTAL FOR CHILD. To the extent not covered by insurance, all deductibles, all medical and dental expenses, including but not limited to necessary orthodontia, eye care (including prescription lenses), psychological care and psychiatric care, shall be shared equally by the parties.

14. SPOUSAL MAINTENANCE. Neither party shall pay temporary or permanent maintenance to the other. The parties have waived the right to have the other pay temporary or permanent maintenance.

By presently waiving their right to receive maintenance, the parties intend to immediately divest the court of jurisdiction to order maintenance in the future. Consideration for this agreement is the parties' mutual waiver of past present and future maintenance. Said consideration is adequate.

15. INSURANCE FOR SPOUSE. Any insurance conversion rights granted under this Judgment and Decree or by state or federal law shall be construed so as to afford to the other party the greatest coverage available to a former spouse under state and federal law or rule.

The parties shall be entitled to medical coverage through the other parties' employer for any period of time for which he or she requests eligibility and is eligible under the state or federal law or insurer's rules, but he or she shall be responsible for paying any premium for said insurance relating to said coverage.

16. HOMESTEAD.

a. Petitioner/~~Respondent~~ shall have all the parties' right, title, interest, and equity in the real property located at <u>1417 Main Street, Saint Paul, Minnesota, Ramsey County</u>

Legal Description: Lot 7, Block 2 Dayton's Addition, County of Ramsey, State of Minnesota

subject to all encumbrances presently against said homestead including mortgages and real estate taxes. ~~He/~~She shall pay to ~~Petitioner/~~Respondent the sum of $30,000 within thirty days of entry of this judgment and decree dissolving the marriage. Respondent shall hold a lien against the property for the remaining balance of his marital interest of $25,000. Said lien shall accrue interest at a rate of six percent per annum.

The parties' previous rights in said homestead are extinguished as of the date of the decree herein, and Petitioner/~~Respondent~~ shall become owner in fee simple simultaneously with the attachment of ~~Petitioner's/~~Respondent's equitable lien.

b. Petitioner/~~Respondent~~ shall be solely liable for the normal maintenance and all monthly payments of principal, interest, taxes and insurance on said homestead, and she shall indemnify and hold ~~Petitioner/~~Respondent harmless from any liability or obligation to make any payment whatsoever regarding said homestead.

c. Upon the happening of any events hereinafter enumerated in Paragraph d herein, said homestead shall be placed on the market for sale (at a price and upon terms to be mutually agreed upon by the parties), and the "net proceeds" from said sale shall be paid to Petitioner/~~Respondent~~ after satisfying any liens or mortgage of the parties in full.

d. The conditions on which said sale shall occur shall be as follows:

(1) Petitioner's/~~Respondent's~~ remarriage, at which time she will have the option of refinancing the home and satisfying the lien owed to Respondent;

(2) Petitioner's/~~Respondent's~~ moving from the premises;

(3) Petitioner's/~~Respondent's~~ death;

(4) Petitioner/~~Respondent~~ becoming more than three (3) months in arrears in any twelve (12) month period on the monthly payment of principal, interest, taxes or insurance for said homestead.

e. The filing of either a certified copy of the Judgment and Decree or a certified copy of a Summary Real Estate Disposition Judgment or a Quit Claim Deed with the <u>Ramsey</u> County Recorder's Office shall operate as a conveyance of ~~Petitioner's/~~Respondent's entire interest in said property to Petitioner/~~Respondent~~. If said real property is Torrens or registered property, then the <u>Ramsey</u> County Registrar of Titles is hereby directed, upon filing such Judgment and Decree, Summary Real Estate Disposition Judgment or Quit Claim Deed, to cancel any Certificate of Title showing both parties herein as registered owners and to issue a new Certificate of Title covering such real property in the sole name of Petitioner/~~Respondent~~ subject to ~~Petitioner's~~/Respondent's lien interest.

f.   Immediately upon entry of the Judgment and Decree herein, ~~Petitioner~~/Respondent shall execute a Quit Claim Deed conveying ~~Petitioner's~~/Respondent's interest in the homestead to Petitioner/~~Respondent~~ subject to his lien interest.

g.   As between the parties, Petitioner shall be entitled, if she chooses, to claim all income tax deductions relating to said property for the year 2001 and all years thereafter.

h.   Said transfer to Petitioner is a transfer of property incident to dissolution of marriage and is therefore not a realization event for income tax purposes.

17.   ERROR IN LEGAL DESCRIPTION.   In the event there is any technical error or omission made in describing the legal title or description to any of the real property referenced herein, the parties are required to make, execute, and deliver to each other any and all documents necessary to correct any such error or omission.

18.   PERSONAL PROPERTY.   The parties have divided the personal property between them except as otherwise set forth herein.

19.   MOTOR VEHICLES.   Petitioner shall have all right, title, interest, and equity, free and clear of any claim on the part of Respondent to the <u>1999 Oldsmobile Silhouette</u> automobile of the parties. Respondent shall, upon entry of judgment, or sooner if he/~~she~~ desires, execute all necessary documents to effect transfer of title.

Respondent shall have all right, title, interest, and equity, free and clear of any claim on the part of Petitioner to the leased <u>1999 Ford Taurus and the 1955 Chevrolet</u> automobiles of the parties. Petitioner shall, upon entry of judgment, or sooner if ~~he/~~she desires, execute all necessary documents to effect transfer of title.

20.   BANK ACCOUNTS.   The parties have divided their bank accounts and cash assets in a manner agreeable to both parties.

21.   STOCK, BOND, AND INVESTMENT ACCOUNTS.   The parties have no stock account. They have equitably divided their bonds between themselves.

22.   RETIREMENT PLANS.   Petitioner is awarded the entire right, title, interest, and equity, free and clear of any claim of Respondent in and to any retirement, pension, profit-sharing, 401(k), Keogh and IRA accounts or plans in her own name.

Respondent is awarded the entire right, title, interest, and equity, free and clear of any claim of Petitioner in and to any retirement, pension, profit-sharing, 401(k), Keogh and IRA accounts or plans in his own name.

23.   INCOME TAX EXEMPTION. The income tax exemptions for the minor children shall be divided as follows:

The parties shall each be entitled to one of the income tax exemptions for the children. At such time as there is only one exemption available to the parties, they shall alternate the exemption with Petitioner claiming the exemption in even-numbered years and Respondent in odd-numbered years.

24.   CURRENT INCOME TAXES. Any refund or payment due to the state or federal government for the filing of the parties joint federal and state income tax returns shall be equally divided between the parties.

25.   WAIVER OF AUTOMATIC STAY. The automatic stay provision of Rule 125 of the General Rules of Practice is hereby waived and the District Court Administrator is hereby ordered to immediately enter Judgment and Decree in this matter.

26.   CAPITAL GAINS TAXES. Each of the parties shall be responsible for their own capital gains taxes.

27.   DEBTS. The parties have satisfied all bills and obligations of the parties incurred during the marriage, not otherwise specified herein which constitute a joint obligation of the parties except the following:

a.   Respondent shall assume and pay the above stated debts to Visa, and he shall indemnify and hold the Petitioner harmless from any obligation to make payment of the same. He shall pay $1,000 to Petitioner's MasterCard account to equalize the debts of the parties.

b.   Petitioner shall assume and pay the above stated debts to MasterCard and Sears, and she shall indemnify and hold the Respondent harmless from any obligation to make payment of the same.

c.   Both of the parties shall assume and pay the debts which each has incurred since their separation.

d.   Any undisclosed debts shall become sole responsibility of the party that incurred it.

28.   FORMER NAME RESTORED. Petitioner does not seek to change her name.

29.	ATTORNEY FEES. The parties shall each pay their own attorney fees, if any.

30.	APPENDIX A. The attached Appendix A is incorporated and made a part of any Judgment and Decree entered based upon this Marital Termination Agreement.

31.	SERVICE. Service of a copy of the final Judgment and Decree entered herein may be made by U.S. Mail on the attorney for each party named herein, in lieu of personal service.

32.	EXECUTION OF DOCUMENTS REQUIRED. Within twenty (20) days each party hereto shall execute any and all documents necessary to transfer real and personal property in the manner described herein without further order of the court. Should either party fail to comply with this provision, the filing with the agency of a certified copy of the judgment and decree shall have the same effect as if the party had executed the necessary documents.

LET JUDGMENT BE ENTERED ACCORDINGLY

RECOMMENDED FOR APPROVAL   APPROVED FOR ENTRY:

Dated:_____		Dated:_____

_____		_____
Referee Anderson				Judge of District Court

I hereby certify that the foregoing Conclusions of Law constitute the Judgment and Decree of the Court. Judgment and Decree entered this _____ day of _____, 20___.

By:_____
    Court Administrator

DISSOLUTION WITH CHILDREN - 4

~~DISSOLUTION WITHOUT CHILDREN - 5~~

STATE OF MINNESOTA

COUNTY OF <u>RAMSEY</u>

DISTRICT COURT

SECOND JUDICIAL DISTRICT

FAMILY COURT DIVISION

_____

In Re the Marriage of:

<u>Jane A. Smith</u>,

         Petitioner,

and

<u>John B. Smith</u>,

         Respondent.

_____

DEFAULT SCHEDULING REQUEST

Court File No. <u>F4-01-3737</u>

Judicial Officer: <u>Referee Anderson</u>

The above-entitled matter is submitted for default scheduling as follows:

(Check all appropriate lines)

___ Approval without hearing pursuant to Minn. Stat. 518.13, subd. 5.

    ___ The marriage includes minor children, each party is represented by a lawyer, and each party has signed a stipulation.

    ___ The marriage does not include minor children and each party has signed a stipulation.

    ___ The marriage does not include minor children, at least 50 days have elapsed since service of the Summons and Petition, and the Respondent has not appeared in the action.

<u>X</u> Default hearing required or requested

    <u>X</u> Marriage includes minor children

Submitted by:

<u>Jane Smith</u>

Name of Party

Dated:_____

By: _____

Name: <u>Jane Smith</u>

Petitioner/~~Respondent~~ *Pro Se*

Address: <u>1417 Main Street</u>

<u>Saint Paul, Minnesota 55106</u>

Telephone No. <u>(651) 771-0050</u>

Attorney Reg.: *Pro Se*

DISSOLUTION WITH CHILDREN - 4

~~DISSOLUTION WITHOUT CHILDREN - 5~~

STATE OF MINNESOTA   DISTRICT COURT

COUNTY OF <u>RAMSEY</u>   <u>SECOND</u>   JUDICIAL DISTRICT

FAMILY COURT DIVISION

_____

In Re the Marriage of:

<u>Jane Smith   </u>,

        Petitioner,

and

<u>John Smith   </u>,

        Respondent.

_____

CONFIDENTIAL INFORMATION FORM

Court File No. <u>F4-01-3737</u>

Judicial Officer: <u>Referee Anderson</u>

	Name	Social Security Number
Petitioner	<u>Jane Smith</u>	<u>470-70-0000</u>
Respondent	<u>John Smith</u>	<u>375-70-0000</u>
Children	<u>Amber Lynn Smith</u>	<u>534-96-0000</u>
	<u>Barbara Ann Smith</u>	<u>474-96-0000</u>

Submitted by:

Dated:_____

By: _____

Name: <u>Jane Smith</u>

Petitioner/~~Respondent~~ *Pro Se*

Address: <u>1417 Main Street</u>

<u>Saint Paul, MN 55106</u>

_____

Telephone No. <u>(651) 771-0050</u>

NOTE: This would not be used in this hypothetical case, but is provided for your information.)

DISSOLUTION WITH CHILDREN - 4

~~DISSOLUTION WITHOUT CHILDREN - 5~~

STATE OF MINNESOTA	DISTRICT COURT
COUNTY OF <u>RAMSEY</u>	<u>SECOND</u> JUDICIAL DISTRICT
	FAMILY COURT DIVISION

In Re the Marriage of:

<u>Jane Smith_____</u>,

             Petitioner,

and

<u>John Smith_____</u>,

             Respondent.

APPLICATION FOR SERVICE BY ALTERNATE MEANS

Court File No. <u>F4-01-3737_____</u>

Judicial Officer: <u>Referee Anderson</u>

The last known address of Respondent is <u>1417 Main Street_____</u>

<u>Saint Paul, Minnesota 55106_____</u>.

Petitioner's most recent contacts with Respondent were as follows:<u>He mailed a birthday present to our youngest daughter two years ago. There was no return address.</u>

The last know location of Respondent's employment was: <u>I heard he was working as a truck driver in Alabama.</u>

The names and locations of Respondent's parents are: <u>His mother is in a nursing home at 1231 Marion Street in Inner Grove Heights. His father is deceased.</u>

The names and locations of Respondent's other siblings and relatives are: <u>His sister lives in Florida. I do not know where. His brother lives at 4700 Wheelock Parkway in Vadnais Heights, MN.</u>

The names and locations of other persons who may know Respondent's whereabouts are: none
_____

_____.

We have made the following efforts to locate other persons who know Respondent's whereabouts: I have contacted truck driver licensing agencies in Alabama, Missouri, and Florida. He has no contact with friends or family that I know of.

_____.

_____

Jane Smith, Affiant

Subscribed and sworn to before me,

this _____ day of _____, _____.

_____

Notary Public

NOTE: This would not be used in this hypothetical case, but is provided for your information.)

DISSOLUTION WITH CHILDREN - 4

~~DISSOLUTION WITHOUT CHILDREN - 5~~

STATE OF MINNESOTA

COUNTY OF <u>RAMSEY</u>

_____

In Re the Marriage of:

<u>Jane Smith</u>_____,

        Petitioner,

and

<u>John Smith</u>_____,

        Respondent.

_____

DISTRICT COURT

<u>SECOND</u> JUDICIAL DISTRICT

FAMILY COURT DIVISION

CERTIFICATE OF DISSOLUTION

Court File No. <u>F4-01-3737</u>_____

Judicial Officer: <u>Referee Anderson</u>

WHEREAS, Petitioner/~~Respondent~~ assumed the name <u>Jane Amanda Smith</u>_____ upon marriage; and

WHEREAS, Petitioner/~~Respondent~~ seeks to have her former name, <u>Jane Amanda Jones</u>, restored as her legal name; and

WHEREAS, Petitioner/~~Respondent~~ has not been known by any other names; and

WHEREAS, Petitioner/~~Respondent~~ seeks this name change solely because of dissolution of marriage and not to defraud or mislead anyone; and

WHEREAS, the marriage of the parties was dissolved by Judgment and Decree of this Court entered on _____, _____.

IT IS HEREBY ORDERED that hereafter Petitioner's/Respondent's legal name shall be <u>Jane Amanda Jones</u>___.

RECOMMENDED FOR ENTRY:

Dated:

BY THE COURT:

Dated:

_____

Referee of District Court

_____

Judge of District Court

185

Appendix B
Blank Forms

The forms that follow include blanks that can be filled in by hand. However, it is better to type. In many cases it is preferable to re-type the forms to meet the needs of your case. They are perforated, and you may want to photocopy them before writing on them in case you make a mistake. As stated elsewhere in this book, it is possible that the forms will not meet the unique circumstances of your case, and you will need to use the forms as a guide. Of course, you should always consult a lawyer if your case is complex or you have issues that are not covered in the forms.

Table of Forms

Child Support Calculation Worksheet

Obligor/Payor Calculation

Gross Monthly Income	$_____
Federal Income Tax	_____
State Income Tax	_____
Social Security/Medicare (.0765)	_____
Pension Deduction	_____
Union Dues	_____
Dependent Health Insurance	_____
Dental Insurance	_____
Individual Health Insurance	_____
Other Child Support	_____
Total Deductions	_____
Net Monthly Income	$_____
Child support multiplier (._____)	_____

Obligee/Recipient Calculation

Gross Monthly Income	$_____
Federal Income Tax (S-2)	_____
State Income Tax(S-2)	_____
FICA (.0765)	_____
Pension Deduction	_____
Union Dues	_____
Dependent Health Insurance	_____
Dental Insurance	_____
Individual Health Insurance	_____
Other Child Support	_____
Total Deductions	_____
Net Monthly Income	$_____

Child Care Calculation Proportion

<u>Obligor</u>

Net income _____

Support Paid (_____)

Total _____

<u>Obligee</u>

Net income _____

Support Rec'd _____

Total _____

Obligor's Total _____

Obligee's Total +_____

Total Income _____

Obligor's Total _____

Total Income ÷_____

Obligor's Percentage _____

Childcare Benefit x .75_____

Childcare Percentage: _____

DISSOLUTION WITH CHILDREN - 4

DISSOLUTION WITHOUT CHILDREN - 5

STATE OF MINNESOTA

COUNTY OF _____

In Re the Marriage of:

DISTRICT COURT

_____ JUDICIAL DISTRICT

FAMILY COURT DIVISION

_____,

Petitioner,

and

SUMMONS

Court File No. _____

Judicial Officer: _____

_____,

Respondent.

_____

THE STATE OF MINNESOTA TO THE ABOVE-NAMED RESPONDENT.

You are hereby summoned and required to serve upon the Petitioner's attorney an Answer to the Petition which is herewith served upon you within thirty (30) days, exclusive of the date of service. If you fail to do so, judgment by default will be taken against you for the relief demanded in the Petition.

This proceeding involves, affects, or brings into question real property situated in the County of _____ and legally described as:

NOTICE OF TEMPORARY RESTRAINING PROVISIONS

UNDER MINNESOTA LAW, SERVICE OF THIS SUMMONS MAKES THE FOL-LOWING REQUIREMENTS APPLY TO BOTH PARTIES TO THIS ACTION, UNLESS THEY ARE MODIFIED BY THE COURT OR THE PROCEEDING DISMISSED;

(1) NEITHER PARTY MAY DISPOSE OF ANY ASSETS EXCEPT (i) FOR THE NECESSITIES OF LIFE OR FOR THE NECESSARY GENERATION OF INCOME OR PRESERVATION OF ASSETS, (ii) BY AN AGREEMENT IN WRITING, OR (iii) FOR RETAINING COUNSEL TO CARRY ON OR TO CONTEST THIS PROCEEDING.

(2) NEITHER PARTY MAY HARASS THE OTHER PARTY; AND

(3) ALL CURRENTLY AVAILABLE INSURANCE COVERAGE MUST BE MAINTAINED AND CONTINUED WITHOUT CHANGE IN COVERAGE OR BENEFICIARY DESIGNATION.

(4) PARTIES TO A MARRIAGE DISSOLUTION PROCEEDING ARE ENCOURAGED TO ATTEMPT ALTERNATIVE DISPUTE RESOLUTION PURSUANT TO MINNESOTA LAW. ALTERNATIVE DISPUTE RESOLUTION INCLUDES MEDIATION, ARBITRATION, AND OTHER PROCESSES AS SET FORTH IN THE DISTRICT COURT RULES. YOU MAY CONTACT THE COURT ADMINISTRATOR ABOUT RESOURCES IN YOUR AREA. IF YOU CANNOT PAY FOR MEDIATION OR ALTERNATIVE DISPUTE RESOLUTION, IN SOME COUNTIES, ASSISTANCE MAY BE AVAILABLE TO YOU THROUGH A NONPROFIT PROVIDER OR A COURT PROGRAM. IF YOU ARE A VICTIM OF DOMESTIC ABUSE OR THREATS OF ABUSE AS DEFINED IN MINNESOTA STATUTES, CHAPTER 518B, YOU ARE NOT REQUIRED TO TRY MEDIATION AND YOU WILL NOT BE PENALIZED BY THE COURT IN LATER PROCEEDINGS.

IF YOU VIOLATE ANY OF THESE PROVISIONS, YOU WILL BE SUBJECT TO SANCTIONS BY THE COURT.

Dated:_____   By: _____

                                              Name:_____

                                              Petitioner *Pro Se*

                                              Address:_____

                                              _____

                                              _____

                                              Telephone No._____

DISSOLUTION WITH CHILDREN - 4

DISSOLUTION WITHOUT CHILDREN - 5

STATE OF MINNESOTA   DISTRICT COURT

COUNTY OF _____   _____ JUDICIAL DISTRICT

In Re the Marriage of: FAMILY COURT DIVISION

_____,   **PETITION FOR DISSOLUTION
OF MARRIAGE**

      Petitioner,   Court File No. _____

and   Judicial Officer: _____

_____,

      Respondent.

_____

    Petitioner for her Petition for Dissolution of Marriage, against the above-named Respondent alleges that:

I.

    The name, address, date of birth, age, and Social Security Number of Petitioner are as follows:

          Name: _____

          Address: _____

                      _____

          County: _____

          Born: _____

          Age: _____

          Social Security Number: <u>Confidential Information Form</u>

    The Petitioner has formerly been known by the following name(s):

_____

II.

The name, address, date of birth, age, and Social Security Number of Respondent are as follows:

Name: _____

Address: _____

_____

County: _____

Born: _____

Age: _____

Social Security Number: <u>Confidential Information Form</u>

The Respondent has formerly been known by the following name(s):

_____

III.

The parties were married to each other on (date) _____ in the City of _____, County of _____, State of _____, and ever since have been and are now husband and wife.

IV.

The parties have the following minor children, including date of birth, age, and social security number:

Name: _____

Born: _____

Age: _____

Social Security Number: <u>Confidential Information Form</u>

Name: _____

Born: _____

Age: _____

Social Security Number: <u>Confidential Information Form</u>

The minor children of the parties are now in the care of (Petitioner/Respondent/both parties). The minor children of the parties are not subject to the jurisdiction of any juvenile court.

_____ Custody of the minor children should be awarded to (Petitioner/Respondent/both parties)

_____ The parties should enter into a parenting plan regarding the care of the minor children.

V.

(Petitioner/Respondent) should pay temporary and permanent support for the care of the minor child of the parties.

VI.

(Petitioner/Respondent/Neither party) should pay temporary or permanent spousal maintenance for the support of the other.

VII.

Petitioner/Respondent provides medical insurance for the benefit of Petitioner.

Petitioner/Respondent provides medical insurance for the benefit of Respondent

Petitioner/Respondent provides medical insurance for the benefit of the minor children.

VIII.

The parties own various items of personal property.

IX.

Petitioner/Respondent has resided within the State of Minnesota for more than 180 days immediately preceding commencement of this proceeding. Petitioner presently resides in _____ County.

X.

The wife is not presently pregnant.

XI.

No separate proceedings for dissolution of marriage or legal separation have been commenced or are pending in any court in the State of Minnesota or elsewhere.

XII.

There has been an irretrievable breakdown of the marriage relationship pursuant to Minn. Stat. § 518.06, as amended, so as to constitute grounds for dissolution of the marriage.

XIII.

Neither party hereto is in the military service of the United States Government so, accordingly, the Soldiers' and Sailors' Relief Act of 1940, as amended, is not applicable in this proceeding.

XIV.

The parties have been separated since _____.

XV.

Petitioner is employed as a _____ by _____.
Petitioner has a net monthly income of approximately $_____.

XVI.

Respondent is employed as a _____ by _____.
Respondent has a net monthly income of approximately $_____.

XVII.

_____ The parties own the following real property:

_____ The parties own no real estate.

XVIII.

The parties own the following motor vehicles:

Year	Make	Model	VIN	Value	Debt

XIX.

The parties are the owners of cash, savings, and checking accounts.

XX.

The parties have incurred miscellaneous debts and obligations during their marriage.

The parties have incurred various individual debts since their separation on _____ for which each party should be responsible.

XXI.

_____ There is an order for protection presently in effect.

_____ There is no order for protection presently in effect.

XXII.

This Petition has been filed in good faith and for the purposes set forth herein.

WHEREFORE, Petitioner prays for the Judgment and Decree of the Court as follows:

_____ 1.   Granting a dissolution of the marriage of Petitioner and Respondent.

_____ 2.   Awarding to (Petitioner/Respondent/the parties jointly) the physical custody of the children. Awarding to (Petitioner/Respondent/the parties jointly) the legal custody of the children.

_____ 3.   Ordering a parenting plan for the care of the minor children of the parties.

_____ 4.   Ordering (Petitioner/Respondent/neither party) to pay child support for the minor child of the parties, as is consistent with Minnesota Child Support Guidelines.

_____ 5.   Granting to (Petitioner/Respondent/neither party) an award of spousal maintenance.

_____ 6.   Ordering (Petitioner/Respondent) to keep in full force and effect medical, health, and hospitalization insurance for the benefit of the minor child of the parties. Further ordering that the (Petitioner/Respondent/both parties) parties pay the cost of any premiums, co-payments, or deductibles for the above mentioned medical, health, and hospitalization insurance.

_____ 7.   Ordering that each party be responsible for their own individual debts incurred or assets purchased since their separation on _____. Further ordering an equitable division of the debts existing prior to the date of separation.

_____ 8.   Awarding to (Petitioner/Respondent) exclusive right, title, and interest in the homestead of the parties.

_____ 9.   Order the homestead sold.

_____ 10.   Awarding to the parties exclusive use and possession of the motor vehicles in his or her individual possession.

_____ 11.   Awarding to Petitioner the following motor vehicles:

Awarding to Respondent the following motor vehicles:

_____ 12. Awarding an equitable division of the personal property of the parties.

_____ 13. Granting such other and further relief as may be just and equitable.

By: _____

Name: _____

Petitioner *Pro Se*

Address: _____

_____

Telephone No.: _____

Attorney Reg.: *Pro Se*

ACKNOWLEDGMENT

The undersigned hereby acknowledges that costs, disbursements, and reasonable attorney and witness fees may be awarded pursuant to Minn. Stat. § 549.21, subd. 2 to the party against whom the allegations in this pleading are asserted.

Dated:_____   By: _____

                                     Name: _____

                                     Petitioner *Pro Se*

                                     Address: _____

                                     _____

                                     Telephone No.: _____

                                     Attorney Reg.: *Pro Se*

VERIFICATION

STATE OF MINNESOTA)

)ss.

COUNTY OF _____)

_____, being first duly sworn upon oath, deposes and states that she is the Petitioner in the above-entitled proceeding; that she has read the foregoing Petition for Dissolution of Marriage and knows the contents thereof; that the same is true to her knowledge except as to those matters therein stated on information and belief, and to those matters she believes them to be true.

                                           _____

                                           Petitioner

Subscribed and sworn to before me

this _____ day of _____, 20___.

_____

Notary Public

DISSOLUTION WITH CHILDREN - 4

DISSOLUTION WITHOUT CHILDREN - 5

STATE OF MINNESOTA

COUNTY OF _____

In Re the Marriage of:

DISTRICT COURT

_____ JUDICIAL DISTRICT

FAMILY COURT DIVISION

_____,

Petitioner,

and

ADMISSION OF SERVICE

Court File No. _____

Judicial Officer: _____

_____,

Respondent.

_____

    I, _____, the Respondent in the above-entitled proceeding, hereby accept service of the Summons and Petition for Dissolution of Marriage. I understand that:

1.   Signing this Admission starts the dissolution process;

2.   Signing this Admission does not mean that I agree with everything in the Petition for Dissolution of Marriage;

3.   I have thirty (30) days from the date I sign this Acknowledgement to serve an Answer to the Petitioner; and

4.   I do not have to sign this Admission; if I do not sign, the Petitioner can begin this action to dissolve the marriage by having the Summons and Petition served upon me.

_____

Respondent

Subscribed and sworn to before me,

this ____ day of _____, 20___.

_____

Notary Public

FORM 104. CERTIFICATE OF REPRESENTATION AND PARTIES

STATE OF MINNESOTA   DISTRICT COURT

COUNTY OF _____   _____ JUDICIAL DISTRICT

CERTIFICATE OF REPRESENTATION AND PARTIES

(ONLY THE INITIAL FILING LAWYER NEEDS TO COMPLETE THIS FORM)

Date Case Filed: _____

<u>In Re the Marriage of:</u> _____

This certificate must be filed pursuant to Rule 104 of the General Rules of Practice for the District Courts, which states: "A party filing a civil case shall, at the time of filing, notify the court administrator in writing of the name, address, and telephone number of all counsel and unrepresented parties, if known (see form 104 appended to these rules). If that information is not then known to the filing party, it shall be provided to the court administrator in writing by the filing party within seven days of learning it. Any party impleading additional parties shall provide the same information to the court administrator. The court administrator shall, upon receipt of the completed certificate, notify all parties or their lawyers, if represented by counsel, of the date of filing the action and the file number assigned."

LIST ALL LAWYERS/PRO SE PARTIES INVOLVED IN THIS CASE.

<u>LAWYER FOR PETITIONER</u>   <u>LAWYER FOR RESPONDENT</u>

                                        (If not known, name party and address)

_____   _____

Name of Party   Name of Party

Pro Se   *Pro Se*

Atty Name   Atty Name

_____   _____

_____   _____

Address   Address

_____   _____

Telephone Number   Telephone Number

N/A   N/A

MN Atty ID No.   MN Atty ID No.

DISSOLUTION WITH CHILDREN - 4

DISSOLUTION WITHOUT CHILDREN - 5

STATE OF MINNESOTA   DISTRICT COURT

COUNTY OF _____   _____ JUDICIAL DISTRICT

In Re the Marriage of: FAMILY COURT DIVISION

_____,   **ANSWER**

        Petitioner,   Court File No. _____

and   Judicial Officer: _____

_____,

        Respondent.

_____

TO: _____, THE ABOVE-NAMED PETITIONER:

1.   That except as expressly admitted or otherwise qualified each and every allegation of the Petition is denied.

2.   Respondent admits the allegations of paragraphs _____

_____.

3.   Respondent is without sufficient knowledge to admit or deny the allegations of paragraph(s) _____.

4.   Respondent denies the allegations of paragraph(s) _____

_____

Dated:_____   By: _____

                                Name: _____

                                Respondent *Pro Se*

                                Address: _____

                                _____

                                Telephone No. _____

DISSOLUTION WITH CHILDREN - 4

DISSOLUTION WITHOUT CHILDREN - 5

STATE OF MINNESOTA

COUNTY OF _____

In Re the Marriage of:

DISTRICT COURT

_____ JUDICIAL DISTRICT

FAMILY COURT DIVISION

_____,

Petitioner,

and

_____,

Respondent.

SCHEDULING INFORMATION STATEMENT

Court File No. _____

Judicial Officer: _____

_____

1.   All parties have/have not been served with process.

2.   All parties have/have not joined in the filing of this form.

3.   The parties are in agreement on all matters and this case will proceed by default.

Yes _____   No _____

____   Default hearing by General Rules of Practice, Rule 306

____   Marriage includes minor children

____   Approval without a hearing pursuant to M.S.A. 518.13, subd. 5.

____   The marriage includes minor children, each party is represented by a lawyer and each party has signed a stipulation.

____   The marriage does not include minor children, at least 50 days has elapsed since service of the Summons and Petition, and the respondent has not appeared in the action.

4.   The case involves the following (check all that apply and supply estimates where indicated):

a. minor children   No ____   Yes ____   number: _____

b. custody dispute   No _____   Yes _____   Specify: _____

_____

_____

c. parenting time dispute   No _____   Yes _____   Specify: _____

_____

_____

Each party will submit a proposal outlining custody and parenting time for each child.

d. marital property   No _____   Yes _____

Identify the asset and requested disposition: _____

_____

_____

e. non-marital property   No _____   Yes _____

Each party shall identify any non-marital claims, their respective positions for the basis for the claim, the method(s) used to arrive at the claimed amount or trace the claim and requested disposition:

_____

_____

_____

f. complex evaluation issues   No _____   Yes _____

5.   It is estimated that discovery specified below can be completed within _____ months from the date of this form. (Check all that apply and supply estimates where indicated.)

a.   Factual Depositions   No _____   Yes _____

Identify the person who will be deposed by either party:

_____

_____

_____

b.   Medical/Vocational Evaluations   No _____   Yes _____

Identify the person who will conduct such evaluations for either party:

_____

_____

_____

c.   Experts   No _____   Yes _____

Identify experts for either party.

_____

_____

6.   The dates and deadlines specified below are suggested.

a. _____ Deadline for motion regarding: _____

b. _____ Deadline for completion and review of property evaluation

c. _____ Deadline for completion and review of custody/parenting time mediation

d. _____ Deadline for completion and review of custody/parenting time evaluation

e. _____ Deadline for submitting _____ to the court.

f. _____ Date for prehearing conference.

g. _____ Date for trial or final hearing.

7.   Estimated trial or final hearing time: _____ days _____ hours (estimates less than a day must be stated in hours).

8.   Alternative dispute resolution is/is not recommended in the form of: _____ (specify, e.g., arbitration, mediation, or other means).

_____ Date for completion of mediation/alternative dispute resolution expected to extend over a period of _____ days/weeks.

9.   Please list any additional information which might be helpful to the court when scheduling this matter, including, e.g., facts which will affect readiness for trial and any issues that significantly affect the welfare of the children.

_____

_____

_____

Dated:_____   By: _____

                                    Name: _____

                                    Petitioner/Respondent *Pro Se*

                                    Address: _____

                                    _____

                                    Telephone No. _____

DISSOLUTION WITH CHILDREN - 4

DISSOLUTION WITHOUT CHILDREN - 5

STATE OF MINNESOTA

COUNTY OF _____

DISTRICT COURT

_____ JUDICIAL DISTRICT

FAMILY COURT DIVISION

In Re the Marriage of:

_____,

Petitioner,

and

NOTICE OF MOTION AND MOTION

Court File No. _____

Judicial Officer: _____

_____,

Respondent.

_____

TO: _____, THE ABOVE NAMED PETITIONER/RESPONDENT,

PLEASE TAKE NOTICE that on _____ at _____ a.m./p.m. or as soon thereafter as counsel can be heard before _____ at _____ _____ the undersigned will move the court for the following relief:

1.

2.

3.

4.

5.

6.

7.   For such other relief as the court deems just and equitable.

This motion is based upon the attached Affidavit and upon all the files and records in the above-entitled action.

PLEASE TAKE FURTHER NOTICE that all responsive pleadings shall be served and mailed to or filed with the court administrator no later than five days prior to the scheduled hearing. The court may, in its discretion, disregard any responsive pleadings served or filed with the court administrator less than five days prior to such hearing in ruling on the motion or matter in question.

Dated:_____

By: _____

Name: _____

Petitioner/Respondent *Pro Se*

Address: _____

_____

Telephone No. _____

<u>ACKNOWLEDGMENT</u>

The undersigned hereby acknowledges that costs, disbursements, and reasonable attorney and witness fees may be awarded pursuant to Minn. Stat. § 549.21, subd. 2 to the party against whom the allegations in this pleading are asserted.

Dated:_____

By: _____

Name: _____

Petitioner/Respondent *Pro Se*

Address: _____

_____

Telephone No. _____

DISSOLUTION WITH CHILDREN - 4

DISSOLUTION WITHOUT CHILDREN - 5

STATE OF MINNESOTA

COUNTY OF _____

In Re the Marriage of:

DISTRICT COURT

_____ JUDICIAL DISTRICT

FAMILY COURT DIVISION

_____,

Petitioner,

and

**APPLICATION FOR
TEMPORARY RELIEF**

Court File No. _____

Judicial Officer: _____

_____,

Respondent.

_____

STATE OF MINNESOTA)

)SS

COUNTY OF _____)

_____, the Petitioner/Respondent, hereinafter called Wife/Husband being first duly sworn, upon oath, respectfully represents to the Court that:

1.   The parties were married on _____; the Wife's age is _____; the Husband's age is _____.

2.   That parties have been separated _____ months during which the Husband/Wife has paid $_____ to the Wife/Husband.

3.   (a) There are _____ children of the parties, aged ___, ___, ___, now in the care of the Wife/Husband/both at _____.

       (b) The family home is owned/rented by the parties and is now occupied by the Wife/Husband/both parties. and _____.

       (c) For the best interests of the minor children, they should be in the temporary custody of the Husband/Wife/both.

(d) The Wife has ___ children of a prior marriage. The amount of support received, paid is $ _____ per month.

(e) The Husband has ___ children of a prior marriage. The amount of support received, paid is $ _____ per month.

4.   The assets of the parties include:

APPROXIMATE VALUE AND ENCUMBRANCE

Item	Wife	Husband	Joint Tenancy	Encumbrances
Cars	_____	_____	_____	$_____
(Year, make)	_____	_____	_____	_____
Stocks, bonds, notes	$_____	$_____	$_____	$_____
Cash and Savings	$_____	$_____	$_____	$_____
Claims	$_____	$_____	$_____	$_____
Accounts Receivable	$_____	$_____	$_____	$_____
Homestead	$_____	$_____	$_____	$_____

5.   Secured Debts, not listed above (excluding homestead):

(a) Creditor	1._____	2._____	3._____	4._____
(b) Total Outstanding	$_____	$_____	$_____	$_____
(c) Monthly Payment	$_____	$_____	$_____	$_____
(d) Party Obligated	_____	_____	_____	_____
(e) Security Pledged	_____	_____	_____	_____

6.   Necessary Monthly Expenses:

	Husband	Child(ren) (if separate)
(a) Rent	$____	$____
(b) Mortgage Payment	$____	$____
(c) Contract for Deed Payment	$____	$____
(d) Homeowner's Insurance	$____	$____
(e) Real Estate Taxes	$____	$____
(f) Utilities	$____	$____
(g) Heat	$____	$____
(h) Food	$____	$____

(i) Clothing	$_____	$_____
(j) Laundry and Dry Cleaning	$_____	$_____
(k) Medical and Dental	$_____	$_____
(l) Transportation (includes car payment)	$_____	$_____
(m) Car Insurance	$_____	$_____
(n) Life Insurance	$_____	$_____
(o) Recreation, Entertainment, Travel	$_____	$_____
(p) Newspapers and Magazines	$_____	$_____
(q) Social and Church Obligations	$_____	$_____
(r) Personal Allowance and Incidentals	$_____	$_____
(s) Babysitting and Child Care	$_____	$_____
(t) Home Maintenance	$_____	$_____
(u) Children School Needs and Allowances	$_____	$_____
(v) Additional Information_____	$_____	$_____
re: Debts and Expenses _____	$_____	$_____
TOTAL:	$_____	$_____

7.   Employment Data: Provide the following data for each employer. Attach prior month's paycheck stub(s) as Exhibit.

	Husband	Wife
(a) Name of Employer	_____	_____
Type of Employment	_____	_____
(b) Income:		
(1) Gross Income per month	$_____	$_____
(2) Statutory Deductions:		
Federal Income Tax	$_____	$_____
State Withholding	$_____	$_____
Social Security (FICA)	$_____	$_____
Pension Deduction	$_____	$_____
Union Dues	$_____	$_____
Dependent Health/Hospitalization	$_____	$_____
Dental Coverage	$_____	$_____
(3) Subtotal of Statutory Deductions	$_____	$_____
(4) Net Income (line 1-line 3)	$_____	$_____
(5) Other Paycheck Deductions		
Specify _____		
_____	$_____	$_____

(6) Subtotal (Other Deductions) $_____ $_____
(7) NET TAKE HOME PAY (Line 4-Line 6) $_____ $_____

(c) Tax withholding figures above are based on Married
    of Single taxpayer with # of deductions
    (Example: M-4 or S-2)   _____   _____

(d) Employer reimbursed expenses $_____ $_____

    Specify _____ $_____ $_____

    _____ $_____ $_____

(e) Other Income:

    (1) Public Assistance (MFIP/GA) $_____ $_____

    (2) Social Security benefits for party or

        child(ren) $_____ $_____

    (3) Unemployment/Worker's Compensation $_____ $_____

    (4) Interest income per _____ $_____ $_____

    (5) Dividend income per _____ $_____ $_____

    (6) Gross Rental Income $_____ $_____

    (7) Other Income _____ $_____ $_____

8.   (a) $_____ is a reasonable amount for temporary support for ___ children per
month.

      (b) $_____ is a reasonable amount for temporary maintenance per month.

      (c) Payment should be made on N/A.

9.   (a) $_____ has been paid on the Wife's attorney fees and costs.

      (b) $_____ has been paid on the Husband's attorney fees and costs.

      (c) $_____ is reasonable for Wife/Husband's attorney fees and costs.

10.   Additional material facts:

WHEREFORE, Petitioner/Respondent prays for an order granting such relief prior to trial as may be just and lawful.

_____

Petitioner/Respondent

Subscribed and sworn to before me

this ____ day of _____, 20___.

_____

Notary Public

DISSOLUTION WITH CHILDREN - 4

DISSOLUTION WITHOUT CHILDREN - 5

STATE OF MINNESOTA

COUNTY OF _____

DISTRICT COURT

_____ JUDICIAL DISTRICT

FAMILY COURT DIVISION

_____

In Re the Marriage of:

_____,

Petitioner,

and

_____,

Respondent.

_____

STATE OF MINNESOTA)

)SS.

COUNTY OF _____)

AFFIDAVIT

Court File No. _____

Judicial Officer: _____

_____, after being duly sworn, upon oath says as follows:

_____

Affiant

Subscribed and sworn to before me,

this ____ day of _____, 20___.

_____

Notary Public

DISSOLUTION WITH CHILDREN - 4

DISSOLUTION WITHOUT CHILDREN - 5

STATE OF MINNESOTA	DISTRICT COURT
COUNTY OF _____	_____ JUDICIAL DISTRICT
_____	FAMILY COURT DIVISION

In Re the Marriage of:

_____,

       Petitioner,

and

_____,

       Respondent.

_____

INTERROGATORIES

Court File No. _____

Judicial Officer: _____

TO: _____, THE ABOVE-NAMED PETITIONER/RESPONDENT:

     YOU WILL PLEASE TAKE NOTICE that Petitioner/Respondent demands Answers under oath by Petitioner/Respondent, within thirty/forty five (30/45) days of the service hereof pursuant to Rules 26 and 33 of the Minnesota Rules of Civil Procedure, the following Interrogatories. If information is discovered by or becomes known to you or to your attorneys or to anyone acting on your behalf, after answering the same and before trial, which would change or add to the answers given, you are hereby directed to promptly furnish such information to the undersigned.

INSTRUCTIONS

     A. These instructions shall be applicable to these and all subsequent interrogatories submitted.

     B. Where any Interrogatory requests you to identify papers, documents, correspondence or any other records or writings, state for all writings, documents, records correspondence or papers sought to be identified:

    1.   The subject matter of the contents of each.

    2.   The date of each.

    3.   The name of the person writing or signing the same, if any.

4.   The full name and last known residential and business address of each person in whose custody such is now being kept or to whose control the same is subject, and the position with said person's employment with his or her employer.

5.   Whether you will attach to your answers these Interrogatories true and correct copies of each of said documents.

C. "Document" shall mean the original and any copy (by any means made) of any written, printed, or graphic matter, however produced or reproduced, including, but not limited to any letter, memorandum, report, check, check stub, handwritten note, diary, paper, inter-office memoranda, interpersonal communication, contract, agreement, computer storage device, or any other medium in the possession of you or your attorney of record.

INTERROGATORIES

1.   Residence. State your present residence address, the type of residence, and identify all other persons residing at your residence address.

2.   Education. Describe in detail your educational background and future plans, and include the names and addresses of all institutions that you have attended or will attend, the dates of attendance, and a description of the degrees or certificates that you have obtained or may obtain.

3.   If you currently lack certification in any field in which you have a degree or have received training, describe in detail any and all requirements you must fulfill in order to obtain certification, how those requirements can be met, the time necessary to fulfill the requirements, and the cost of fulfilling the requirements.

4.   Employment. Describe each position of employment held by you since January 1, 20___, and include the name and address of your employer, the dates of your employment, your official title, if any, a description of all compensation that you received including bonuses, and any benefits provided by the employment.

5.   Other income. Describe in detail all of your sources of income or compensation, whether or not reported on any Tax Return, since January 1, 20___.

6.   State whether you are receiving or have taken any action since the date of your separation to qualify for or secure Social Security benefits, workers' compensation benefits, unemployment compensation benefits, free legal services, or any other form of public assistance, and if so, describe in detail the action taken, the results of such action, any benefits you received, and the anticipated duration of any benefits.

7.   Assets. Set forth in detail each and all of your assets value exceeds $_____.

8.   <u>Household Property</u>. Identify any particular household goods, furnishings, or other assets to which you assert a specific claim or right, and state the factual grounds upon which any such specific claim or right is based.

9.   <u>Gifts</u>. If any sales, assignments, gifts, or gifts of real or personal property were made by you during the preceding three years whose value exceeded $100, set forth:

   a.   a full description of any such real or personal property sold, assigned or gifted; the date thereof; the name and address of the purchaser, assignee, or beneficiary; the price, if any, charged therefor; and the terms of any such transaction, including the nature of the pay-off to you, if any, as to each such asset sold, assigned or gifted; and

   b.   the complete details as to the disposition by you of the proceeds of any sale referred to in Subpart "a" of this interrogatory.

10. If any person, corporation, partnership or entity of any nature owes you any money, then for each debtor state:

   a.   the name and address of the debtor;

   b.   the amount due as of the date of these Interrogatories, the basis for the indebtedness, whether there is written evidence of the indebtedness, the date the indebtedness was incurred, the manner in which the indebtedness is to be satisfied, and the date for such satisfaction; and

   c.   whether the obligation is contingent and a description of any such contingency.

11. <u>Creditors</u>. Set forth the name and address of each of your creditors.

12. <u>Asset accounts</u>. Set forth the name and address of each depository in which you have had any checking account, savings account, money market account, certificate of deposit, trust certificate, and any other account in your name, or with any other party.

13. <u>Other accounts</u>. If during the past three years there have been any bank accounts or depositories on which your name did not appear and in which you have deposited any money, state the place of the deposit, the address of the depository, the name of the account owner, the date of your deposits, and the reason for the deposit by you in the account.

14. <u>Safe deposit boxes</u>. If you have any safe deposit boxes, state where they are located, when first rented, and give a detailed description of the contents of each such box on January 1 of this year and as of the date of the Answers to these Interrogatories.

15. Describe each policy of life insurance on your life and/or your spouse's life, setting forth the name of the company issuing the policy; the number of each policy; the face amount of each policy; the type of insurance, whether whole, endowment, level term, reducing term, or otherwise.

16. State whether or not you have any beneficial interest in any profit sharing, pension, or retirement plan and describe the plan in detail, indicating the gross amount of your beneficial interest, whether vested or unvested; and the present fair market value of your interest.

17. <u>Medical and dental insurance</u>. With respect to health and dental insurance available through your union, employer, or other source state:

    a. the name of the insurance carrier(s) and the basic coverage provided by each;

    b. the premiums charged you for health coverage for yourself, and the premiums charged for dependent coverage; and

    c. the type of dental coverage available and the cost for yourself and for dependents.

18. Set forth the names and addresses of the accountants or accounting firms who have done accounting work for you personally or for any business in which you have had an interest during the preceding five years.

19. Set forth the names and addresses of all stockbrokers with whom you have done business during the preceding five years.

20. Describe in detail any and all written appraisals made or caused to be made by you or on your behalf with respect to any of your assets listed in response to the preceding Interrogatories. In lieu thereof, copies of the written appraisals may be attached hereto.

21. <u>Non-marital property</u>. Identify each item of real or personal property which you claim to be "non-marital" as defined by Minn. Stat. § 518.54, Subd. 5.

22. <u>Non-marital debt</u>. Identify each debt incurred during the marriage by either party which you claim to be "non-marital" as defined by Minn. Stat. § 518.54, Subd. 5.

23. For each automobile, recreational vehicle, snowmobile, trailer, motor, boat, etc. owned or used by you, state the:

    a. make, model, and year;

    b. owner;

    c. license plate number and state of issue;

  d. fair market value;

  e. name of the secured party;

  f. balance of any encumbrance thereon;

  g. amount of monthly payment; and

  h. names of all person using it.

24. Set forth with particularity an itemized schedule of your average monthly living expenses (stating separately, wherever possible, expenses relating to the minor child[ren]).

25. Expense sharing. If any other person or source assists you in meeting your monthly living expenses, state what expenses are contributed to and the amount received.

26. If you anticipate an increase or decrease in your income or any of your expenses, state the nature and amount of the increase or decrease, the reason, and the date you expect it to occur.

27. State the permanent legal and physical custody arrangements that you believe are in the best interests of the minor child(ren) of the parties, and specifically address the time that each parent should have with said child(ren).

28. Describe in detail the parenting responsibilities assumed by each party during the marriage and subsequent to the separation of the parties, and specifically set forth the time spent by each party with the minor child(ren) during the marriage and subsequent to the separation of the parties.

29. If you or any of the minor child(ren) of the parties have been seen, tested, evaluated, or treated within the last _____ years by any professional person such as a psychiatrist, psychologist, sociologist, social worker, family counselor, or other professional, identify the professional by name, address and area of practice, state the date of each contact with the professional, explain the purpose of each contact, and indicate whether the contacts are continuing.

30. If you have been involved in any criminal or civil legal proceedings of any kind since January 1, 20___, for each matter state the:

  a. type of matter and nature of the claims;

  b. names of the involved parties;

  c. date proceedings were commenced; and

  d. venue, case caption, and case number of any such proceedings.

31.   State the name and address of each witness, expert or otherwise, that you intend to call on your behalf in this proceeding, and for each such witness, state:

    a.   the substance of the facts and opinions to which the witness is expected to testify;

    b.   a summary of the grounds for each opinion; and

    c.   the contents of any documents upon which the witness will rely.

Dated:

By: _____

Name: _____

Petitioner/Respondent *Pro Se*

Address: _____

_____

_____

Telephone No. _____

DISSOLUTION WITH CHILDREN - 4

DISSOLUTION WITHOUT CHILDREN - 5

STATE OF MINNESOTA

COUNTY OF _____

_____

In Re the Marriage of:

_____,

Petitioner,

and

_____,

Respondent.

_____

DISTRICT COURT

_____ JUDICIAL DISTRICT

FAMILY COURT DIVISION

REQUEST FOR PRODUCTION

Court File No. _____

Judicial Officer: _____

TO: _____, THE ABOVE-NAMED PETITIONER/RESPONDENT:

PLEASE TAKE NOTICE that pursuant to Rules 26 and 34 of the Minnesota Rule of Civil Procedure, you are hereby requested to produce and permit Petitioner/Respondent herein, to inspect and copy the following documents.

1.   All personal Federal and State Income Tax returns, including all schedules, tables, and other attachment, signed by you for years _____ to the present.

2.   All documents which will be used to prepare your tax returns for the current year.

3.   All documents that reflect any income received by you from January 1, 20___ to the present such as W-2 forms, paycheck stubs, bonus check stubs, income receipts or vouchers, expense reimbursement records, dividend or interest statements, rental income records, copies of checks or check stubs, and deposit records.

4.   All documents that detail or reflect any interest that you have in any vested and unvested employment benefits including, but not limited to, bonus or incentive plans, benefit booklets, health and life insurance coverage, stock option plans, deferred compensation plans, profit sharing plans, or statements of account, any other retirement plans or statements of account, and summary descriptions.

5.   All financial statements prepared from January 1, 20___ to the present by you or on your behalf.

6.   All personal check account records from January 1, 20___ to the present, specifically including account statements, canceled checks and check registers for any joint or separate accounts used by you or in which you have or claim to have any interest.

7.   All statements from January 1, 20___ to the present for each bank account, savings account, money market account, liquid asset account, credit union account, insurance account, brokerage firm account, and depository in which you have had or claim to have any interest.

8.   All documents relating to any joint and/or separate interest you have or have had in and to any stock, bonds, debentures, Treasury Bills, notes, or other investments from January 1, 20___ to the present.

9.   All documents relating to real property in which you have had any interest since January 1, 20___, jointly or individually, specifically including purchase agreements, closing documents, warranty deeds, mortgage statements, appraisals, and market analyses.

10.   All documents relating to insurance assets to which you have had any interest since January 1, 20___, jointly or individually, specifically including copies of each policy, loan statements, premium statement, and statements of actual or projected cash value.

11.   All documents pertaining to motor vehicles, boats, or other recreational vehicles in which you have any interest.

12.   All documents relating to any contingent assets or other expectancies, such as annuities, trusts, wills, probate and estate records and evidence of distributions.

13.   All documents, records, notes and files, not already provided in response to any of the foregoing requests, relating to any assets worth more than $200.00 that you have owned from January 1, 20___ to the present.

14.   All documents evidencing any debts that you have incurred, jointly or individually, since January 1, 20___, specifically including promissory notes, invoices, bills, and account statements.

15.   All documents, records, notes and files that establish or support any claims or non-marital contributions or entitlement of _____.

16.   All pleadings relating to any litigation or Court proceedings in which you are involved, other than this proceeding.

17.   All resumes, transcripts, diplomas, certificates, or other evidence of your academic accomplishments and employability, including evidence of any job offers or efforts to obtain employment.

18.   All documents or records that evidence your inability to obtain or maintain employment, including but not limited to medical records, school records and assessments.

19.   All records or reports relating to any medical or mental health care or treatment that you have received since January 1, 20___.

20.   Copies of all expert reports and any documents, records, notes and files that served as a basis for the expert's opinion.

21.   Copies of all exhibits that you intend to offer at trial.

Dated:

By: _____

Name: _____

Petitioner/Respondent *Pro Se*

Address: _____

_____

_____

Telephone No. _____

DISSOLUTION WITH CHILDREN - 4

DISSOLUTION WITHOUT CHILDREN - 5

STATE OF MINNESOTA

DISTRICT COURT

COUNTY OF _____

_____ JUDICIAL DISTRICT

In Re the Marriage of:

FAMILY COURT DIVISION

_____,

PREHEARING STATEMENT

Petitioner,

Court File No. _____

and

Judicial Officer: _____

_____,

Respondent.

_____

1.   **PERSONAL INFORMATION**

	HUSBAND	WIFE
Full Name	_____	_____
Present Mailing Address	_____	_____
	_____	_____
Employer	_____	_____
Street Address	_____	_____
City, State, ZIP	_____	_____
Birthdate	_____ Age: _____	_____ Age: _____
Marriage Date	_____	_____
Separation Date (Different Residences)	_____	_____
Date of Temporary Order(s), if any	_____	_____

Minor children born to this marriage or who will be affected by this legal action:

FULL NAME   BIRTHDATE   AGE   LIVING WITH:

_____

_____

_____

_____

Is the wife pregnant now? _____ no _____ yes-due date _____

Is the issue of custody contested? _____ yes _____ no

If custody is disputed, each party shall submit proposals for custody and parenting time for each child as Exhibit 1A.

2. **EMPLOYMENT**: Provide the following data for each employer.

	HUSBAND	WIFE
a) Name of Employer	_____	_____
Length of Employment	_____	_____
Income:		
(1) Gross income per month	_____	_____
Statutory Deductions		
Federal Income Tax	$_____	$_____
State Withholding	$_____	$_____
Social Security (FICA)	$_____	$_____
Pension Deduction	$_____	$_____
Union Dues	$_____	$_____
Dependent Health/Hospitalization Coverage	$_____	$_____
Dental Coverage	$_____	$_____
(2) Subtotal of statutory deductions	$_____	$_____
(3) Net income (line 1-Line2)	$_____	$_____
Other paycheck deductions:	$_____	$_____
Specify: _____	$_____	$_____
_____	$_____	$_____
(4) Subtotal of Other Deductions	$_____	$_____
(5) NET TAKE HOME PAY PER MONTH (line 3-line 4)	_____	_____
Tax withholding figures above are based upon Married or Single taxpayer with # of exemptions	_____	_____

(example M-4 or S-2)

Attach prior month's paycheck stub(s) as Exhibit 2A

(b)   Employment benefits: identify all benefits in addition to wages including bonus paid or due, automobile or travel expense reimbursement, other per diem compensation, memberships paid by the employer.

_____   _____

_____   _____

_____   _____

Will medical and dental insurance coverage be available for your spouse after the dissolution?

____ yes _____ no

(c) Other income

    (1) Public assistance (MFIP/GA) $_____ $_____

    (2) Social Security benefits for party or child(ren) $_____ $_____

    (3) Unemployment/Workers Comp. $_____ $_____

    (4) Interest income per month $_____ $_____

    (5) Dividend income per month $_____ $_____

    (6) Other income: _____ $_____ $_____

    (7) Last Year's Tax Refunds   Federal _____   Federal _____

                                        State _____   State _____

3.   **CHILD SUPPORT/SPOUSAL MAINTENANCE**

(a)   Does either party receive child support or spousal maintenance from a separate proceeding? ____ yes _____ no

    If yes, specify the $ _____ received each month for child support/alimony for _____ by the order of _____, County dated _____.

(b)   Child Support or Spousal Maintenance established by court order for person(s) not included in this proceeding currently being paid:

_____   _____

_____   _____

    To whom is this obligation owed? _____

(c)   Current Monthly Child Support or Spousal Maintenance Order established by temporary order for either party and minor children in this proceeding:

Child Support: $ _____ Spousal Maintenance $ _____

Any claim or arrearages claimed under existing court order(s): ____ yes _____ no

If yes, specify the amount(s) claimed: Child Support $ _____

Spousal Maintenance $ _____

4.   LIVING EXPENSES

Your estimated monthly expenses: $_____

(Attach an itemization as Exhibit 4A)

5.   REAL PROPERTY

	HOMESTEAD	OTHER*
(a) Date Acquired	_____	_____
(b) Purchase Price	$_____	$_____
(c) Present Fair Market Value	$_____	$_____
(d) First Mortgage Balance	$_____	$_____
(e) Second Mortgage Balance or Home Improvement Loan	$_____	$_____
(f) Net Value	$_____	$_____
(g) Monthly Payment (PITI)	$_____	$_____
(h) Rental Income, if any	$_____	$_____

* Other Real Estate: Provide the same information for other real property such as rental property, lake cabin, etc. as Exhibit 5C.

6.   PERSONAL PROPERTY: Fair Market Value

In possession of:

	Husband	Wife	Joint
(a) Household Contents	_____	_____	_____
(b) Stocks, bonds, etc._____	$_____	$_____	$_____
_____	$_____	$_____	$_____
(c) Checking Accounts	$_____	$_____	$_____
Savings Accounts	$_____	$_____	$_____
(d) Receivables and Claims	$_____	$_____	$_____
_____	$_____	$_____	$_____

(e) Motor Vehicles: year/make/model

	(1) _____	(2) _____	(3)_____
Market Value	$_____	_____	_____
Encumbrance	$_____	_____	_____
Net Value	$_____	_____	_____
Monthly Payment	$_____	_____	_____
In Possession of :	_____	_____	_____

(f) Boats, Motors, Campers, Snowmobiles, Trailers, etc.:

	(1)_____	(2)_____	(3)_____
Market Value	$_____	$_____	$_____
Encumbrance	$_____	$_____	$_____
Net Value	$_____	$_____	$_____
Monthly Payment	$_____	$_____	$_____
In Possession of :	_____	_____	$_____

(g)　　Other: (such as power equipment, tools, guns, valuable animals, etc.)

Description: _____　　Fair Market Value: $_____

Encumbrance: $_____

Net Value: $_____

7.　　NON-MARITAL CLAIMS:

(a)　　Description: (1) _____　(2) _____

(b)　　Amount claimed: $_____$_____

Set forth the basis for and method used to arrive at your claims to be attached as Exhibit 7A.

8.　　LIFE INSURANCE:

	a) _____	b) _____	c) _____
Company	_____	_____	_____
Policy Number	_____	_____	_____
Type of Insurance	_____	_____	_____
Face Amount	$_____	$_____	$_____
Cash Value	$_____	$_____	$_____
Loans	$_____	$_____	$_____
Insured	_____	_____	_____
Beneficiary	_____	_____	_____
Owner	_____	_____	_____

9. PENSION PLAN AND/OR PROFIT SHARING PLAN:

	HUSBAND	WIFE
a) Through Employment		
1) Present Cash Value	_____	_____
2) Vested or Nonvested	_____	_____
(b) Private Plans		
(IRA, Keogh, SEP, etc.)	_____	_____
Present cash value	_____	_____
(c) Deferred Compensation	_____	_____
(d) Military Pension or Disability	Yes ____ No_____	Yes ____ No ____

10. DEBTS: (Not listed in 4 or 5 above)

(a)　　All secured debts:

	1)	2)	3)
Creditor	_____	_____	_____
Total Amount Owing	$_____	$_____	$_____
Total Monthly Payment	$_____	$_____	$_____
When Incurred	_____	_____	
Party Obligated (H, W, J)	_____	_____	
Reason for debt	_____	_____	
Totals	H:_____	W:_____	J:_____

(b)　　Unsecured Debts: Attach a separate schedule showing the creditor, balance, owed, monthly payment, etc. to be attached as Exhibit 9B. Include attorney fees and costs.

Total　Husband: $_____　Wife: $_____　Joint: $_____

Dated: _____　The statements contained herein are true and complete to the best of my knowledge.

_____
Petitioner/Respondent

EXHIBIT 1A

RESPONDENT'S CUSTODY/PARENT ACCESS SCHEDULE PROPOSAL

EXHIBIT 4A

PETITIONER'S/RESPONDENT'S MONTHLY LIVING EXPENSES

	Husband	Child(ren) (if separate)
(a) Rent	$	$
(b) Mortgage Payment	$	$
(c) Contract for Deed Payment	$	$
(d) Homeowner's Insurance	$	$
(e) Real Estate Taxes	$	$
(f) Utilities	$	$
(g) Heat	$	$
(h) Food	$	$
(i) Clothing	$	$
(j) Laundry and Dry Cleaning	$	$
(k) Medical and Dental	$	$
(l) Transportation (includes car payment)	$	$
(m) Car Insurance	$	$
(n) Life Insurance	$	$
(o) Recreation, Entertainment, Travel	$	$
(p) Newspapers and Magazines	$	$
(q) Social and Church Obligations	$	$
(r) Personal Allowance and Incidentals	$	$
(s) Babysitting and Child Care	$	$
(t) Home Maintenance	$	$
(u) Children School Needs and Allowances	$	$
(v) Additional Information_____	$	$
re: Debts and Expenses _____	$	$
TOTAL:	$	$

EXHIBIT 7A
NON-MARITAL CLAIMS

EXHIBIT 9B

UNSECURED DEBTS OF PARTIES

Debt	Payment	Amount Owing	Party Obligated
_____	$_____	$_____	_____
_____	$_____	$_____	_____
_____	$_____	$_____	_____
_____	$_____	$_____	_____
_____	$_____	$_____	_____
_____	$_____	$_____	_____
_____	$_____	$_____	_____
_____	$_____	$_____	_____
_____	$_____	$_____	_____
_____	$_____	$_____	_____
_____	$_____	$_____	_____
_____	$_____	$_____	_____
TOTALS:	$_____	$_____	_____

DISSOLUTION WITH CHILDREN - 4

DISSOLUTION WITHOUT CHILDREN - 5

STATE OF MINNESOTA

COUNTY OF _____

_____

In Re the Marriage of:

_____,

          Petitioner,

and

_____,

          Respondent.

_____

DISTRICT COURT

_____ JUDICIAL DISTRICT

FAMILY COURT DIVISION

MARITAL   TERMINATION AGREEMENT

Court File No._____

Judicial Officer: _____

WHEREAS, Petitioner has commenced the above-entitled proceeding for dissolution of the marriage relationship with Respondent; and

WHEREAS, on _____ [DATE] a copy of the Summons and Petition for Dissolution of Marriage were served upon Respondent; and

WHEREAS, it appears to both parties hereto that efforts toward reconciliation would not be fruitful; and

WHEREAS, the parties desire to settle their differences amicably with regard to questions of custody, maintenance, property division, attorneys' fees , and other related matters; and

WHEREAS, each party has fully disclosed to the other party all of his or her income, including any and all income which he or she has in the name of a third person, but which is under his or her control; and

WHEREAS, each party has fully disclosed to the other party all of his or her assets, both real and personal, including any and all assets which he or she has in the name of a third person, but which are under his or her control; and

NOW, THEREFORE, IT IS HEREBY STIPULATED AND AGREED by and between the parties to the above-entitled proceeding as follows:

1.   <u>MARITAL STATUS</u>. The bonds of matrimony heretofore existing between the parties shall be dissolved.

2   MILITARY SERVICE. Neither party is entitled to the protections of the Soldier's and Sailor's Civil Relief Act of 1940 as amended.

3.   COMPLETE AGREEMENT. The parties have made this agreement intending that it be a full, complete, and final settlement and satisfaction of any and all claims of any kind, nature, or description which involve issues addressed in the marital termination agreement to which either party may be entitled or may claim to be entitled, now or in the future, against the other. Except as is expressly provided herein to the contrary, each is released from any and all further liability whatsoever to the other.

4.   M.T.A. AS EVIDENCE. Respondent will not appear in these proceedings, save and except through this Marital Termination Agreement. Petitioner may proceed with said dissolution as by default. As a part of these proceedings, Petitioner will submit this agreement to the above-entitled court. If said dissolution is not granted, the terms of this agreement shall be of no effect. If this agreement is not approved by the court, Respondent shall be advised and shall be given the opportunity to appear and present his arguments, witnesses, and testimony. If this agreement is approved by the court and if the court grants a dissolution to the Petitioner herein, the terms of this agreement shall be made by reference a part of any decree issued, whether or not each and every portion of this agreement is literally set forth in said decree.

5.   UNIFORM CHILD CUSTODY JURISDICTION. Minnesota is the proper jurisdiction within the contemplation of the Uniform Child Custody Jurisdiction and Enforcement Act, Minnesota Statutes Section 518D to enter an order regarding the custody, care, and control of the minor child[ren].

6.   CUSTODY. The Parenting Plan attached as Appendix B shall be incorporated into any Judgment and Decree and shall control all issues related to access to the children.

6.   CUSTODY. [Petitioner/Respondent/Both parties] shall have physical custody, care, and control of the minor child of the parties.

[Petitioner/Respondent/Both parties] legal custody of the minor child of the parties.

Respondent shall have parenting time as set forth in the attached Appendix B.

7.   PARENTING PLAN. The parties have entered into a parenting plan which is attached as Appendix B.

8.   UNDERSTANDING AS TO DECISIONS AFFECTING THE CHILDREN. We agree that the actual residence of the children may be changed at any time as the parties mutually agree or as allowed by order of the Court.

We further agree that all decisions pertaining to the education, discipline, health, extracurricular or summer activities, religious training, medical and dental care will be decided by both of us after reasonable and adequate discussion. We also agree that the parent with actual physical custody shall make day-to-day decisions affecting the children, including any medical or dental emergencies. We agree that if we are unable to reach agreement on any decisions affecting our children, we will use the services of a mediator (as discussed below) to resolve our differences.

We further agree that each parent has the right to know of any circumstances or decisions that affect the children and that each of us has the right to any medical, dental, or school records of our children. Neither of us will knowingly do anything to hamper or interfere with the natural and continuing relationship between our children and the other parent, nor will we allow others to interfere.

Further, we recognize that the well-being of our children is of paramount importance, and, therefore, we agree that our children should have as much contact as possible with the parent that does not have physical custody and our children may visit the non-custodial parent as often as may be agreed upon.

9.   MEDIATION. Any claim or controversy involving visitation or any other issue involving the children (other than child support) which cannot be resolved by the parties through direct communication without mediation, shall be promptly submitted to mediation.

    a.   Definition of Mediation. Mediation is a voluntary process entered into by the parties. In this process, the parties continue direct communication with each other, but with the assistance of a neutral person who is the mediator. The mediator has no authority to require any concession or agreement. A good faith effort shall be made between the parties to resolve any claim or controversy.

    b.   Selection of Mediator. The mediator shall be named by mutual agreement of the parties or by obtaining a list of five qualified persons from the Court and by alternately striking names.

    c.   Duties and Responsibilities of Mediator. The mediator shall have the duty to assist the parties in resolving visitation issues.

    d.   Duty to Cooperate and Complete. Both parties agree to cooperate and act in good faith to resolve the disputes with the assistance of the mediator.

    e.   Payment of Costs. The parties shall share the costs of mediation equally unless they mutually agree otherwise.

    f.   Exhaustion of Remedies. The above procedure shall be followed before either party may apply to the Court for relief.

10.   CHILD SUPPORT. Neither party shall pay child support to the other. The parties shall have joint legal and physical custody of the child with each sharing equally in the time of custody and support of the minor child pursuant to a Parenting Plan.

10. CHILD SUPPORT. [Petitioner/Respondent/Neither] shall pay as child support for the benefit of the minor children of the parties the sum of $_____ per month in equal installments consistent with his/her pay periods through Automatic Income Withholding (AIW). Said obligation shall continue until one of the parties' minor children either attains the age of eighteen (18) is married, emancipated, self-supporting, deceased, or in the Armed Forces of the United States of America, whichever shall occur first, unless at such time the child is still attending high school, in which case, child support shall continue until the earlier of the child's graduation from high school or the child's 20th birthday if the child is still in high school. At such time, the child support obligation shall be reduced pursuant to the Minnesota Child Support Guidelines.

Until Automatic Income Withholding of the aforesaid child support obligation commences, [Petitioner/Respondent] shall make all child support payments required of him/her herein directly to [Petitioner/Respondent] at such times and in such amounts as set forth above.

Any child support arrearages shall not merge into the Judgment and Decree.

11. INSURANCE FOR CHILD SUPPORT. In order to insure that funds are available for the support of minor children of the parties, for so long as there exists an obligation of support, the parties shall maintain in full force and effect, and not borrow against the value of same, life insurance on his and her own life for the benefit of the minor children in the amount of $_____.

12. MEDICAL COVERAGE FOR CHILD. As additional child support, during the time that the child of the parties is a minor, Petitioner/Respondent maintain in full force and effect and pay the premium cost for all medical insurance available to him/her through his/her employer he/she shall be responsible for notifying his/her employer. Petitioner/Respondent shall be responsible for dental coverage.

13. UNINSURED MEDICAL AND DENTAL FOR CHILD. To the extent not covered by insurance, all deductibles, all medical and dental expenses, including but not limited to necessary orthodontia, eye care (including prescription lenses), psychological care and psychiatric care, shall be shared equally by the parties.

13. UNINSURED MEDICAL AND DENTAL FOR CHILD. Petitioner shall pay _____% and Respondent shall pay ____% of any medical and dental expenses of the children that are not covered by insurance.

14. SPOUSAL MAINTENANCE. Neither party shall pay temporary or permanent maintenance to the other, and the parties hereby waive the right to have the other pay temporary or permanent maintenance.

By presently waiving their right to receive maintenance, the parties intend to immediately divest the court of jurisdiction to order maintenance in the future. Consideration for this agreement is the parties' mutual waiver of past present and future maintenance.

14. SPOUSAL MAINTENANCE. Petitioner/Respondent shall pay to Petitioner/Respondent as spousal maintenance the sum of $_____ per month through Automatic Income Withholding [for ____ consecutive months/as temporary maintenance].

The court shall retain jurisdiction to modify the award of spousal maintenance.

The parties agree that the obligation incurred by Respondent by this agreement to pay Petitioner periodic payments of support shall not be dischargeable in any bankruptcy proceedings. Further, the parties agree that any judgment that may result from failure to pay said support shall likewise not be discharged in any bankruptcy proceeding.

Any arrearages claimed under an existing order shall not merge into the Judgment and Decree.

15. INSURANCE FOR SPOUSE. Any insurance conversion rights granted under the Judgment and Decree or state or federal law shall be construed so as to afford to the former spouse the greatest coverage available to a former spouse under state and federal law or rule.

[Petitioner/Respondent] shall be entitled to medical coverage through [Petitioner's/Respondent's] employer for any period of time for which he/she requests eligibility and is eligible under the state or federal law or insurer's rules, but he/she shall be responsible for paying any premium for said insurance relating to said coverage.

16. HOMESTEAD.

   a. Petitioner/Respondent shall have all the parties' right, title, interest, and equity in the real property located at _____, Minnesota, _____ County

Legal Description:

subject to all encumbrances presently against said homestead including mortgages and real estate taxes. He/She shall pay to Petitioner/Respondent the sum of $_____ within ____ months of entry of this judgment and decree dissolving the marriage. Petitioner/Respondent shall hold a lien against the property for the remaining balance of his/her marital interest of $_____. Said lien shall accrue interest at a rate of six percent per annum.

The parties' previous rights in said homestead are extinguished as of the date of the decree herein, and Petitioner/Respondent shall become owner in fee simple simultaneously with the attachment of Petitioner's/Respondent's equitable lien.

b. Petitioner/Respondent shall be solely liable for the normal maintenance and all monthly payments of principal, interest, taxes and insurance on said homestead, and he/she shall indemnify and hold Petitioner/Respondent harmless from any liability or obligation to make any payment whatsoever regarding said homestead.

c. Upon the happening of any events hereinafter enumerated in Paragraph d herein, said homestead shall be placed on the market for sale (at a price and upon terms to be mutually agreed upon by the parties), and the "net proceeds" from said sale shall be paid to Petitioner/Respondent after satisfying any liens or mortgage of the parties in full.

d. The conditions on which said sale shall occur shall be as follows:

(1) Petitioner's/Respondent's remarriage, at which time she will have the option of refinancing the home and satisfying the lien owed to Respondent;

(2) Petitioner's/Respondent's moving from the premises;

(3) Petitioner's death;

(4) Petitioner/Respondent becoming more than three (3) months in arrears in any twelve (12) month period on the monthly payment of principal, interest, taxes or insurance for said homestead.

e. The filing of either a certified copy of the Judgment and Decree or a certified copy of a Summary Real Estate Disposition Judgment or a Quit Claim Deed with the _____ County Recorder's Office shall operate as a conveyance of Respondent's entire interest in said property to Petitioner. If said real property is Torrens or registered property, then the Ramsey County Registrar of Titles is hereby directed, upon filing such Judgment and Decree, Summary Real Estate Disposition Judgment or Quit Claim Deed, to cancel any Certificate of Title showing both parties herein as registered owners and to issue a new Certificate of Title covering such real property in the sole name of Petitioner/Respondent subject to Petitioner's/Respondent's lien interest.

f. Immediately upon entry of the Judgment and Decree herein, Petitioner/Respondent shall execute a Quit Claim Deed conveying Petitioner's/Respondent's interest in the homestead to Petitioner/Respondent subject to his lien interest.

g. As between the parties, Petitioner/Respondent shall be entitled if she chooses to claim all income tax deductions relating to said property for the year 2001 and all years thereafter.

h. Said transfer to Petitioner/Respondent is a transfer of property incident to dissolution of marriage and is therefore not a realization event for income tax purposes

17. <u>ERROR IN LEGAL DESCRIPTION</u>. In the event there is any technical error or omission made in describing the legal title or description to any of the real property referenced herein, the parties are required to make, execute, and deliver to each other any and all documents necessary to correct any such error or omission.

18. <u>PERSONAL PROPERTY</u>. The parties have divided the personal property between them except:

18. <u>PERSONAL PROPERTY</u>. The parties shall have all right, title, interest, and equity in and to the personal property now in their individual possession.

19. <u>MOTOR VEHICLES</u>. Petitioner shall have all right, title, interest, and equity, free and clear of any claim on the part of Respondent to the _____ automobile of the parties. Respondent shall, upon entry of judgment, or sooner if he desires, execute all necessary documents to effect transfer of title.

Respondent shall have all right, title, interest, and equity, free and clear of any claim on the part of Petitioner to the _____ automobile of the parties. Petitioner shall, upon entry of judgment, or sooner if he/she desires, execute all necessary documents to effect transfer of title.

20. <u>BANK ACCOUNTS</u>. The parties have divided their bank accounts and cash assets in a manner agreeable to both parties.

21. <u>STOCK, BOND, AND INVESTMENT ACCOUNTS</u>. The parties have no stock account. They have equitably divided their bonds between themselves.

21. <u>STOCK, BOND, AND INVESTMENT ACCOUNTS</u>. The parties have divided their stock, bond, and investment accounts in a manner agreeable to both parties.

21. <u>STOCK, BOND, AND INVESTMENT ACCOUNTS</u>.

a. Petitioner shall have all of the parties' right title, interest, and equity in the following stock bond and investment accounts:

b. Respondent shall have all of the parties' right title, interest, and equity in the following stock bond and investment accounts:

22. <u>RETIREMENT PLANS</u>. Petitioner is awarded the entire right, title, interest, and equity, free and clear of any claim of Respondent in and to any retirement, pension, profit-sharing, 401(k), Keogh, and IRA accounts or plans in her own name

Respondent is awarded the entire right, title, interest, and equity, free and clear of any claim of Petitioner in and to any retirement, pension, profit-sharing, 401(k), Keogh and IRA accounts or plans in his own name.

22. <u>RETIREMENT PLANS</u>. The parties' retirement plans shall be divided pursuant to separate qualified domestic relations orders as follows:

23. <u>INCOME TAX EXEMPTIONS</u>. The parties shall each be entitled to one of the income tax exemptions for the children. At such time as there is only one exemption available to the parties, they shall alternate the exemption with Petitioner claiming the extra exemption in even-numbered years and Respondent in odd-numbered years.

23. <u>INCOME TAX EXEMPTIONS</u>. The income tax exemptions for the minor children shall be divided as follows:

24. <u>CURRENT INCOME TAXES</u>. Any refund or payment due to the state or federal government for the filing of the parties joint federal and state income tax returns shall be equally divided between the parties.

24. <u>CURRENT INCOME TAXES</u>. The parties shall file separately and each shall be responsible for his or her own payments or receive his or her own refund.

25. <u>WAIVER OF AUTOMATIC STAY</u>. The automatic stay provision of Rule 125 of the General Rules of Practice is hereby waived and the District Court Administrator is hereby ordered to immediately enter Judgment and Decree in this matter.

26. <u>CAPITAL GAINS TAXES</u>. Each of the parties shall be responsible for their own capital gains taxes.

27. DEBTS. The parties have satisfied all bills and obligations of the parties incurred during the marriage, not otherwise specified herein which constitute a joint obligation of the parties except the following:

   a. Petitioner shall assume and pay the above stated debts to _____, _____, _____, _____, and _____, and he/she shall indemnify and hold the Respondent harmless from any obligation to make payment of the same.

   b. Respondent shall assume and pay the above stated debts to _____, _____, _____, _____, and _____, and he/she shall indemnify and hold the Petitioner harmless from any obligation to make payment of the same.

   c. Both of the parties shall assume and pay the debts which each has incurred since their separation.

   d. Any undisclosed debts shall become sole responsibility of the party that incurred it.

28. FORMER NAME RESTORED. Petitioner/Respondent does not seek to change his/her name.

28. FORMER NAME RESTORED. Petitioner/Respondent shall have his/her former name, _____ restored. Petitioner/Respondent seeks this name change solely because of the marriage dissolution and not to defraud or mislead anyone. He/She has not gone through bankruptcy, nor has he/she been convicted of any felonies.

29. ATTORNEY FEES. The parties shall each pay their own attorney fees, if any.

30. APPENDIX A. The attached Appendix A is incorporated and made a part of any Judgment and Decree entered based upon this Marital Termination Agreement.

31. SERVICE. Service of a copy of the final Judgment and Decree entered herein may be made by U.S. Mail on each party named herein, in lieu of personal service.

32. EXECUTION OF DOCUMENTS REQUIRED. Within twenty (20) days of entry of the judgment and decree each party hereto shall execute any and all documents necessary to transfer real and personal property in the manner described herein without further order of the court. Should either party fail to comply with this provision, the filing with the agency of a certified copy of the judgment and decree shall have the same effect as if the party had executed the necessary documents.

33. RELEASE. Except as hereinbefore provided, each party hereto releases and waives any claim in and to the property of the other, provided the existence of that property was fully disclosed in this proceeding.

34. <u>DISCLOSURE</u>. Each party warrants to the other that there has been an accurate, complete, and current disclosure of all income, assets, debts, and liabilities. Both parties understand and agree that the deliberate failure to provide complete disclosure constitutes perjury. The property referred to in this agreement represents all the property which either party has any interest in full or in part by either party, separately or jointly.

This agreement is founded upon complete financial disclosure by each party.

35. <u>UNDERSTANDING</u>. The parties have read this agreement and understand its contents. This agreement was signed by the parties after they had given it serious thought and consideration. This agreement is fair, just, and equitable under the circumstances. This agreement was signed by the parties after it was definitely understood between them that there could be no reconciliation. This agreement was made in aid of an orderly and just termination of property settlement in this matter satisfactory to the parties, with the further mutual understanding and agreement between the parties that this agreement shall be made a part of any judgment and decree of dissolution to be entered in this matter if Petitioner is granted a decree of dissolution as prayed for in [his/her] petition.

IT IS FURTHER STIPULATED AND AGREED that the signing of this agreement shall not be construed as an appearance by Respondent and that Petitioner may proceed to place this matter upon the default calendar and try this matter as by default.

IT IS FURTHER STIPULATED AND AGREED that this agreement may be approved by the court without notice to the parties.

Dated: Dated:

_____   _____

Petitioner   Respondent

Subscribed and sworn before me,   Subscribed and sworn before me,

this ___ day of _____, 20___.   this ___ day of _____, 20___.

_____   _____

Notary Public   Notary Public

FORM 3. APPENDIX A

NOTICE IS HEREBY GIVEN TO THE PARTIES:

I. PAYMENTS TO PUBLIC AGENCY. PURSUANT TO MINNESOTA STATUTES, SECTION 518.551, SUBDIVISION 1, PAYMENTS ORDERED FOR MAINTENANCE AND SUPPORT MUST BE PAID TO THE PUBLIC AGENCY RESPONSIBLE FOR CHILD SUPPORT ENFORCEMENT AS LONG AS THE PERSON ENTITLED TO RECEIVE THE PAYMENTS IS RECEIVING OR HAS APPLIED FOR PUBLIC ASSISTANCE OR HAS APPLIED FOR SUPPORT AND MAINTENANCE COLLECTION SERVICES. MAIL PAYMENTS TO: _____

MN Child Support Payment Center, PO Box 64326, St. Paul, MN 55164-0326

II. DEPRIVING ANOTHER OF CUSTODIAL OR PARENTAL RIGHTS – A FELONY. A PERSON MAY BE CHARGED WITH A FELONY WHO CONCEALS A MINOR CHILD OR TAKES, OBTAINS, RETAINS, OR FAILS TO RETURN A MINOR CHILD FROM OR TO THE CHILD'S PARENT (OR PERSON WITH CUSTODIAL OR VISITATION RIGHTS), PURSUANT TO MINNESOTA STATUTES, SECTION 609.26. A COPY OF THAT SECTION IS AVAILABLE FROM ANY COURT ADMINISTRATOR.

III. RULES OF SUPPORT, MAINTENANCE AND VISITATION.

A. Payment of support or spousal maintenance is to be as ordered, and the giving of gifts or making purchases of food, clothing, and the like will not fulfill the obligation.

B. Payment of support must be made as it becomes due, and failure to secure or denial of rights of visitation is NOT an excuse for nonpayment, but the aggravated party must seek relief through a proper motion filed with the court.

C. Nonpayment of support is not grounds to deny visitation. The party entitled to receive support may apply for support and collection services, file a contempt motion, or obtain a judgment as provided in Minnesota Statutes, section 548.091.

D. The payment of support or spousal maintenance takes priority over payment of debts and other obligations.

E. A party who accepts additional obligations of support does so with the full knowledge of the party's prior obligation under this proceeding.

F. Child support or maintenance is based on annual income, and it is the responsibility of a person with seasonal employment to budget income so that payments are made throughout the year as ordered.

G.   If there is a layoff or pay reduction, support may be reduced as of the time of the lay-off or reduction if a motion to reduce the support is served and filed with the court at that time, but any such reduction must be ordered by the court. The court is not permitted to reduce support retroactively, except as provided in Minnesota Statutes, section 518.64, subdivision 2, part (c).

IV.   PARENTAL RIGHTS FROM MINNESOTA STATUTES, SECTION 518.17, SUBDIVISION 3. UNLESS OTHERWISE PROVIDED BY THE COURT:

A.   **Each party has the right to access to, and receive copies of, school, medical, dental, religious training, and other important records and information about the minor children. Each party has the right of access to information regarding health or dental insurance available to the minor children. Presentation of a copy of this order to the custodian of a record or other information about he minor children constitutes sufficient authorization for the release of a record or information to the requesting party.**

B.   Each party shall keep the other informed as to the name and address of the school of attendance of the minor children. Each party has the right to be informed by school officials about the children's welfare, educational progress and status, and to attend school and parent teacher conferences. The school is not required to hold a separate conference for each party.

C   In case of an accident or serious illness of a minor child, each party shall notify the other party of the accident or illness, and the name of the health care provider and the place of treatment.

D.   Each party has the right of reasonable access and telephone contact with the minor children.

V.   WAGE AND INCOME DEDUCTION OF SUPPORT AND MAINTENANCE. CHILD SUPPORT AND/OR SPOUSAL MAINTENANCE MAY BE WITHHELD FROM INCOME, WITH OR WITHOUT NOTICE TO THE PERSON OBLIGATED TO PAY, WHEN THE CONDITIONS OF MINNESOTA STATUTES, SECTIONS 518.611 AND 518.613, HAVE BEEN MET. A COPY OF THOSE SECTIONS IS AVAILABLE FROM ANY COURT ADMINISTRATOR.

VI.   CHANGE OF ADDRESS OR RESIDENCE. UNLESS OTHERWISE ORDERED, THE PERSON RESPONSIBLE TO MAKE SUPPORT OR MAINTE-NANCE PAYMENTS SHALL NOTIFY THE PERSON ENTITLED TO RECEIVE THE PAYMENT AND THE PUBLIC AUTHORITY RESPONSIBLE FOR COLLECTION.

IF APPLICABLE, OF A CHANGE OF ADDRESS OR RESIDENCE WITHIN 60 DAYS OF THE ADDRESS OR RESIDENCE CHANGE.

VII. **COST OF LIVING INCREASE OF SUPPORT AND MAINTENANCE.** CHILD SUPPORT AND/OR SPOUSAL MAINTENANCE MAY BE ADJUSTED EVERY TWO YEARS BASED UPON A CHANGE IN THE COST OF LIVING (USING THE U.S. DEPARTMENT OF LABOR, BUREAU OF LABOR STATISTICS, CONSUMER PRICE INDEX MPLS. ST. PAUL, FOR ALL URBAN CONSUMERS (CPI-U), UNLESS OTHERWISE SPECIFIED IN THIS ORDER) WHEN THE CONDITIONS OF MINNESOTA STATUTES, SECTION 518.641ARE MET. COST OF LIVING INCREASES ARE COMPOUNDED. A COPY OF MINNESOTA STATUTES, SECTION 518.641, AND FORMS NECESSARY TO REQUEST OR CONTEST A COST OF LIVING INCREASE ARE AVAILABLE FROM ANDY COURT ADMINISTRATOR.

VIII. **JUDGMENTS FOR UNPAID SUPPORT; INTEREST.** PURSUANT TO MINNESOTA STATUTES, SECTION 548.091:

A. If a person fails to make a child support payment, the payment owed becomes a judgment against the person responsible to make the payment by operation of law on or after the date the payment is due, and the person entitled to receive the payment or the public agency may obtain entry and docketing of the judgment without notice to the person responsible to make the payment.

B. Interest begins accruing on a payment or installment of child support whenever the unpaid amount due is greater than the current support due.

IX. **JUDGMENTS FOR UNPAID MAINTENANCE.** A JUDGMENT FOR UNPAID SPOUSAL MAINTENANCE MAY BE ENTERED WHEN THE CONDITIONS OF MINNESOTA STATUTES, SECTION 548.091, ARE MET. A COPY OF THAT SECTION IS AVAILABLE FROM ANY COURT ADMINISTRATOR.

X. **ATTORNEY FEES AND COLLECTION COSTS FOR ENFORCEMENT OF CHILD SUPPORT.** A JUDGMENT FOR ATTORNEY FEES AND OTHER COLLECTION COSTS INCURRED IN ENFORCING A CHILD SUPPORT ORDER WILL BE ENTERED AGAINST THE PERSON RESPONSIBLE TO PAY SUPPORT WHEN THE CONDITIONS OF MINNESOTA STATUTES. SECTION 518.14, SUBDIVISION 2, ARE MET. A COPY OF THAT SECTION AND FORMS NECESSARY TO REQUEST OR CONTEST THESE ATTORNEY FEES AND COLLECTION COSTS ARE AVAILABLE FROM ANY COURT ADMINISTRATOR.

XI. **CAPITAL GAIN ON SALE OF PRINCIPAL RESIDENCE.** INCOME TAX LAWS REGARDING THE CAPITAL GAIN TAX MAY APPLY TO THE SALE OF THE PARTIES' PRINCIPAL RESIDENCE AND THE PARTIES MAY WISH TO CONSULT WITH AN ATTORNEY OR TAX ADVISOR CONCERNING THE APPLICABLE LAWS. THESE LAWS MAY INCLUDE, BUT ARE NOT LIMITED TO, THE EXCLUSION AVAILABLE ON THE SALE OF A PRINCIPAL RESIDENCE FOR THOSE OVER A CERTAIN AGE UNDER SECTION 121 OF THE INTERNAL REVENUE CODE OF 1986, OR OTHER APPLICABLE LAW.

XII. **VISITATION EXPEDITER PROCESS.** ON REQUEST OF EITHER PARTY OR ON ITS OWN MOTION, THE COURT MAY APPOINT A VISITATION EXPEDITER TO RESOLVE VISITATION DISPUTES UNDER MINNESOTA STATUTES, SECTION 518.1751. A COPY OF THAT SECTION AND A DESCRIPTION OF THE EXPEDITER PROCESS IS AVAILABLE FROM ANY COURT ADMINISTRATOR.

XIII. **VISITATION REMEDIES AND PENALTIES.** REMEDIES AND PENALTIES FOR WRONGFUL DENIAL OF VISITATION RIGHTS ARE AVAILABLE UNDER MINNESOTA STATUTES, SECTION 518.175. SUBDIVISION 6. THESE INCLUDE COMPENSATORY VISITATION; CIVIL PENALTIES; BOND REQUIREMENTS; CONTEMPT; AND REVERSAL OF CUSTODY. A COPY OF THAT SUBDIVISION AND FORMS FOR REQUESTING RELIEF ARE AVAILABLE FORM ANY COURT ADMINISTRATOR.

WAIVER OF COUNSEL

I, _____, acknowledge that I have been told that I have a right to be represented by counsel of my choice and that I know that I am not represented in this matter. I am of sound mind. I have freely and voluntarily chosen to waive my right to be represented by counsel for the purpose of this agreement.

_____
Petitioner

Subscribed and sworn to before me

this ____ day of _____, 20___

_____
Notary Public

I, _____, acknowledge that I have been told that I have a right to be represented by counsel of my choice and that I know that I am not represented in this matter. I am of sound mind. I have freely and voluntarily chosen to waive my right to be represented by counsel for the purpose of this agreement.

_____
Respondent

Subscribed and sworn to before me

this ____ day of _____, 20___

_____
Notary Public

DISSOLUTION WITH CHILDREN - 4

STATE OF MINNESOTA

COUNTY OF _____

DISTRICT COURT

_____ JUDICIAL DISTRICT

FAMILY COURT DIVISION

_____

In Re the Marriage of:

_____,

Petitioner,

and

_____,

Respondent.

_____

PARENTING PLAN

Court File No. _____

Judicial Officer: _____

This parenting plan applies to the following children:

<u>Name</u>   <u>Birthdate</u>

RESIDENTIAL SCHEDULE

Unless the parents agree otherwise, the following provisions set forth where the child(ren) shall reside each day of the year and what contact the child(ren) shall have with each parent:

PRESCHOOL SCHEDULE

____   There are no children of preschool age

____   Prior to enrollment in school, the children shall reside or be with

    ____   father the following days and times

from _____ to _____

    ____   every week   ____   every other week

and

    ____   from _____ to _____

    ____   every week   ____   every other week

___ mother the following days and times

from _____ to _____

___ every week   ___ every other week

and

___ from _____ to _____

___ every week   ___ every other week

___ other (specify) _____

SCHOOL SCHEDULE

Unless the parents agree otherwise, upon enrollment in school, the child(ren) shall reside or be with the

___ father the following days and times

from _____ to _____

___ every week   ___ every other week

and

___ from _____ to _____

___ every week   ___ every other week

___ mother the following days and times

from _____ to _____

___ every week   ___ every other week

and

___ from _____ to _____

___ every week   ___ every other week

___ other (specify) _____

The school schedule will start when each child begins

___ kindergarten   ___ first grade   ___ other (specify)

_____

SCHOOL BREAKS

Unless the parents agree otherwise, the child(ren) shall reside with the parents during winter breaks as follows:

    ___   With father every year

    ___   With mother every year

    ___   With father alternate   ___ odd   ___ even years

    ___   With mother alternate   ___ odd   ___ even years

    ___   With father the first half   ___ odd   ___ even years

    ___   With mother the second half ___ odd   ___ even years

    ___   Other (specify) _____.

The children shall reside with the parents as follows during the spring break as follows:

    ___   With father every year

    ___   With mother every year

    ___   With father alternate   ___ odd   ___ even years

    ___   With mother alternate   ___ odd   ___ even years

    ___   With father the first half   ___ odd   ___ even years

    ___   With mother the second half ___ odd   ___ even years

    ___   Other (specify) _____.

SUMMER SCHEDULE

Unless the parents agree otherwise, upon completion of the school year, the child(ren) shall reside with the

    ___   father the following days and times

    ___   from _____ to _____

    ___   every week   ___   every other week

                    and

    ___   from ___day/time_____ to _____day/time_____

___ every week   ___ every other week

___ mother the following days and times

___ from _____ to _____

___ every week   ___ every other week

and

___ from ___day/time_____ to ____day/time_____

___ every week   ___ every other week

___ same as school year schedule

___ other (specify)_____

VACATION WITH EACH PARENT

___ Does not apply

___ Unless the parents agree otherwise, the schedule for vacation with parents is as follows:

___ One week per year

___ Two weeks per year

    ___ Consecutive

    ___ Non-consecutive

___ Summer only

___ Other (specify) _____

SCHEDULE FOR HOLIDAYS

(Parents may include any religious or cultural holidays they wish to observe.) Unless the parents agree otherwise, the residential schedule for the child(ren) for the holidays listed below is as follows:

	With Mother	With Father
	(Specify Year Odd/Even/Every)	(Specify Year Odd/Even/Every)
New Years Day		
Easter		
Memorial Day Weekend		
July 4th		

Labor Day Weekend

Thanksgiving Day

Christmas Eve (overnight
until 10:00 a.m.)

Christmas Day

For purposes of this plan, a holiday shall begin and end as follows (set forth times):

_____

_____

_____

___   Holidays which fall on a Friday or Monday shall include Saturday and Sunday

___   Other (specify) _____

SCHEDULE FOR SPECIAL OCCASIONS

Unless the parents agree otherwise, the residential schedule for the child(ren) for the following special occasions is as follows:

	With Mother (Specify Year Odd/Even/Every)	With Father (Specify Year Odd/Even/Every)
Mother's Day	Every	
Father's Day		Every
Child's Birthday		
Child's Birthday		
Father's Birthday		Every
Mother's Birthday	Every	

PRIORITIES UNDER THE RESIDENTIAL SCHEDULE

___   Does not apply

___   Holidays have priority over vacations

___   Special occasions have priority over vacations

___   Vacations have priority over regular residential time

___   Other (specify) _____

TRANSPORTATION ARRANGEMENTS

Unless the parents agree otherwise, transportation arrangements for the children between the parents shall be as follows:

    ___   Father shall pick up as follows: _____

    ___   Father shall drop off as follows _____

    ___   Mother shall pick up as follows _____

    ___   Mother shall drop off as follows: _____

    ___   Parents will meet at the following location _____

    ___   Other (specify): _____

The parents will share equally in the transportation necessary to effectuate the Parenting Plan.

TELEPHONE CONTACTS

    ___   Reasonable   ___   Mother   ___   Father

    ___   Specific   ___   Mother   ___   Father

Days and times _____

RESTRICTIONS

___   Does not apply

___   The ___ Father's ___ Mother's residential time with the child(ren) shall be limited due to the following factor(s): _____

_____

The following restrictions shall apply when the child(ren) spend time with this parent: _____

_____

_____

___   Contact shall be supervised by:

    ___   A mutually agreed upon third party

    ___   Specify: _____

DECISION MAKING

Major decisions regarding the child(ren) shall be made as follows:

Health care   ___   father   ___ mother   ___   joint

Education   ___   father   ___ mother   ___   joint

Religious Upbringing   ___   father   ___ mother   ___   joint

Extracurricular Act   ___   father   ___ mother   ___   joint

     ___   father shall be solely responsible for making decisions in the following specific areas: _____

     ___   mother shall be solely responsible for making decisions in the following specific areas: _____

     ___   father and mother shall share responsibility for making decisions in the following specific areas: _____

ADDITIONAL ARRANGEMENTS

Should any decisions involve additional expenses not covered by child support, we agree to:

     ___   share them equally

     ___   share them in the following way (specify): _____

     ___   have father be solely responsible for the following additional expenses: _____

                    _____

     ___   have mother be solely responsible for the following additional expenses: _____

                    _____

OTHER

RIGHT OF FIRST REFUSAL

If a parent named in this parenting plan is unable to care for the children for a period of five (5) hours, the other parent shall have the option of the residential placement of the children. If the non-residential parent is unavailable, the residential parent will make appropriate child care arrangements. The parents agree not to advise the children of any changes or negotiations until the matter is settled. Each parent shall give the other parent at least 24 hours notice if he/she is unable to comply with the regular schedule.

SICK CHILD

When a child is ill

____ the residential schedule shall remain in effect

____ the residential schedule shall not remain in effect

____ the child will remain with the residential parent with make-up time for the nonresidential parent

____ other (specify) _____

DISPUTE RESOLUTION

Disputes between the parents, other than child support disputes, shall be submitted to:

____ Counseling by _____

____ Mediation by _____

____ Arbitration by:_____

There shall be mediation followed by arbitration. It is intended that this persons role is consistent with the role of a "Visitation Expediter".

The cost of this process shall be allocated between the parties as determined in the dispute resolution process.

The dispute resolution process shall be commenced by notifying the other parent by:

____ written request

____ certified mail

____ other (specify) _____

____ No dispute resolution process, except court action, shall be ordered because the following limiting factor applies (specify): _____

_____

In the dispute resolution process:

1. Preference shall be given to carrying out this Parenting Plan.

2. Unless an emergency exists, the parents shall use the designated process to resolve disputes relating to implementation of the plan.

3. A written record of any agreement reached in counseling or mediation and of each arbitration award shall be provided to each party.

SICK CHILD

When a child is ill

____ the residential schedule shall remain in effect

____ the residential schedule shall not remain in effect

____ the child will remain with the residential parent with make-up time for the nonresidential parent

____ other (specify) _____

DISPUTE RESOLUTION

Disputes between the parents, other than child support disputes, shall be submitted to:

____ Counseling by _____

____ Mediation by _____

____ Arbitration by: _____

There shall be mediation followed by arbitration. It is intended that this persons role is consistent with the role of a "Visitation Expediter".

The cost of this process shall be allocated between the parties as determined in the dispute resolution process.

The dispute resolution process shall be commenced by notifying the other parent by:

____ written request

____ certified mail

____ other (specify) _____

____ No dispute resolution process, except court action, shall be ordered because the following limiting factor applies (specify): _____

_____

In the dispute resolution process:

1. Preference shall be given to carrying out this Parenting Plan.

2. Unless an emergency exists, the parents shall use the designated process to resolve disputes relating to implementation of the plan.

3. A written record of any agreement reached in counseling or mediation and of each arbitration award shall be provided to each party.

DECISION MAKING

Major decisions regarding the child(ren) shall be made as follows:

Health care ___ father ___ mother ___ joint

Education ___ father ___ mother ___ joint

Religious Upbringing ___ father ___ mother ___ joint

Extracurricular Act ___ father ___ mother ___ joint

___ father shall be solely responsible for making decisions in the following specific areas: _____

___ mother shall be solely responsible for making decisions in the following specific areas: _____

___ father and mother shall share responsibility for making decisions in the following specific areas: _____

ADDITIONAL ARRANGEMENTS

Should any decisions involve additional expenses not covered by child support, we agree to:

___ share them equally

___ share them in the following way (specify): _____

___ have father be solely responsible for the following additional expenses: _____

_____

___ have mother be solely responsible for the following additional expenses: _____

_____

OTHER

RIGHT OF FIRST REFUSAL

If a parent named in this parenting plan is unable to care for the children for a period of five (5) hours, the other parent shall have the option of the residential placement of the children. If the non-residential parent is unavailable, the residential parent will make appropriate child care arrangements. The parents agree not to advise the children of any changes or negotiations until the matter is settled. Each parent shall give the other parent at least 24 hours notice if he/she is unable to comply with the regular schedule.

4. If the court finds a parent has use or frustrated the dispute resolution process in bad faith, the court may alter the parenting plan and/or award attorney's fees and financial sanctions to the other parent.

OTHER PROVISIONS

___   There are no other provisions

___   The following other provisions apply:

Neither parent shall take the children out of the State of Minnesota without notice to the other parent. The other parent will not be able to prohibit travel.

Neither party will take the children out of school without the agreement of the other party except for scheduled appointments.

DESIGNATION OF CUSTODIAN

Solely for the purpose of state and federal statutes which require a designation or determination of custody the ___ father ___ mother ___ both are designated the custodian of the children.

_____   _____
Petitioner   Respondent

Subscribed and sworn to before me,   Subscribed and sworn to before me,
this ___ day of _____, 20___.   this ___ day of _____, 20___.

_____   _____
Notary Public   Notary Public

The foregoing constitutes the Parenting Plan Order of the Court:

RECOMMENDED FOR APPROVAL   APPROVED FOR ENTRY:

Dated: _____   Dated: _____

_____   _____
Referee   Judge of District Court

DISSOLUTION WITH CHILDREN - 4

DISSOLUTION WITHOUT CHILDREN - 5

STATE OF MINNESOTA

COUNTY OF _____

DISTRICT COURT

_____ JUDICIAL DISTRICT

FAMILY COURT DIVISION

_____

In Re the Marriage of:

_____,

Petitioner,

and

_____,

Respondent.

_____

FINDINGS OF FACT, CONCLUSIONS OF LAW, ORDER FOR JUDGMENT, AND JUDGMENT AND DECREE

Court File No. _____

Judicial Officer: _____

The above-entitled matter came on for default hearing before the Honorable _____, Judge/Referee of _____ County District Court, Family Division on _____. Petitioner/Respondent/Neither party appeared personally.

Based upon the complete file and the written Marital Termination Agreement of the parties, the Court makes the following Findings of Fact, Conclusions of Law, and Order for Judgment:

FINDINGS OF FACT

I.

The name, address, date of birth, age, and Social Security Number of Petitioner are as follows:

Name: _____

Address: _____

_____

County: _____

Born: _____

Age: _____

Social Security Number: <u>Confidential Information Form</u>

The Petitioner has formerly been known by the following name(s):

_____

II.

The name, address, date of birth, age, and Social Security Number of Respondent are as follows:

Name: _____

Address: _____

_____

County: _____

Born: _____

Age: _____

Social Security Number: <u>Confidential Information Form</u>

The Respondent has formerly been known by the following name(s):

_____

III.

The parties were married to each other on (date) _____ in the City of _____, County of _____, State of _____, and ever since have been and are now husband and wife.

IV.

The parties have the following minor children, including date of birth, age, and social security number

Name: _____

Born: _____

Age: _____

Social Security Number: <u>Confidential Information Form</u>

Name: _____

Born: _____

Age: _____

Social Security Number: <u>Confidential Information Form</u>

The minor children of the parties are now in the care of [Petitioner/Respondent/both parties]. The minor children of the parties are not subject to the jurisdiction of any juvenile court.

_____ It is in the best interests of the children that custody should be awarded to (Petitioner/Respondent/both parties)

_____ It is in the best interests of the children that the parties enter into a parenting plan regarding the care of the minor children.

V.

It is in the best interests of the children that neither party pay support to the other as their incomes are comparable and they will have the children approximately equal amounts of time. Each of the parties has sufficient income to allow each to provide for the children while they are in his or her care.

V.

(Petitioner/Respondent) should pay child support for the care of the minor child of the parties.

VI.

(Petitioner/Respondent/Neither party) should pay temporary or permanent spousal maintenance for the support of the other party.

VII.

Petitioner/Respondent provides medical insurance for the benefit of Petitioner.

Petitioner/Respondent provides medical insurance for the benefit of Respondent

Petitioner/Respondent provides medical insurance for the benefit of the minor children.

VIII.

The parties own various items of personal property which they have divided between themselves.

IX.

Petitioner/Respondent has resided within the State of Minnesota for more than 180 days immediately preceding commencement of this proceeding. Petitioner presently resides in _____ County.

CONCLUSIONS OF LAW

1. <u>MARITAL STATUS</u>. The bonds of matrimony heretofore existing between the parties are hereby dissolved.

2. <u>MILITARY SERVICE</u>. Neither party is entitled to the protections of the Soldier's and Sailor's Civil Relief Act of 1940 as amended.

3. <u>RELEASE</u>. Except as is expressly provided herein to the contrary, by agreement, each party is released from any and all further liability whatsoever to the other.

4. <u>MARITAL TERMINATION AGREEMENT INCORPORATED</u>. The terms of the Marital Termination Agreement are hereby incorporated into the Judgment and Decree, whether or not each and every portion of this agreement is literally set forth in said decree.

5. <u>UNIFORM CHILD CUSTODY JURISDICTION</u>. Minnesota is the proper jurisdiction within the contemplation of the Uniform Child Custody Jurisdiction and Enforcement Act, Minnesota Statutes Section 518D, to enter an order regarding the custody, care, and control of the minor child[ren].

6. <u>CUSTODY</u>. [Petitioner/Respondent/Both parties] shall have physical custody, care, and control of the minor child of the parties. [Petitioner/Respondent/Both parties] legal custody of the minor child of the parties. Petitioner/Respondent shall have parenting time as set forth in the attached Appendix B.

6. <u>PARENTING PLAN</u>. The parenting plan attached as Appendix B shall be incorporated into any Judgment and Decree and shall control all issues related to access to the children.

7. <u>PARENT ACCESS</u>. The Parenting Plan attached as Appendix B shall be incorporated into any Judgment and Decree and shall control all issues related to access to the children.

8. <u>UNDERSTANDING AS TO DECISIONS AFFECTING THE CHILDREN</u>. The actual residence of the children may be changed at any time as the parties mutually agree or as allowed by order of the Court.

    All decisions pertaining to the education, discipline, health, extracurricular or summer activities, religious training, medical and dental care will be decided by both parties after reasonable and adequate discussion. The parent with actual physical custody shall make day-to-day decisions affecting the children, including any medical or dental emergencies. If the parties are unable to reach agreement on any decisions affecting the children, they shall use the services of a mediator (as discussed below) to resolve their differences.

Each parent has the right to know of any circumstances or decisions that affect the children and each of us has the right to any medical, dental, or school records of the children. Neither of party may knowingly do anything to hamper or interfere with the natural and continuing relationship between the children and the other parent, nor allow others to interfere.

The well-being of the children is of paramount importance, and, therefore, the children shall have as much contact as possible with each parent.

9.   MEDIATION. Any claim or controversy involving visitation or any other issue involving the children (other than child support) which cannot be resolved by the parties through direct communication without mediation, shall be promptly submitted to mediation.

   a.   Definition of Mediation. Mediation is a voluntary process entered into by the parties. In this process, the parties continue direct communication with each other, but with the assistance of a neutral person who is the mediator. The mediator has no authority to require any concession or agreement. A good faith effort shall be made between the parties to resolve any claim or controversy.

   b.   Selection of Mediator. The mediator shall be named by mutual agreement of the parties or by obtaining a list of five qualified persons from the Court and by alternately striking names.

   c.   Duties and Responsibilities of Mediator. The mediator shall have the duty to assist the parties in resolving visitation issues.

   d.   Duty to Cooperate and Complete. Both parties agree to cooperate and act in good faith to resolve the disputes with the assistance of the mediator.

   e.   Payment of Costs. The parties shall share the costs of mediation equally unless they mutually agree otherwise.

   f.   Exhaustion of Remedies. The above procedure shall be followed before either party may apply to the Court for relief.

10.   CHILD SUPPORT. Neither party shall pay child support to the other. The parties shall have joint legal and physical custody of the child with each sharing equally in the time of custody and support of the minor child. In light of the relative incomes of the parties, such an arrangement is in the best interests of the children.

10. <u>CHILD SUPPORT</u>. [Petitioner/Respondent] shall pay as child support for the benefit of the minor children of the parties the sum of $_____ per month in equal installments consistent with his/her pay periods through Automatic Income Withholding (AIW). Said obligation shall continue until one of the parties' minor children either attains the age of eighteen (18) is married, emancipated, self-supporting, deceased, or in the Armed Forces of the United States of America, whichever shall occur first, unless at such time the child is still attending high school, in which case, child support shall continue until the earlier of the child's graduation from high school or the child's 20th birthday if the child is still in high school. At such time, the child support obligation shall be reduced pursuant to the Minnesota Child Support Guidelines.

Until Automatic Income Withholding of the aforesaid child support obligation commences, [Petitioner/Respondent] shall make all child support payments required of him herein directly to [Petitioner/Respondent] at such times and in such amounts as set forth above.

Any child support arrearages shall not merge into the Judgment and Decree.

11. <u>INSURANCE FOR CHILD SUPPORT</u>. In order to insure that funds are available for the support of minor children of the parties, for so long as there exists an obligation of support the parties shall maintain life insurance in the amount of $50,000 and each shall name the other party as beneficiary thereof.

11. <u>INSURANCE FOR CHILD SUPPORT</u>. In order to insure that funds are available for the support of minor children of the parties, for so long as there exists an obligation of support, the parties shall maintain in full force and effect, and not borrow against the value of same, life insurance on his and her own life for the benefit of the minor children in the amount of $_____.

12. <u>MEDICAL COVERAGE FOR CHILD</u>. As additional child support, during the time that the child(ren) of the parties is a minor, Petitioner/Respondent maintain in full force and effect and pay the premium cost for all medical insurance available to him/her through his/her employer he/she shall be responsible for notifying his/her employer. Petitioner/Respondent shall be responsible for dental coverage.

12. <u>MEDICAL COVERAGE FOR CHILD</u>. Petitioner/Respondent shall keep in full force and effect medical, dental, and hospitalization insurance for the benefit of the minor child(ren) of the parties either through his employment, union, or private policy until such time as the obligation to pay child support shall cease.

13. UNINSURED MEDICAL AND DENTAL FOR CHILD. To the extent not covered by insurance, all deductibles, all medical and dental expenses, including but not limited to necessary orthodontia, eye care (including prescription lenses), psychological care and psychiatric care, shall be shared equally by the parties.

13. UNINSURED MEDICAL AND DENTAL FOR CHILD. Petitioner shall pay _____% and Respondent shall pay ____% of any medical and dental expenses of the children that are not covered by insurance.

14. SPOUSAL MAINTENANCE. Neither party shall pay temporary or permanent maintenance to the other. The parties have waived the right to have the other pay temporary or permanent maintenance.

By presently waiving their right to receive maintenance, the parties intend to immediately divest the court of jurisdiction to order maintenance in the future. Consideration for this agreement is the parties' mutual waiver of past present and future maintenance. Said consideration is adequate.

14. SPOUSAL MAINTENANCE. Petitioner/Respondent shall pay to Petitioner/Respondent as spousal maintenance the sum of $_____ per month through Automatic Income Withholding [for ____ consecutive months/as permanent maintenance].

The court shall retain jurisdiction to modify the award of spousal maintenance.

The parties agree that the obligation incurred by Respondent by this agreement to pay Petitioner periodic payments of support shall not be dischargeable in any bankruptcy proceedings. Further, the parties agree that any judgment that may result from failure to pay said support shall likewise not be discharged in any bankruptcy proceeding.

Any arrearages claimed under an existing order shall not merge into the Judgment and Decree.

15. INSURANCE FOR SPOUSE. Any insurance conversion rights granted under the Judgment and Decree or state or federal law shall be construed so as to afford to the former spouse the greatest coverage available to a former spouse under state and federal law or rule.

[Petitioner/Respondent] shall be entitled to medical coverage through [Petitioner's/Respondent's] employer for any period of time for which she requests eligibility and is eligible under the state or federal law or insurer's rules, but he/she shall be responsible for paying any premium for said insurance relating to her coverage.

16. <u>HOMESTEAD.</u>

    a.   Petitioner/Respondent shall have all the parties' right, title, interest, and equity in the real property located at _____, Minnesota, _____ County

Legal Description:

subject to all encumbrances presently against said homestead including mortgages and real estate taxes and subject to a lien interest in favor of Petitioner/Respondent in the amount of $_____ payable within _____ months of entry of the decree of dissolution. Further Petitioner/Respondent shall satisfy or refinance so as to remove Petitioner/Respondent from any obligation on the property.

b. Petitioner/Respondent shall be solely liable for the normal maintenance and all monthly payments of principal, interest, taxes and insurance on said homestead, and he/she shall indemnify and hold Petitioner/Respondent harmless from any liability or obligation to make any payment whatsoever regarding said homestead.

c. Upon the happening of any events hereinafter enumerated in Paragraph d herein, said homestead shall be placed on the market for sale (at a price and upon terms to be mutually agreed upon by the parties), and the "net proceeds" from said sale shall be paid to Petitioner/Respondent after satisfying any liens or mortgage of the parties in full. In the event Petitioner/Respondent remarries she shall have the option of refinancing (rather than selling) the homestead mortgage thereby removing Petitioner/Respondent from any and all liability on the homestead.

d. The conditions on which said sale shall occur and said lien mortgage shall mature shall be as follows:

(1) Petitioner/Respondent's remarriage, at which time she will have the option of refinancing the homestead mortgage as discussed in (c) above;

(2) Petitioner/Respondent's moving from the premises;

(3) Petitioner/Respondent's death;

(4) Petitioner/Respondent becoming more than three (3) months in arrears in any twelve (12) month period on the monthly payment of principal, interest, taxes or insurance for said homestead.

(5) Petitioner/Respondent failing to satisfy the lien interest in favor of the former spouse as set forth above.

e. The filing of either a certified copy of the Judgment and Decree or a certified copy of a Summary Real Estate Disposition Judgment or a Quit Claim Deed with the _____ County Recorder's Office shall operate as a conveyance of Petitioner's/Respondent's entire interest in said property to Petitioner. If said real property is Torrens or registered property, then the _____ County Registrar of Titles is hereby directed, upon filing such Judgment and Decree, Summary Real Estate Disposition Judgment or Quit Claim Deed, to cancel any Certificate of Title showing both parties herein as registered owners and to issue a new Certificate of Title covering such real property in the sole name of Petitioner/Respondent.

f. Immediately upon entry of the Judgment and Decree herein, Petitioner/Respondent shall execute a Quit Claim Deed conveying his interest in the homestead to Petitioner/Respondent.

17. <u>ERROR IN LEGAL DESCRIPTION</u>. In the event there is any technical error or omission made in describing the legal title or description to any of the real property referenced herein, the parties are required to make, execute, and deliver to each other any and all documents necessary to correct any such error or omission.

18. <u>PERSONAL PROPERTY</u>. The parties shall have all right, title, interest, and equity in and to the personal property now in their individual possession.

19. <u>MOTOR VEHICLES</u>. Petitioner shall have all right, title, interest, and equity, free and clear of any claim on the part of Respondent to the _____ automobile of the parties. Respondent shall, upon entry of judgment, or sooner if he desires, execute all necessary documents to effect transfer of title.

Respondent shall have all right, title, interest, and equity, free and clear of any claim on the part of Petitioner to the _____ automobile of the parties. Petitioner shall, upon entry of judgment, or sooner if he/she desires, execute all necessary documents to effect transfer of title.

20. <u>BANK ACCOUNTS</u>. The parties have divided their bank accounts and cash assets in a manner agreeable to both parties.

21. <u>STOCK, BOND, AND INVESTMENT ACCOUNTS</u>. The parties have divided their stock bond and investment account in a manner agreeable to both parties.

21. <u>STOCK, BOND, AND INVESTMENT ACCOUNTS</u>.

a. Petitioner shall have all of the parties' right title, interest, and equity in the following stock, bond, and investment accounts:

b. Respondent shall have all of the parties' right title, interest, and equity in the following stock bond and investment accounts:

22. <u>RETIREMENT PLANS</u>. Petitioner is awarded the entire right, title, interest, and equity, free and clear of any claim of Respondent in and to any retirement, pension, profit-sharing, 401(k), Keogh and IRA accounts or plans in her own name.

Respondent is awarded the entire right, title, interest, and equity, free and clear of any claim of Petitioner in and to any retirement, pension, profit-sharing, 401(k), Keogh and IRA accounts or plans in his own name.

22. <u>RETIREMENT PLANS</u>. The parties' retirement plans shall be divided pursuant to a separate qualified domestic relations order as follows:

23. <u>INCOME TAX EXEMPTION</u>. The income tax exemptions for the minor children shall be divided as follows:

24. <u>CURRENT INCOME TAXES</u>. Any refund or payment due to the state or federal government for the filing of the parties joint federal and state income tax returns shall be equally divided between the parties.

24. <u>CURRENT INCOME TAXES</u>. The parties shall file separately and each shall be responsible for his or her own payments or receive his or her own refund.

25. <u>WAIVER OF AUTOMATIC STAY</u>. The automatic stay provision of Rule 125 of the General Rules of Practice is hereby waived and the District Court Administrator is hereby ordered to immediately enter Judgment and Decree in this matter.

26. <u>CAPITAL GAINS TAXES</u>. Each of the parties shall be responsible for their own capital gains taxes.

27. <u>DEBTS</u>. The parties have satisfied all bills and obligations of the parties incurred during the marriage, not otherwise specified herein which constitute a joint obligation of the parties except the following:

   a. Petitioner shall assume and pay the above stated debts to _____, _____, _____, _____, and _____, and he/she shall indemnify and hold the Petitioner harmless from any obligation to make payment of the same.

   b. Respondent shall assume and pay the above stated debts to _____, _____, _____, _____, and _____, and he/she shall indemnify and hold the Respondent harmless from any obligation to make payment of the same.

   c. Both of the parties shall assume and pay the debts which each has incurred since their separation.

   d. Any undisclosed debts shall become sole responsibility of the party that incurred it.

28. <u>FORMER NAME RESTORED</u>. Petitioner does not seek to change her name.

28. <u>FORMER NAME RESTORED</u>. Petitioner/Respondent shall have his/her former name, _____ restored. Petitioner/Respondent seeks this name change solely because of the marriage dissolution and not to defraud or mislead anyone. He/She has not gone through bankruptcy, nor has she been convicted of any felonies.

29. <u>ATTORNEY FEES</u>. The parties shall each pay their own attorney fees, if any.

30. <u>APPENDIX A</u>. The attached Appendix A is incorporated and made a part of any Judgment and Decree entered based upon this Marital Termination Agreement.

31. <u>SERVICE</u>. Service of a copy of the final Judgment and Decree entered herein may be made by U.S. Mail on each party named herein, in lieu of personal service.

32. <u>EXECUTION OF DOCUMENTS REQUIRED</u>. Within twenty (20) days each party hereto shall execute any and all documents necessary to transfer real and personal property in the manner described herein without further order of the court. Should either party fail to comply with this provision, the filing with the agency of a certified copy of the judgment and decree shall have the same effect as if the party had executed the necessary documents.

LET JUDGMENT BE ENTERED ACCORDINGLY

RECOMMENDED FOR APPROVAL   APPROVED FOR ENTRY:

Dated:_____   Dated:_____

_____   _____

Referee   Judge of District Court

I hereby certify that the foregoing Conclusions of Law constitute the Judgment and Decree of the Court. Judgment and Decree entered this _____ day of _____, 20___.

By:_____

Court Administrator

DISSOLUTION WITH CHILDREN - 4

DISSOLUTION WITHOUT CHILDREN - 5

STATE OF MINNESOTA

COUNTY OF _____

_____

In Re the Marriage of:

_____,

Petitioner,

and

_____,

Respondent.

_____

DISTRICT COURT

_____ JUDICIAL DISTRICT

FAMILY COURT DIVISION

AFFIDAVIT OF PERSONAL SERVICE

Court File No. _____

Judicial Officer: _____

STATE OF MINNESOTA)

)SS.

COUNTY OF _____)

_____, after being duly sworn, upon oath says: that on _____ 20___, [s]he served the attached _____ _____ upon _____ by handing to and leaving with (him) (her) a true and correct copy thereof.

_____

Affiant

Subscribed and sworn to before me,

this ____ day of _____, 20___.

_____

Notary Public

DISSOLUTION WITH CHILDREN - 4

DISSOLUTION WITHOUT CHILDREN - 5

STATE OF MINNESOTA

COUNTY OF _____

_____

In Re the Marriage of:

_____,

Petitioner,

and

_____,

Respondent.

_____

DISTRICT COURT

_____ JUDICIAL DISTRICT

FAMILY COURT DIVISION

AFFIDAVIT OF SERVICE BY MAIL

Court File No. _____

Judicial Officer: _____

STATE OF MINNESOTA)

)SS.

COUNTY OF _____)

_____, after being duly sworn, upon oath says: that on _____ 20___, [s]he served the attached _____ _____ on the following named person by mailing to (him) (her) (each of them) a copy thereof, enclosed in an envelope, postage prepaid, and by depositing the same in the United States Mail, directed to said person as follows:

_____

Affiant

Subscribed and sworn to before me,

this ____ day of _____, 20___.

_____

Notary Public

DISSOLUTION WITH CHILDREN - 4

DISSOLUTION WITHOUT CHILDREN - 5

STATE OF MINNESOTA

COUNTY OF _____

DISTRICT COURT

_____ JUDICIAL DISTRICT

FAMILY COURT DIVISION

_____

In Re the Marriage of:

_____,

Petitioner,

and

_____,

Respondent.

DEFAULT SCHEDULING REQUEST

Court File No. _____

Judicial Officer: _____

_____

The above-entitled matter is submitted for default scheduling as follows:

(Check all appropriate lines)

____ Approval without hearing pursuant to Minn. Stat. 518.13, subd. 5.

    ____ The marriage includes minor children, each party is represented by a lawyer, and each party has signed a stipulation.

    ____ The marriage does not include minor children and each party has signed a stipulation.

    ____ The marriage does not include minor children, at least 50 days have elapsed since service of the Summons and Petition, and the Respondent has not appeared in the action.

____ Default hearing required or requested

    ____ Marriage includes minor children

Submitted by:

_____

Name of Party

Dated:_____

By: _____

Name: _____

Petitioner/Respondent *Pro Se*

Address: _____

_____

Telephone No. _____

Attorney Reg.: *Pro Se*

```
          Barnes & Noble Bookseller
              15 First Street SW
              Rochester MN 55902
                 (50  ) 288-3848
          05-25-04 SO2555 R005


CUSTOMER RECEIPT COPY


BARNES & NOBLE MEMBER   EXP: 10-31 04


Child Custody Made Simpl      .75
09       34
DISCOUNT      21.95 - 2.20
Your Right to Child Cust    22.45
1572   806
DISCOUNT      24.95 - 2.50
How to File for Balance      .75
1572481420
DISCOUNT         - 2.20


SUBTOTAL                    6 .95
SALES TAX                   4.34
TOTAL                      66.29
AMOUNT TENDERED
VISA                       66.29
CARD #:          ********    9 17
AMOUNT          66.29
AUTH CODE       009612



MEMBER SAVINGS              6.90


TOTAL PAYMENT              66.29
        Thank you for Shopping at
        Barnes & Noble Booksellers
#216921 05-25-04 01:31P Becky
```

bn.com with a bn.com receipt for store credit at the bn.com price.

Full refund issued for new and unread books and unopened music within 30
days with a receipt from any Barnes & Noble store.
Store Credit issued for new and unread books and unopened music after 30
days or without a sales receipt. Credit issued at <u>lowest sale price</u>.
We gladly accept returns of new and unread books and unopened music from
bn.com with a bn.com receipt for store credit at the bn.com price.

Full refund issued for new and unread books and unopened music within 30
days with a receipt from any Barnes & Noble store.
Store Credit issued for new and unread books and unopened music after 30
days or without a sales receipt. Credit issued at <u>lowest sale price</u>.
We gladly accept returns of new and unread books and unopened music from
bn.com with a bn.com receipt for store credit at the bn.com price.

Full refund issued for new and unread books and unopened music within 30
days with a receipt from any Barnes & Noble store.
Store Credit issued for new and unread books and unopened music after 30
days or without a sales receipt. Credit issued at <u>lowest sale price</u>.
We gladly accept returns of new and unread books and unopened music from
bn.com with a bn.com receipt for store credit at the bn.com price.

Full refund issued for new and unread books and unopened music within 30
days with a receipt from any Barnes & Noble store.
Store Credit issued for new and unread books and unopened music after 30
days or without a sales receipt. Credit issued at <u>lowest sale price</u>.
We gladly accept returns of new and unread books and unopened music from
bn.com with a bn.com receipt for store credit at the bn.com price.

Full refund issued for new and unread books and unopened music within 30
days with a receipt from any Barnes & Noble store.
Store Credit issued for new and unread books and unopened music after 30.

DISSOLUTION WITH CHILDREN - 4

DISSOLUTION WITHOUT CHILDREN - 5

STATE OF MINNESOTA

COUNTY OF _____

_____

In Re the Marriage of:

_____,

        Petitioner,

and

_____,

        Respondent.

_____

DISTRICT COURT

_____ JUDICIAL DISTRICT

FAMILY COURT DIVISION

CONFIDENTIAL INFORMATION FORM

Court File No. _____

Judicial Officer: _____

	Name	Social Security Number
Petitioner	_____	_____
Respondent	_____	_____
Children	_____	_____
	_____	_____
	_____	_____
	_____	_____
	_____	_____
	_____	_____

Submitted by:

Dated:_____

By: _____

Name: _____

Petitioner/Respondent *Pro Se*

Address: _____

_____

_____

Telephone No. _____

DISSOLUTION WITH CHILDREN - 4

DISSOLUTION WITHOUT CHILDREN - 5

STATE OF MINNESOTA

DISTRICT COURT

COUNTY OF _____

_____ JUDICIAL DISTRICT

_____

FAMILY COURT DIVISION

In Re the Marriage of:

_____,

APPLICATION FOR SERVICE BY ALTERNATE MEANS

Petitioner,

Court File No. _____

and

Judicial Officer: _____

_____,

Respondent.

_____

The last known address of Respondent is _____

_____.

Petitioner's most recent contacts with Respondent were as follows:_____

_____

_____

_____.

The last know location of Respondent's employment was:_____

_____.

The names and locations of Respondent's parents are:_____

_____.

The names and locations of Respondent's other siblings and relatives are:_____

_____

_____

_____.

The names and locations of other persons who may know Respondent's whereabouts are:_____

_____.

We have made the following efforts to locate other persons who know Respondent's whereabouts:_____

_____.

_____
Affiant

Subscribed and sworn to before me,

this _____ day of _____, _____.

_____
Notary Public

DISSOLUTION WITH CHILDREN - 4

DISSOLUTION WITHOUT CHILDREN - 5

STATE OF MINNESOTA
DISTRICT COURT

COUNTY OF _____
_____ JUDICIAL DISTRICT

_____
FAMILY COURT DIVISION

In Re the Marriage of:

_____,
CERTIFICATE OF DISSOLUTION

Petitioner,
Court File No. _____

and
Judicial Officer: _____

_____,

Respondent.

_____

    WHEREAS, Petitioner/Respondent assumed the name _____ upon marriage; and

    WHEREAS, Petitioner/Respondent seeks to have her former name, _____, restored as her legal name; and

    WHEREAS, Petitioner/Respondent has not been known by any other names; and

    WHEREAS, Petitioner/Respondent seeks this name change solely because of dissolution of marriage and not to defraud or mislead anyone; and

    WHEREAS, the marriage of the parties was dissolved by Judgment and Decree of this Court entered on _____, _____.

    IT IS HEREBY ORDERED that hereafter Petitioner's/Respondent's legal name shall be _____.

RECOMMENDED FOR ENTRY:
BY THE COURT:

Dated:
Dated:

_____
_____

Referee of District Court
Judge of District Court

INDEX

SPHINX® PUBLISHING ORDER FORM

BILL TO:		SHIP TO:		
Phone #	**Terms**	**F.O.B.**	Chicago, IL	**Ship Date**

Charge my: ☐ VISA ☐ MasterCard ☐ American Express

☐ **Money Order or Personal Check**

Credit Card Number [ ][ ][ ][ ][ ][ ][ ][ ][ ][ ][ ][ ][ ][ ][ ][ ] **Expiration Date**

Qty	ISBN	Title	Retail	Ext.	Qty	ISBN	Title	Retail	Ext.
		SPHINX PUBLISHING NATIONAL TITLES				1-57071-345-6	Most Valuable Bus. Legal Forms You'll Ever Need (2E)	$19.95	
	1-57248-148-X	Como Hacer su Propio Testamento	$16.95			1-57071-346-4	Most Valuable Corporate Forms You'll Ever Need (2E)	$24.95	
	1-57248-147-1	Como Solicitar su Propio Divorcio	$24.95			1-57248-130-7	Most Valuable Personal Legal Forms You'll Ever Need	$19.95	
	1-57071-342-1	Debtors' Rights (3E)	$14.95			1-57248-098-X	The Nanny and Domestic Help Legal Kit	$22.95	
	1-57248-139-0	Grandparents' Rights (3E)	$24.95			1-57248-089-0	Neighbor v. Neighbor (2E)	$16.95	
	1-57248-087-4	Guia de Inmigracion a Estados Unidos (2E)	$24.95			1-57071-348-0	The Power of Attorney Handbook (3E)	$19.95	
	1-57248-103-X	Help Your Lawyer Win Your Case (2E)	$14.95			1-57071-337-5	Social Security Benefits Handbook (2E)	$16.95	
	1-57071-164-X	How to Buy a Condominium or Townhome	$19.95			1-57071-399-5	Unmarried Parents' Rights	$19.95	
	1-57071-223-9	How to File Your Own Bankruptcy (4E)	$19.95			1-57071-354-5	U.S.A. Immigration Guide (3E)	$19.95	
	1-57248-132-3	How to File Your Own Divorce (4E)	$24.95			1-57248-138-2	Winning Your Personal Injury Claim (2E)	$24.95	
	1-57248-100-5	How to Form a DE Corporation from Any State	$24.95			1-57248-097-1	Your Right to Child Custody, Visitation and Support	$22.95	
	1-57248-083-1	How to Form a Limited Liability Company	$22.95				**CALIFORNIA TITLES**		
	1-57248-101-3	How to Form a NV Corporation from Any State	$24.95			1-57248-150-1	CA Power of Attorney Handbook (2E)	$18.95	
	1-57248-099-8	How to Form a Nonprofit Corporation	$24.95			1-57248-151-X	How to File for Divorce in CA (3E)	$26.95	
	1-57248-133-1	How to Form Your Own Corporation (3E)	$24.95			1-57071-356-1	How to Make a CA Will	$16.95	
	1-57071-343-X	How to Form Your Own Partnership	$22.95			1-57248-145-5	How to Probate and Settle an Estate in California	$26.95	
	1-57248-119-6	How to Make Your Own Will (2E)	$16.95			1-57248-146-3	How to Start a Business in CA	$18.95	
	1-57071-331-6	How to Negotiate Real Estate Contracts (3E)	$18.95			1-57071-358-8	How to Win in Small Claims Court in CA	$16.95	
	1-57071-332-4	How to Negotiate Real Estate Leases (3E)	$18.95			1-57071-359-6	Landlords' Rights and Duties in CA	$21.95	
	1-57248-124-2	How to Register Your Own Copyright (3E)	$21.95				**FLORIDA TITLES**		
	1-57248-104-8	How to Register Your Own Trademark (3E)	$21.95			1-57071-363-4	Florida Power of Attorney Handbook (2E)	$16.95	
	1-57071-349-9	How to Win Your Unemployment Compensation Claim	$19.95			1-57248-093-9	How to File for Divorce in FL (6E)	$24.95	
	1-57248-118-8	How to Write Your Own Living Will (2E)	$16.95			1-57071-380-4	How to Form a Corporation in FL (4E)	$24.95	
	1-57071-344-8	How to Write Your Own Premarital Agreement (2E)	$21.95			1-57248-086-6	How to Form a Limited Liability Co. in FL	$22.95	
	1-57071-333-2	Jurors' Rights (2E)	$12.95			1-57071-401-0	How to Form a Partnership in FL	$22.95	
	1-57071-400-2	Legal Research Made Easy (2E)	$14.95			1-57248-113-7	How to Make a FL Will (6E)	$16.95	
	1-57071-336-7	Living Trusts and Simple Ways to Avoid Probate (2E)	$22.95			1-57248-088-2	How to Modify Your FL Divorce Judgment (4E)	$24.95	

Form Continued on Following Page   **SUBTOTAL**

To order, call Sourcebooks at 1-800-432-7444 or FAX (630) 961-2168 (Bookstores, libraries, wholesalers—please call for discount)
Prices are subject to change without notice.

SPHINX® PUBLISHING ORDER FORM

Qty	ISBN	Title	Retail	Ext.
_____	1-57248-081-5	How to Start a Business in FL (5E)	$16.95	_____
_____	1-57071-362-6	How to Win in Small Claims Court in FL (6E)	$16.95	_____
_____	1-57248-123-4	Landlords' Rights and Duties in FL (8E)	$21.95	_____

GEORGIA TITLES

Qty	ISBN	Title	Retail	Ext.
_____	1-57248-137-4	How to File for Divorce in GA (4E)	$21.95	_____
_____	1-57248-075-0	How to Make a GA Will (3E)	$16.95	_____
_____	1-57248-140-4	How to Start a Business in Georgia (2E)	$16.95	_____

ILLINOIS TITLES

Qty	ISBN	Title	Retail	Ext.
_____	1-57071-405-3	How to File for Divorce in IL (2E)	$21.95	_____
_____	1-57071-415-0	How to Make an IL Will (2E)	$16.95	_____
_____	1-57071-416-9	How to Start a Business in IL (2E)	$16.95	_____
_____	1-57248-078-5	Landlords' Rights & Duties in IL	$21.95	_____

MASSACHUSETTS TITLES

Qty	ISBN	Title	Retail	Ext.
_____	1-57248-128-5	How to File for Divorce in MA (3E)	$24.95	_____
_____	1-57248-115-3	How to Form a Corporation in MA	$24.95	_____
_____	1-57248-108-0	How to Make a MA Will (2E)	$16.95	_____
_____	1-57248-106-4	How to Start a Business in MA (2E)	$16.95	_____
_____	1-57248-107-2	Landlords' Rights and Duties in MA (2E)	$21.95	_____

MICHIGAN TITLES

Qty	ISBN	Title	Retail	Ext.
_____	1-57071-409-6	How to File for Divorce in MI (2E)	$21.95	_____
_____	1-57248-077-7	How to Make a MI Will (2E)	$16.95	_____
_____	1-57071-407-X	How to Start a Business in MI (2E)	$16.95	_____

NEW YORK TITLES

Qty	ISBN	Title	Retail	Ext.
_____	1-57248-141-2	How to File for Divorce in NY (2E)	$26.95	_____
_____	1-57248-105-6	How to Form a Corporation in NY	$24.95	_____
_____	1-57248-095-5	How to Make a NY Will (2E)	$16.95	_____
_____	1-57071-185-2	How to Start a Business in NY	$16.95	_____
_____	1-57071-187-9	How to Win in Small Claims Court in NY	$16.95	_____
_____	1-57071-186-0	Landlords' Rights and Duties in NY	$21.95	_____
_____	1-57071-188-7	New York Power of Attorney Handbook	$19.95	_____
_____	1-57248-122-6	Tenants' Rights in NY	$21..95	_____

NORTH CAROLINA TITLES

Qty	ISBN	Title	Retail	Ext.
_____	1-57071-326-X	How to File for Divorce in NC (2E)	$22.95	_____
_____	1-57248-129-3	How to Make a NC Will (3E)	$16.95	_____
_____	1-57248-096-3	How to Start a Business in NC (2E)	$16.95	_____
_____	1-57248-091-2	Landlords' Rights & Duties in NC	$21.95	_____

OHIO TITLES

Qty	ISBN	Title	Retail	Ext.
_____	1-57248-102-1	How to File for Divorce in OH	$24.95	_____

PENNSYLVANIA TITLES

Qty	ISBN	Title	Retail	Ext.
_____	1-57248-127-7	How to File for Divorce in PA (2E)	$24.95	_____
_____	1-57248-094-7	How to Make a PA Will (2E)	$16.95	_____
_____	1-57248-112-9	How to Start a Business in PA (2E)	$18.95	_____
_____	1-57071-179-8	Landlords' Rights and Duties in PA	$19.95	_____

TEXAS TITLES

Qty	ISBN	Title	Retail	Ext.
_____	1-57071-330-8	How to File for Divorce in TX (2E)	$21.95	_____
_____	1-57248-114-5	How to Form a Corporation in TX (2E)	$24.95	_____
_____	1-57071-417-7	How to Make a TX Will (2E)	$16.95	_____
_____	1-57071-418-5	How to Probate an Estate in TX (2E)	$22.95	_____
_____	1-57071-365-0	How to Start a Business in TX (2E)	$16.95	_____
_____	1-57248-111-0	How to Win in Small Claims Court in TX (2E)	$16.95	_____
_____	1-57248-110-2	Landlords' Rights and Duties in TX (2E)	$21.95	_____

SUBTOTAL THIS PAGE _____

SUBTOTAL PREVIOUS PAGE _____

Shipping — $5.00 for 1st book, $1.00 each additional _____

Illinois residents add 6.75% sales tax _____

Connecticut residents add 6.00% sales tax _____

TOTAL _____

To order, call Sourcebooks at 1-800-432-7444 or FAX (630) 961-2168 (Bookstores, libraries, wholesalers—please call for discount)

Prices are subject to change without notice.